# IRELAND: 1841/1851
## CENSUS ABSTRACTS
### (Republic of Ireland)

Josephine Masterson

Genealogical Publishing Co., Inc.

Published by Genealogical Publishing Co., Inc.
1001 N. Calvert St., Baltimore, MD 21202

Library of Congress Catalogue Card Number 98-75211
International Standard Book Number 0-8063-1586-5
*Made in the United States of America*

Extracts from official documents are published
with permission of The National Archives,
Dublin, Ireland, The Chief Herald of Ireland,
Dublin, The Public Record Office of Northern
Ireland, Belfast.

# TABLE OF CONTENTS

## Part Three

## Part Four

# INTRODUCTION

The earliest complete census available for Ireland is for the year 1901. For census years 1841 and 1851, fragments of the original censuses, transcriptions, certified copies of portions of some returns and secondary census information from Old Age Pension records are readily available for only some areas of the country. This is due mainly to the loss of records in the fire of 1922 at the Public Record Office (now the National Archives) in Dublin. From these sources, selected 1841 and 1851 Census information for 75,000 persons, of possible genealogical value, was transcribed and indexed, most of it found on LDS film.

A limited amount of filmed 1841 and 1851 Census information, for Republic of Ireland locations, was available for this compilation at the time these records were being collected (1992-1993). Of the various abstracts in this book (records for 5800 persons), data for 2600 persons, in these Republic of Ireland counties, were found in the Old Age Pension summary books held in Belfast by the Public Record Office of Northern Ireland (PRONI). A larger body of material from this source was available for the 6 northern counties, therefore, the records have been divided, due to the volume of information and its uneven distribution. Census abstracts for 23,000 persons (20,000 from OAP records) are in another collection by this author, *Ireland: 1841/1851 Census Abstracts (Northern Ireland)*.

Other sources of 1841 and 1851 Census abstracts, for locations in the present-day Republic of Ireland, used for this compilation, in addition to the Old Age Pension records, include:

1. Original census records for the night of June 6, 1841, held at the National Archives, Dublin, consisting of the Parish of Killeshandra (15,000 persons), the only surviving parish-wide census record for 1841, and a few 1841 burnt fragments for Counties Cork, Fermanagh and Waterford (171 persons); a transcription of the latter is included herein. The Parish of Killeshandra records have been transcribed from LDS film. Copies of the transcription and index (by William G. Masterson and Josephine Masterson) are available at the Allen County Public Library in Fort Wayne, IN, the Family History Library in Salt Lake City, UT, the Pennsylvania Historical Society, Philadelphia, PA, the National Library of Ireland, Dublin, and the County Cavan Library, Cavan Town, County Cavan, Ireland. A list of surnames only from the 1841 Killeshandra Parish Census is included in this book.

2. Some family transcriptions such as the 1841 and 1851 E. Walsh Kelly transcriptions (1600 persons), held at the Genealogical Office, Dublin, and the 1841 and 1851 Thrift Genealogical Abstracts (560 for Republic of Ireland locations), held at the National Archives, found on film and included herein. Not found on LDS film, but acquired from the National Archives, are the 1841 Census abstracts for Loughrea, County Galway (63 persons).

3. A xeroxed copy of a photostatted written transcription of some 1851 County Cork Census records (for the Union of Kilworth) obtained by this author from the National Archives which was transcribed and indexed (4000 persons). This was published in 1994 in paperback as *County Cork, Ireland – A Collection of 1851 Census Records*, by the Clearfield Company, Baltimore, MD. This material is not available on LDS film. List of surnames only on p. 135.

4. Certified Copies of portions of some returns, used to determine the age of the applicant, available at PRONI and the National Archives, not all found on LDS film. Of these, only selected records were used, due to the fragmentary nature of the information, which is, in the majority of cases, related only to the pension applicant and his parents.

# Old Age Pension Records

The Old Age Pension was introduced in 1908, but as civil registration of births, marriages and deaths was not begun in Ireland until 1864, birth certificates were not available for persons of eligible age (70 years).

In the case of persons applying to the local Pensions Office without supplying proof of age, the Pensions Officer sent the particulars of claimants on Form 37 for checking in the 1841 and/or 1851 Censuses held in the Public Record Office of Ireland at the Four Courts in Dublin. The details were checked and completed forms returned to the Pensions Officer. This checking was done before the Public Record Office fire of 1922. Consequently there is a partial census record available for some families in which a member filed for a pension in the early 1900s.

Only a portion of the Old Age Pension records (about one fourth) are in Belfast, with the balance at the National Archives in Dublin. The National Archives census search records, which were not found on LDS film in 1993, are under their general reference no. Cen/S/1-32.

The Old Age Pension records in Belfast are mainly for the Counties of Antrim, Armagh, Down, Fermanagh, Londonderry and Tyrone, which are in Northern Ireland and not included in this volume. However, a large number of records are for the County of Donegal, which is presently located in the Republic of Ireland, with a small number of records for other counties in the Republic. The locations in the Republic have been sorted out for this collection.

The Old Age Pension records summary books, in general, have brief notes in them, recording whether a census record was found for the applicant and his family or not, and what ages were reported on the census. About one in 40 application summaries contains useful census information listing the names of the entire family from the 1841 Census and about one in 10 contains family information from the 1851 Census. Absentee and deceased persons are often recorded, but not the cause of death. Servants, visitors and lodgers are occasionally listed. Baptismal records and marriage records were used in some cases to establish age, so a few parish reports are on these films.

Upon application the person gave the Pensions Officer the place of residence of his/her family on June 6, 1841 or March 30, 1851, the names of his/her parents (sometimes including the maiden name of the mother) and the names of the applicant's brothers and sisters, their order of birth and ages, in order to identify the family and confirm the applicant's age. If a record were not found in the location given, another search was sometimes requested. A fee was charged for each search. In some cases the investigator (Search Officer) was asked to obtain complete details about the family, in which case there is a substantial amount of information about them for that particular year.

A major part of the Old Age Pension records summary book consists of records of applications for pension in which the family was not found in the censuses at the location given by the applicant, or if found, the record consists of the name and age of the person found in the census, to verify his/her age for that year, the names of the parents and where they lived. This type of fragmentary material was not used for this transcription.

Because these records are in books, some tightly bound, some of the information could not be extracted because the filming did not cover the extreme edge of the page.

A possible relationship to the claimant was necessary for a family to be listed in the OAP records. Recorded for families for which complete details were requested are the following: (1) the name of the head of the family, rarely the occupation; (2) often the marriage date; (3) the wife's name, her maiden name if supplied by the claimant; (4) the place of residence of the family for that year; (5) the children and their ages; (6) other members of the family living in the household; (7) occasionally the names of servants, lodgers and visitors; and (8) persons deceased in the 10 years prior to the census (the latter not always recorded).

For this compilation standardization was attempted for the spellings of counties, baronies, parishes and townlands. The names of the townlands, as given by the applicant or spelled by the Pensions Officer, are in many cases phonetically spelled or the spelling transposed. The spellings of the townlands were compared with the spellings in *Census of Ireland, 1871, General Alphabetical Index to the Townlands and Towns, Parishes and Baronies of Ireland* because that document was available on film. Some of the names of townlands, as submitted by the applicant or the Pensions Officer, could not be found in that listing. An 1851 list was available at the Allen County Public Library, Fort Wayne, IN, in book form, and that was also consulted. Some spellings and/or locations were not found in either index.

The researcher should be aware that this is a transcription of secondary census information, and that somewhere along the line inaccuracies may have occurred, even if the original census information were correct. Most researchers are aware of discrepancies in census information. One of the frequently found errors was that grandchildren were listed as nephews and nieces.

Some Certified Copies of portions of some returns from the 1841 and 1851 Censuses, held in Belfast and Dublin, were found on film. Additional Certified Copies, not found on LDS film, were obtained from the National Archives, in the form of xeroxed copies. In most cases the whole household is not listed, as in the OAP summary books, but concerns the person applying for pension, his parents, and the location of the family at the time of the census. However, there is additional information, not found in the OAP summary books, such as the occupation, education and place of birth. Some records selected from this source were those from locations for which there is otherwise little data available, or because they contain possibly useful information such as the ages and marriage dates of the parents. Certified Copies were obtained for Old Age Pension purposes, to verify ages of applicants.

Guide to the Use of the Old Age Pension Abstracts

1. The 0258500 and 0993000 series are numbers of LDS films from which these records were transcribed. The films were rented from the Family History Library in Salt Lake City, Utah, and transcribed at a local LDS Family History Center. If one should wish to consult this source the films may be ordered and reviewed at a local center.

2. The spelling of the surname may differ from the 1841 to the 1851 Census record for the same family. The preferred spelling used for this transcription was the one copied by the investigator from the census and noted in the OAP record books. In most cases the notation was that the parents were found but no census spelling of the surname was given, in which case the spelling supplied by the applicant was used. Because this is a transcription, the standardization of the spelling of common surnames was not considered. The researcher should be aware of this, allowing for variations.

3. In some cases where more than one record was found for a family, they sometimes differed from one another to some extent. In one case there were four records found. When the census record was not found by the investigator in the location given by the claimant, another attempt was made to find it in another location, under another surname spelling, or the age verified through baptismal or marriage records, so several records may be in the books for the same applicant; this information has been combined into one entry.

4. In a large number of cases the marriage date given in the census was different in 1841 from the marriage date given in the 1851 Census for the same individuals; usually it was only different by one year.

5. The claimant is identified in this compilation because this individual stayed in Ireland and had applied for an Old Age Pension. Of particular interest are people not listed as claimants, persons who may have emigrated to the United States.

6. The entries are cross-indexed for relatives, lodgers, visitors and servants but the cross-indexing for the married names of wives and claimants is in a separate listing. The maiden name of the mother, which was supplied by the applicant, is not usually part of the census information. In cases where the claimant was not found in the census, the maiden name of the mother is suspect, indicated as "per claimant not found" and thus was not used in the cross-indexing of married names.

7. The Appendix was used for census records of families in which there were several different surnames, the parents were recently married and had only one child at the time, part of the record was illegible, the location given was confusing or two locations were given, or for some reason the record was unsuitable for inclusion in the larger alphabetized family groupings which comprise the greater part of this work.

Contents of this compilation by county:

1841 Households (354)

| | |
|---|---|
| Carlow | 2 (Crawford p. 36, and McCall p. 25) |
| Cavan | 5 (Brice, Keaney, Lynch, Somers, Turner) |
| Cork | 24 |
| Donegal | 84 |
| Dublin | 11 (Derm, Earley, Fea, Flanagan, Guiness/Costello, Kennedy [3], McKnalley, Robinson, Wade) |
| Galway | 56 |
| Kildare | 1 (Bourke) |
| Kings | 1 (Berry) |
| Kilkenny | 92 |
| Leitrim | 5 (Cassidy, Flynn, Finly, O'Donel, Tiernan) |
| Limerick | 11 (Doody, Elmes, Farr, Feore [3], Foer, Fraher [2], Harnett, Phayer) |
| Longford | 1 (Geraghty) |
| Louth | 1 (Kearney) |
| Mayo | 5 (Bland, Carey, Mullanney, McGuire p. 25, Philips) |

| | |
|---|---|
| Meath | 1 (Mullin p. 25) |
| Monaghan | 11 (Carville, Crawford p. 5, Finnegan, Kelly, McArdle, McNally, Norris [3], Rooney, Short/McQuade/Simple) |
| Queens | 2 (Carroll, Casey) |
| Roscommon | 28 |
| Sligo | 1 (Jordan/Burrows/Green p. 18) |
| Tipperary | 1 (Walsh p. 26) |
| Waterford | 7 (Cronin, Darly, Flannigan, Power, Walsh/Hamilton p. 35, Dower p. 35 [2]) |
| Westmeath | 2 (Carberry, Colgan) |
| Wicklow | 2 (Doran, Ireton) |

## 1851 Households (513)

| | |
|---|---|
| Cavan | 6 (Brennan, Gillece, McKernan, Thompson p. 93, Smyth, Wilson/Kelly p. 93) |
| Clare | 1 (Ryan) |
| Cork | 1 (Swete) |
| Donegal | 234 |
| Dublin | 23 |
| Galway | 4 (Lally, Martin, Murrey, Spellman) |
| Kerry | 4 (Ashe, Daly, Perry, Sullivan) |
| Kildare | 1 (Carr p. 94) |
| Kilkenny | 100 |
| Kings | 2 (Berry p. 115, Cunningham p. 115) |
| Leitrim | 9 (Caine, Hunt [2], Maguire, Mulvey, McHugh, Peacock, Wynne [2]) |
| Limerick | 10 (Elmes, Feore [5], O'Grady, Phayer, Scanlon, Wallace) |
| Longford | 1 (Eagan) |
| Louth | 2 (Cunningham p. 93, McGuinness p. 81) |
| Mayo | 5 (Cannon, Curry, Eagan, Hogan, Mulreany) |
| Meath | 3 (Connell, Gilleran, Mullady) |
| Monaghan | 21 |
| Queens | 1 (Ryan) |
| Roscommon | 39 |
| Sligo | 8 (Callaghan, Daly, Dwyer, Gorman, Heaver, Savage, Shannon, Towey) |
| Tipperary | 2 (Mulcahy, Noonan) |
| Waterford | 31 |
| Wexford | 3 (Lamberd/Dugan, Murphy p. 97, Walsh p. 98) |
| Wicklow | 2 (Kearans, Moran) |

Total 867 households (approximately 5800 persons)


Surnames only in the 1841 Census of Killeshandra Parish, County Cavan (15,000 names)

Surnames only in the 1851 Census of the Union of Kilworth, County Cork (4000 names)

## Abbreviations

| | | |
|---|---|---|
| (sic) = as written | lab = laborer | V = village |
| na = not available | h serv = house servant | Up = upper |
| ABS = absent | boar = boarder | Lr = lower |
| DEC = deceased | appren = apprentice | Rel = relationship |
| b. = born | hk = housekeeper | rel. = relative |
| m. = married | E&I = English & Irish | dau = daughter |
| d. = died | RW = reads & writes | gr/dau = granddaughter |
| n.m. = not married | Co = county | moth = mother |
| wid = widow/widower | T = town | fath = father |
| Cl. = claimant | Tnld = townland | M/L = mother-in-law |
| fd = found | E/W/N/S = east, west, | p. = page |
| visi = visitor | north & south | no. = number |

OAP = Old Age Pension
PRONI = Public Record Office of Northern Ireland, Belfast
NA = National Archives, Dublin
LDS = The Church of Jesus Christ of Latter-day Saints, Salt Lake City, Utah

PART ONE

1841 Irish Census Abstracts from Old Age Pension records, Republic of Ireland locations

Combined 1841/1851 Irish Census Abstracts from Old Age Pension Records

Miscellaneous 1841 Irish Census Abstracts

Confirmation of age from the 1841 and 1851 Censuses of Ireland, County Donegal

| Surname | Given | Rel | Age | Marr | Film | Remarks | Location |
|---------|-------|-----|-----|------|------|---------|----------|
| ANDERSON | James | head | na | 1820 | 0258547 | | Donegal |
| ANDERSON | Sally | wife | na | 1820 | | nee ILLEN | Raphoe S |
| ANDERSON | Isabella | dau | 20 | | | not listed in 1851 | Urney |
| ANDERSON | William | son | 18 | | | 28 in 1851, in America | Alt |
| ANDERSON | John | son | 16 | | | 26 in 1851, in America | |
| ANDERSON | James | son | 14 | | | 24 in 1851, in America | |
| ANDERSON | Samuel | son | 12 | | | not listed in 1851 | |
| ANDERSON | David | son | 10 | | | Dan? 20 in 1851, in America | |
| ANDERSON | Robert | son | 8 | | | claimant, 18 in 1851 | |
| ANDERSON | Thomas | son | 6 | | | 16 in 1851 | |
| ANDERSON | Allen | son | 4 | | | 13 in 1851 | |
| | | | | | | | |
| BARR | Andrew | head | na | na | 0258545 | | Donegal |
| BARR | Mary | wife | na | na | | | Inishowen W |
| BARR | Nellie | dau | 19 | | | | Fahan Lr |
| BARR | Mick | son | 16 | | | | Connaghkinnagoe |
| BARR | Owen | son | 14 | | | | |
| BARR | Andy | son | 12 | | | | |
| BARR | William | son | 11 | | | | |
| BARR | Daniel | son | 10 | | | | |
| BARR | Ann | dau | 7 | | | | |
| BARR | Patrick | son | 6 | | | | |
| BARR | Fanny | dau | 4 | | | | |
| BARR | Neal | son | 18m | | | | |
| * BAXTER | Rebecca | M/L | 71 | na | 0258546 | wid, mother of Betty SLEVAN | |
| BLAND | Wm. C. | head | na | na | 0258547 | Wm. Clough BLAND, farmer | Mayo |
| BLAND | Sarah | wife | na | na | | nee HILDEBRAND | Murrisk |
| BLAND | Sarah | dau | 5 | | | 15 in 1851 | Oughaval |
| BLAND | Llewellyn | son | 4 | | | 14 in 1851 | Westport |
| BLAND | Margaret | dau | 3 | | | 13 in 1851 | High St. |
| BLAND | Charlotte | dau | 11m | | | claimant, 10 in 1851 | |
| BLAND | Elizabeth | dau | 0 | | | 8 in 1851 | |
| BLAND | Howard | son | 0 | | | 5 in 1851 | |
| BLAND | Grace | dau | 0 | | | 4 mo in 1851, twin | |
| BLAND | Geraldine | dau | 0 | | | 4 mo in 1851, twin | |
| BLAND | George | son | 0 | | | died 8 mo in 1851 | |
| BONNER | Patrick | head | 34 | 1835 | 0258547 | or CRAMPSIE, 48 in 1851 | Donegal |
| BONNER | Mary | wife | 30 | 1835 | | 34 in 1851 | Raphoe |
| BONNER | Catherine | dau | 3 | | | 13 in 1851 | Clonleigh |
| BONNER | Bridget | dau | 2 | | | d. 1838/40 | Churchtown |
| BONNER | William | son | 1 | | | 11 in 1851 | |
| BONNER | Jane | dau | 0 | | | 9 in 1851 | |
| BONNER | John | son | 0 | | | 7 in 1851 | |
| BONNER | Bridget | dau | 0 | | | claimant, 5 in 1851, m. McSORLEY | |
| BONNER | James | son | 0 | | | 3 in 1851 | |
| BONNER | Bridget | dau | na | | | d. 1846 age 15 (mo?) | |
| BOURKE | Thomas | head | na | 1808 | 0258545 | m. 1808/1828 | Kildare |
| BOURKE | Catherine | wife | na | 1828 | | nee LUCAS | Narragh & Reban E |

| | | | | | | |
|---|---|---|---|---|---|---|
| BOURKE | Mary | dau 22 | | | half sister of claimant | Tomolin |
| BOURKE | Michael | son 12 | | | 22 in 1851 | Ballitore Town |
| BOURKE | Thomas | son 8 | | | 18 in 1851 | |
| BOURKE | Patrick | son 6 | | | claimant, 15 in 1851 | |
| | | | | | | |
| BRADLY | Michael | head 45 | 1818 0258547 | | | Donegal |
| BRADLY | Margaret | wife 45 | 1818 | | nee PATTON or PEYTON | Raphoe S |
| BRADLY | Pat | son 21 | | | absent | Donaghmore |
| BRADLY | John | son 19 | | | absent | Carn/Templecarn |
| BRADLY | Ann | dau 15 | | | | |
| BRADLY | Michael | son 14 | | | | |
| BRADLY | Hugh | son 12 | | | absent | |
| BRADLY | William | son 12 | | | | |
| BRADLY | Jane | dau 10 | | | | |
| BRADLY | James | son 6 | | | claimant, spells BRADLEY | |
| BRADLY | Margaret | dau 2 | | | | |
| BRADLY | Margaret | dau 4 | | | d. 1835 | |
| | | | | | | |
| BRENNAN | John | head 45 | 1836 0258546 | | age 60 in 1851 | Donegal |
| BRENNAN | Mary | wife 30 | 1836 | | 40 in 1851 | Boylagh |
| BRENNAN | Dan | son 3 | | | died age 12 in 1851 | Templecrone |
| BRENNAN | Mary | dau 5 | | | 14 in 1851 | Meenacross |
| BRENNAN | Catherine | dau 1 | | | 10 in 1851 | |
| BRENNAN | Hanagh | dau 0 | | | 8 in 1851 | |
| BRENNAN | Nelly | dau 0 | | | Ellen claimant, 8 in 1851 | |
| BRENNAN | Nancy | dau 0 | | | 6 in 1851 | |
| BRENNAN | Louesa | dau 0 | | | 5 in 1851 | |
| | | | | | | |
| BRICE | William | head 41 | 1828 0258547 | | apothecary, 51 in 1851, m. 1828/39 | Cavan |
| BRICE | Ann | wife 34 | 1839 | | 46 in 1851, claimant says Martha | Loughtee Up |
| BRICE | Eliza | dau 12 | | | Elizabeth claimant, 21 in 1851 m. | Urney |
| | | | | | MALCOMSON | Cavan Town |
| BRICE | Fred A. | son 11 | | | Fredrick A. 20 in 1851 | Main St. |
| BRICE | Wm. Henry | son 9 | | | Henry 19 in 1851, absent | |
| BRICE – See | | | | | John JOHNSTON, son | |
| | | | | | | |
| | | | | | | Donegal |
| CALLAGHAN | Michael | head na | na | 0258547 | | Inishowen W |
| CALLAGHAN | Margaret | wife na | na | | | Fahan Lr |
| CALLAGHAN | Patrick | son 7 | | | | Keeloges, |
| CALLAGHAN | Biddy | dau 5 | | | | Beauville & |
| CALLAGHAN | Margaret | dau 2 | | | claimant, m. McDAID | Clongash |
| | | | | | | |
| CASSIDY | John | head na | 1828 0258547 | | Owen? | Leitrim |
| CASSIDY | Mary | wife na | 1828 | | | Rosclogher |
| CASSIDY | James | son 10 | | | Jane? | Rossinver |
| CASSIDY | Mary | dau 9 | | | 9 months? | Tawly |
| CASSIDY | Andrew | son 8 | | | | |
| CASSIDY | Bridget | dau 5 | | | ages off page for 1851 | |
| CASSIDY | Patrick | son 1 | | | | |
| CASSIDY | Anne | dau 0 | | | Cl., 5 in 1851? m. MULLIGAN | |
| | | | | | | |
| CAVANAGH | Anthony | head na | na | 0258547 | | Donegal |
| CAVANAGH | Ann | wife na | na | | nee DOHERTY | Inishowen E |
| CAVANAGH | Charles | son 9 | | | 20 in 1851 | Donagh |
| CAVANAGH | William | son 7 | | | 16 in 1851 | Carrowblagh |
| CAVANAGH | Cornelius | son 4 | | | 16 in 1851 | |
| CAVANAGH | Edward | son 3 | | | 13 in 1851 | |
| CAVANAGH | Mary | dau 1 | | | claimant, 14 in 1851 | |

| Surname | Name | Rel | Age | | Film | Notes | Location |
|---|---|---|---|---|---|---|---|
| CAVANAGH | Anthony | son | 0 | | | 8 in 1851 | |
| CAVANAGH | Nancy | dau | 0 | | | Annie, d. 1845, age 1 yr. | |
| | | | | | | | |
| COLGAN | Patrick | head | na | na | 0258547 | | Westmeath |
| COLGAN | Mary | wife | na | na | | nee NIXON | Moycashel |
| COLGAN | James | son | 9 | | | | Newtown |
| COLGAN | John | son | 7 | | | | Killavally |
| COLGAN | Michael | son | 5 | | | | |
| COLGAN | Eliza | dau | 3 | | | claimant, m. FORSYTHE | |
| | | | | | | | |
| COOK | James | head | 29 | 1832 | 0258547 | 38 in 1851 | Donegal |
| COOK | Mary | wife | 28 | 1832 | | 35 in 1851 | Raphoe |
| COOK | Robert | son | 8 | | | 18 in 1851 | Taughboyne |
| COOK | Catherine | dau | 6 | | | d. 1851 age 16 | Creatland |
| COOK | Mary | dau | 3 | | | 14 in 1851 | |
| COOK | John | son | 1 | | | 12 in 1851 | |
| COOK | Jain | dau | 0 | | | Cl., 10 in 1851 m. JOHNSTON | |
| COOK | Alexander | son | 0 | | | 8 in 1851 | |
| COOK | David | son | 0 | | | 3 in 1851 | |
| COOK | James | son | 0 | | | 1 in 1851 | |
| COOK | Sarah | dau | 0 | | | 1 in 1851 | |
| | | | | | | | |
| COYLE | Henry | head | na | na | 0258546 | | Donegal |
| COYLE | Mary | wife | na | na | | | Inishowen W |
| COYLE | Ann | dau | 6 | | | 16 in 1851 | Fahan Up |
| COYLE | Neal | son | 4 | | | 15 in 1851 | Gortnaskea |
| COYLE | Patrick | son | 2 | | | 11 in 1851 | |
| COYLE | Jane | dau | 0 | | | claimant, 9 in 1851 | |
| COYLE | Henry | son | 0 | | | 7 in 1851 | |
| COYLE | Mary | dau | 0 | | | 5 in 1851 | |
| COYLE | Catherine | dau | 0 | | | 3 in 1851 | |
| COYLE | Elizabeth | dau | 0 | | | 1 in 1851 | |
| COYLE | James | son | 1 | | | d. 1841 at age 1 | |
| | | | | | | | |
| COYLE | Henry | head | 30 | 1837 | 0258546 | 40 in 1851, COIL in 1851 | Donegal |
| COYLE | Sally | wife | 28 | 1837 | | Sara, 36 in 1851 | Inishowen W |
| COYLE | James | son | 3 | | | 11 in 1851 | Fahan Lr |
| COYLE | Hugh | son | 1 | | | 9 in 1851 | Foffanagh |
| COYLE | Mary | dau | 0 | | | claimant, 7 in 1851 m. SCANLAN | |
| COYLE | Ellen | dau | 0 | | | 6 in 1851 | |
| COYLE | Catherin | dau | 0 | | | 5 in 1851 | |
| COYLE | Sally | dau | 0 | | | 3 in 1851 | |
| COYLE | Ann | dau | 0 | | | 1 in 1851 | |
| | | | | | | | |
| CRAWFORD | Thomas | head | na | na | 0258545 | | Monaghan |
| CRAWFORD | Jane | wife | na | na | | | Monaghan |
| CRAWFORD | William | son | 3 | | | 12 in 1851 | Monaghan |
| CRAWFORD | Mary | dau | 1 | | | 10 in 1851 | Annahagh |
| CRAWFORD | Elizabeth | dau | 0 | | | claimant, 10 in 1851 | 1851:Coolshannah |
| | | | | | | | |
| CURREN | Edward | head | na | na | 0258547 | | Donegal |
| CURREN | Mary | wife | na | na | | | Kilmacrenan |
| CURREN | Daniel | son | 7 | | | | Tullaghobegly |
| CURREN | Sophia | dau | 6 | | | | Meenaclady |
| CURREN | Manus | son | 4 | | | | |

1841 and 1851 combined Irish Census Abstracts (locations in the Republic of Ireland) from Old Age Pension records held in Belfast by the Public Record Office of Northern Ireland, transcribed from LDS film – see also 1851 Census Abstracts and Appendix.

| DEAN | John | head | na | na | 0258546 | | Donegal |
|---|---|---|---|---|---|---|---|
| DEAN | Elizabeth | wife | na | na | | nee GUY | Inishowen W |
| DEAN | Ellen | dau | 13 | | | died young | Inch |
| DEAN | Mary | dau | 11 | | | died young | Glack or |
| DEAN | Eliza Ann | dau | 9 | | | 18 in 1851 | Bohullion |
| DEAN | John | son | 6 | | | claimant, 16 in 1851 | |
| | | | | | | | |
| DOHERTY | Charles | head | 42 | 1827 | 0258547 | 50 in 1851 | Donegal |
| DOHERTY | Sara | wife | 39 | 1827 | | Sally in 1851, age 48 | Raphoe S |
| DOHERTY | James | son | 13 | | | 23 in 1851, in England | Urney |
| DOHERTY | Hugh | son | 8 | | | 19 in 1851 | Cormakilly |
| DOHERTY | Edward | son | 6 | | | 17 in 1851 | |
| DOHERTY | Sara Anne | dau | 5 | | | 15 in 1851 | |
| DOHERTY | Margaret | dau | 3 | | | 13 in 1851 | |
| DOHERTY | Mary | dau | 7 m | | | 11 in 1851 | |
| DOHERTY | Jane | dau | 0 | | | claimant, 7 in 1851 m. GREER | |
| DOHERTY | Biddy | dau | 0 | | | 5 in 1851 | |
| | | | | | | | |
| DOHERTY | James | head | 50 | 1821 | 0258546 | married twice | Donegal |
| DOHERTY | Margaret | wife | 30 | na | | | Inishowen W |
| DOHERTY | John | son | 19 | | | absent 1841, 25 absent 1851 | Fahan Lr |
| DOHERTY | Denis | son | 17 | | | absent 1841, 23 in 1851 | Meenagory |
| DOHERTY | James | son | 15 | | | absent 1841, absent 21 in 1851 | |
| DOHERTY | George | son | 13 | | | absent 1841, 20 in 1851 | |
| DOHERTY | Michael | son | 11 | | | | |
| DOHERTY | Mary | dau | 6 | | | | |
| DOHERTY | Daniel | son | 0 | | | claimant, 7 in 1851 | |
| DOHERTY | Catherine | dau | 0 | | | 6 in 1851 | |
| DOHERTY | Joseph | son | 0 | | | d. age 1 per 1851 Census | |
| DOHERTY | Catherine | wife | 30 | | | d. 1847 | |
| | | | | | | | |
| DOHERTY | John | head | 50 | na | 0258546 | | Donegal |
| DOHERTY | Isabella | wife | na | na | | | Inishowen W |
| DOHERTY | Sarah | dau | na | | | listed in 1841 | Desertegny |
| DOHERTY | James | son | 6 | | | 15 in 1851 | Tonduff |
| DOHERTY | Patrick | son | 4 | | | 13 in 1851 | |
| DOHERTY | John | son | 3 m | | | claimant, 10 in 1851 | |
| DOHERTY | Michael | son | na | | | listed in 1841 | |
| DOHERTY | Catherine | dau | 8 | | | d. age 18, 1851 | |
| | | | | | | | |
| DOHERTY | Michael | head | na | na | 0258546 | | Donegal |
| DOHERTY | Jane | wife | na | na | | | Inishowen W |
| DOHERTY | Nancy | dau | 13 | | | | Muff |
| DOHERTY | Jane | dau | 10 | | | | Ardmore |
| DOHERTY | Margaret | dau | 9 | | | | |
| DOHERTY | Patrick | son | 8 | | | | |
| DOHERTY | George | son | 6 | | | | |
| DOHERTY | Mary | dau | 3 | | | claimant | |
| DOHERTY | Sarah | dau | 3 m | | | | |
| | | | | | | | |
| DOHERTY | Patrick | head | na | na | 0258547 | | Donegal |
| DOHERTY | Susan | wife | na | na | | 2nd wife | Inishowen W |
| DOHERTY | Patrick | son | 13 | | | 20 in 1851 | Muff |
| DOHERTY | Edward | son | 11 | | | 19 in 1851 | Three Trees |
| DOHERTY | Catherine | dau | 6 | | | 15 in 1851 | |
| DOHERTY | Sophia | dau | 3 | | | 13 in 1851 | |
| DOHERTY | Margaret | dau | 6 m | | | 10 in 1851, children of 2nd marriage | |
| DOHERTY | Michael | son | 0 | | | claimant, 9 in 1851 | |
| DOHERTY | Monasses | son | 0 | | | 8 in 1851 | |
| DOHERTY | John | son | 0 | | | 6 in 1851 | |

| DOHERTY | Charles | son | 0 | | | 5 in 1851 | |
|---------|---------|-----|---|---|---|-----------|---|
| DOHERTY | Bridget | dau | 0 | | | 3 in 1851 | |
| DOHERTY | Susan | dau | 0 | | | claimant, 1 in 1851 | |
| | | | | | | | |
| DOHERTY | William | head | na | na | 0258547 | | Donegal |
| DOHERTY | Bridget | wife | na | na | | | Inishowen E |
| DOHERTY | Lizzie | dau | na | | | Elizabeth, listed, 15 in 1851 | Donagh |
| DOHERTY | John | son | na | | | listed in 1841, 13 in 1851 | Cardonaghy/ |
| DOHERTY | Mary | dau | na | | | listed, claimant, 11 in 1851 | Churchland Qtrs |
| DOHERTY | Hannah | dau | na | | | listed in 1841, 9 in 1851 | |
| DOHERTY | James | son | na | | | listed in 1841, 5 in 1851 | |
| DOHERTY | Bridget | dau | na | | | listed in 1841, not in 1851 | |
| DOHERTY | James | son | 3 m | | | d. 1841 | |
| | | | | | | | |
| DONNEL | John | head | 30 | na | 0258547 | 40 in 1851 | Donegal |
| DONNEL | Eliza | wife | 28 | na | | 42 in 1851 | Raphoe |
| DONNEL | Anton | son | 10 | | | 18 in 1851 | Raphoe |
| DONNEL | John | son | 8 | | | 15 in 1851 | Muntertinny |
| DONNEL | James | son | 6 | | | Cl., 12 in 1851, absent, DONNELL | |
| DONNEL | Robert | son | 4 | | | 10 in 1851 | |
| DONNEL | Roseanna | dau | 0 | | | 7 in 1851 | |
| DONNEL | Bernard | son | 0 | | | 5 in 1851 | |
| | | | | | | | |
| DOUGHERTY | William | head | 44 | 1825 | 0258546 | widower 52 in 1851 | Donegal |
| DOUGHERTY | Catherine | wife | 34 | 1825 | | died age 42 | Raphoe S |
| DOUGHERTY | William | son | 14 | | | 24 in 1851 | Urney |
| DOUGHERTY | James | son | 12 | | | 22 in 1851 | Tullyard |
| DOUGHERTY | Mary | dau | 10 | | | 20 in 1851 | |
| DOUGHERTY | Catherine | dau | 8 | | | 18 in 1851 | |
| DOUGHERTY | Biddy | dau | 6 | | | Bridget, 16 in 1851 | |
| DOUGHERTY | Ann | dau | 4 | | | 14 in 1851 | |
| DOUGHERTY | Neal | son | 18m | | | 12 in 1851 | |
| DOUGHERTY | John | son | 0 | | | claimant, 7/8 in 1851, DOHERTY | |
| | | | | | | | |
| DUGGAN | William | head | na | na | 0258546 | at service, Police Barracks | Donegal |
| DUGGAN | Mary | wife | na | na | | | Raphoe S |
| DUGGAN | Pat | son | 6 | | | | Kilteevoge |
| DUGGAN | Neil | son | 4 | | | | Brockagh |
| DUGGAN | Cormac | son | 2 | | | | (Cloghanay?) |
| | | | | | | | |
| FAULKNER | George | head | na | na | 0993108 | (3 records found for this family) | Donegal |
| FAULKNER | Isabella | wife | na | na | | | Inishowen E |
| FAULKNER | John | son | 22 | | | not listed in 1851 | Moville Up |
| FAULKNER | Mary Anne | dau | 19 | | | 26/30 in 1851 | Carrowkeel |
| FAULKNER | William | son | 17 | | | not listed in 1851 | |
| FAULKNER | Catherine | dau | 15 | | | 24 in 1851 | |
| FAULKNER | Sarah | dau | 13 | | | 23 in 1851 | |
| FAULKNER | Thomas | son | 12 | | | 20 in 1851 | |
| FAULKNER | George | son | 10 | | | claimant, 18 in 1851 | |
| FAULKNER | Patrick | son | 8 | | | 15 in 1851 | |
| | | | | | | | |
| FINLY | Edward | head | 41 | 1821 | 0258547 | 50 in 1851 m. 1826? | Leitrim |
| FINLY | Mary | wife | 39 | | | d. 1847, age 46 | Rosclogher |
| FINLY | James | son | 14 | | | 24 in 1851, absent | Rossinver |
| FINLY | Lucy | dau | 13 | | | 23 in 1851, absent | Derryherk |
| FINLY | Honor | dau | 9 | | | d. age 20 in 1850 | |
| FINLY | Mary | dau | 6 | | | 18 in 1851, absent | |
| FINLY | Bridget | dau | 3 | | | 14 in 1851 | |

| FINLY | Anne | dau | 3 m | | | 12 in 1851 | |
|-------|------|-----|-----|---|---|-----------|---|
| FINLY | Sarah | dau | 0 | | | claimant, 10 in 1851, FINLAY | |
| | | | | | | | |
| FINNEGAN | Patrick | head | 40 | 1833 | 0258547 | | Monaghan |
| FINNEGAN | Mary | wife | 40 | 1833 | | | Farney |
| FINNEGAN | Owen | son | 7 | | | | Donaghmoyne |
| FINNEGAN | Anne | dau | 3 | | | | Drumaconvern |
| FINNEGAN | Michael | son | 3 | | | d. 1839 | |
| FINNEGAN | Bridget | dau | 2 | | | d. 1839 | |
| | | | | | | | |
| GALLAGHER | Charles | head | 32 | 1835 | 0258546 | | Donegal |
| GALLAGHER | Celia | wife | 27 | 1835 | | nee GILLESPIE per Cl. not found | Boylagh |
| GALLAGHER | Mary | dau | 5 | | | | Inishkeene |
| GALLAGHER | James | son | 9 m | | | | Mass |
| GALLAGHER | Owen | son | 1 m | | | d. 1840 | |
| | | | | | | | |
| GALLAGHER | Manus | head | 35 | na | 0993108 | | Donegal |
| GALLAGHER | Naby | wife | 30 | na | 0258547 | | Raphoe S |
| GALLAGHER | Hugh | son | 10 | | | | Kilteevoge |
| GALLAGHER | Catherine | dau | 9 | | | | Kilrean |
| GALLAGHER | Biddy | dau | 7 | | | | |
| GALLAGHER | Peggy | dau | 5 | | | claimant | |
| | | | | | | | |
| GALLAGHER | William | head | na | na | 0258546 | | Donegal |
| GALLAGHER | Letitia | wife | na | na | | | Inishowen W |
| GALLAGHER | James | son | 17 | | | | Burt |
| GALLAGHER | Margaret | dau | 15 | | | | Mulleny |
| GALLAGHER | Mary | dau | 11 | | | | |
| GALLAGHER | Catherine | dau | 12 | | | | |
| GALLAGHER | Letitia | dau | 9 | | | | |
| GALLAGHER | Eliza | dau | 5 | | | | |
| GALLAGHER | John | son | 2 | | | | |
| GALLAGHER | Hugh | son | na | | | listed in 1841, no age | |
| GALLAGHER | William | son | na | | | claimant, listed in 1841, no age | |
| | | | | | | | |
| GALLEN | Maurice | head | 28 | 1838 | 0258547 | or Morris; 32 in 1851, absent | Donegal |
| GALLEN | Ann | wife | 40? | 1838 | | 30 in 1851 (sic) | Raphoe S |
| GALLEN | Ann | dau | 9 m | | | 9 in 1851 | Donaghmore |
| GALLEN | John | son | 1 w | | | d. 1839 | Cronalaghey |
| GALLEN | Mary | dau | 0 | | | claimant, 8 in 1851 | |
| GALLEN | Margaret | dau | 0 | | | 5 in 1851 | |
| GALLEN | Catherine | dau | 0 | | | 2 in 1851 | |
| GALLEN | Catherine | dau | 0 | | | d. 1846, 18 months | |
| | | | | | | | |
| GILLASPY | John | head | 45 | 1837 | 0258547 | GILLESPIE/60 in 1851, m. 1816? | Donegal |
| GILLASPY | Jean | wife | 40 | 1837 | 0993107 | Jane, 50 in 1851 | Banagh |
| GILLASPY | Cathrine | dau | 15 | | | 22 absent in Donegal | Inishkeel |
| GILLASPY | John | son | 13 | | | Owen 20 absent in Donegal | Cloghboy |
| GILLASPY | Dinness | son | 11 | | | Dennis 17 absent in Donegal | |
| GILLASPY | Maggy | dau | 8 | | | 16 in 1851 | |
| GILLASPY | Elener | dau | 2 | | | Ellen, claimant 13, m. McELWEE | |
| GILLASPY | male | son | 3 | | | d. 1837 | |
| | | | | | | | |
| GRANY | James | head | na | na | 0258546 | d. 1844 per 1851 Census | Donegal |
| GRANY | Catherine | wife | na | na | | GRANNEY in 1851 | Inishowen |
| GRANY | Bridget | dau | 18 | | | 24 in 1851 | Fahan Up |
| GRANY | James | son | 17 | | | 22 in 1851 | Gortnaskea |
| GRANY | Mary | dau | 15 | | | 20 in 1851 | |

| GRANY | Charles | son | 13 | | | not in 1851 Census | |
|---|---|---|---|---|---|---|---|
| GRANY | William | son | 11 | | | 16 in 1851 | |
| GRANY | Catherine | dau | 10 | | | 14 in 1851 (ages sic) | |
| GRANY | Roseanne | dau | 9 | | | 12 in 1851 | |
| GRANY | Ellen | dau | 5 | | | 16 in 1851 | |
| GRANY | John | son | 0 | | | claimant, 8 in 1851, spells GRANT | |
| | | | | | | | |
| GUBBIN | Jeremiah | head | na | na | 0258547 | or Darby | Donegal |
| GUBBIN | Mary | wife | na | na | | | Inishowen |
| GUBBIN | Hugh | son | 11 | | | claimant | Clonmany |
| GUBBIN | Michael | son | 10 | | | 18 in 1851 | Roosky |
| GUBBIN | Charles | son | 8 | | | | |
| GUBBIN | John | son | 6 | | | claimant, 16 in 1851 | |
| GUBBIN | Shane | son | 4 | | | | |
| GUBBIN | Eleanor | dau | 1 | | | | |
| GUBBIN | Philip | son | 0 | | | 6 in 1851 listed "Fil" | |
| GUBBIN | Sally | dau | 0 | | | 4 in 1851 | |
| GUBBIN | Bridget | dau | 0 | | | d. 1846 age 9 months | |
| | | | | | | | |
| * HAGGERTY | Margaret | moth | 62 | na | 0258546 | wid, mother of James SLEVAN | |
| | | | | | | | |
| HAMILTON | John | head | na | 1834 | 0258547 | | Donegal |
| HAMILTON | Biddy | wife | na | 1834 | | | Inishowen W |
| HAMILTON | Mary | dau | 17 | | | should be 7? | Burt |
| HAMILTON | Mathew | son | 2 | | | claimant, 10 in 1851 | Bohullion Up |
| | | | | | | | |
| HAMILTON | Robert | head | na | na | 0258546 | | Donegal |
| HAMILTON | Margaret | wife | na | na | | | Tirhugh |
| HAMILTON | Mary | dau | 19 | | | | Templecarn |
| HAMILTON | James | son | 14 | | | | Grousehill |
| HAMILTON | Ann | dau | 7 | | | | |
| HAMILTON | Rebecca | dau | 5 | | | | |
| HAMILTON | Robert | son | 2 | | | | |
| | | | | | | | |
| * HAMLIN | John | serv | 15 | | 0258545 | abs., listed with McNALLY family | |
| | | | | | | | |
| HARPER | Samuel | head | 36 | 1840 | 0258547 | 46 in 1851, m. date 1841 | Donegal |
| HARPER | Letitia | wife | 24 | 1840 | | 30 in 1851, absent | Raphoe S |
| HARPER | Stephen | son | 0 | | | claimant, 7 in 1851 | Donaghmore |
| HARPER | Hugh | son | 0 | | | 5 in 1851 | Cloonarrell |
| HARPER | George | son | 0 | | | 3 in 1851 | |
| HARPER | Jane | dau | 0 | | | 9 mo in 1851 | |
| HARPER | Mary Ann | dau | 0 | | | 5 mo in 1851, absent | |
| HARPER | Anne | moth | 75 | na | | d. 1845 | |
| | | | | | | | |
| HAUGHEY | Charles | head | na | na | 0258547 | deceased 1851 | Donegal |
| HAUGHEY | Catherine | wife | na | na | | deceased 1851 | Tirhugh |
| HAUGHEY | Bridget | dau | 19 | | | 28 in 1851 | Templecarn |
| HAUGHEY | Mary | dau | 17 | | | 24 in 1851 | Lettercran |
| HAUGHEY | Andrew | son | 15 | | | deceased 1851 | |
| HAUGHEY | John | son | 13 | | | 22 in 1851 | |
| HAUGHEY | Catherine | dau | 11 | | | 20 in 1851 | |
| HAUGHEY | Neal | son | 9 | | | deceased 1851 | |
| HAUGHEY | Thomas | son | 7 | | | 13 in 1851 | |
| HAUGHEY | Eleanor | dau | 3 | | | Ellen, claimant, 11 in 1851, m. McCRORY | |

1841 and 1851 combined Irish Census Abstracts (locations in the Republic) from Old Age Pension records held at PRONI in Belfast, transcribed from LDS film – see also 1851 Census Abstracts and Appendix.

| HAUGHEY | Francis | head na | na | 0258546 | | Donegal |
|---------|---------|---------|-----|---------|---|---------|
| HAUGHEY | Margaret | wife na | na | | | Tirhugh |
| HAUGHEY | Jane | dau 12 | | | | Templecarn |
| HAUGHEY | Neal | son 10 | | | | Crilly |
| HAUGHEY | Mary | dau 8 | | | | |
| HAUGHEY | Francis | son 6 | | | | |
| HAUGHEY | Margaret | dau 3 | | | | |
| | | | | | | |
| HEGERTY | James | head na | 1835 | 0258547 | 1851 HEGARTY, m. 1836 | Donegal |
| HEGERTY | Eliza | wife na | 1835 | | Betty in 1851, nee RUSH? | Raphoe S |
| HEGERTY | James | son 5 | | | 14 in 1851 | Urney |
| HEGERTY | Sarah | dau 3 | | | 13 in 1851 | Graffy |
| HEGERTY | Nancy A. | dau 0 | | | Anne, Cl. 7 in 1851, m. KINNEAR | |
| HEGERTY | Mary E. | dau 0 | | | 6 in 1851 | |
| HEGERTY | Eliza | dau 0 | | | 3 in 1851 | |
| HEGERTY | James | fath 61 | | | d. 1848 | |
| HEGERTY – See | | | | | Sally RUSH, M/L | |
| | | | | | | |
| JACK | Peter | head na | 1832 | 0258547 | JACKSON? | Donegal |
| JACK | Nancy | wife na | 1832 | | nee DAVIS | Raphoe S |
| JACK | Ann | dau 8 | | | 17 in 1851 | Urney |
| JACK | Catherine | dau 7 | | | Cl. 15 in 1851, m. ANDERSON | Drumdoit |
| JACK | Isabella | dau 5 | | | 13 in 1851 | |
| JACK | Henry | son 4 | | | 12 in 1851 | |
| JACK | Andy | son 2 | | | 10 in 1851 | |
| JACK | Eliza | dau 0 | | | 8 in 1851 | |
| JACK | James | son 0 | | | 6 in 1851 | |
| JACK | Robert | son 0 | | | 2 in 1851 | |
| JACK | Peter | son 0 | | | d. 1848 age 1 | |
| | | | | | | |
| * JOHNSTON | John | son 1 | | 0258547 | with William BRICE, 1841 only | |
| | | | | | | |
| KEARNEY | James | head na | 1831 | 0258547 | m. 1836? 1851 Census | Louth |
| KEARNEY | Mary | wife na | 1831 | | nee GRIBBEN | Dundalk Lr |
| KEARNEY | John | son 8 | | | 15 in 1851 | Carlingford |
| KEARNEY | Ann | dau 5 | | | 13 in 1851 | Cornamucklagh |
| KEARNEY | Alice | dau 3 | | | 11 in 1851 | |
| KEARNEY | Patrick | son 6 m | | | claimant, 9 in 1851, b. Nov 8, 1840 | |
| KEARNEY | Mary | dau 0 | | | 7 in 1851 | |
| KEARNEY | Michael | son 0 | | | 5 in 1851 | |
| KEARNEY | Catherine | dau 0 | | | 3 in 1851 | |
| KEARNEY | Rose | dau 0 | | | age 1 in 1851 | |
| | | | | | | |
| KELLY | Frank | head na | 1832 | 0258546 | | Donegal |
| KELLY | Biddy | wife na | 1832 | | | Inishowen W |
| KELLY | Cornelius | son 12 | | | 21 in 1851 | Fahan Lr |
| KELLY | James | son 10 | | | not listed in 1851 | Illies |
| KELLY | John | son 8 | | | 14 in 1851 | |
| KELLY | Biddy | dau 6 | | | 18 in 1851 | |
| KELLY | Cicely | dau 4 | | | claimant, 11 in 1851 | |
| KELLY | Susan | dau 11m | | | 12 in 1851 | |
| | | | | | | |
| KELLY | James | head na | na | 0258547 | | Donegal |
| KELLY | Catherine | wife na | na | | | Inishowen E |
| KELLY | John | son 11 | | | | Moville Up |
| KELLY | Paddy | son 7 | | | | |

| Surname | Name | Rel | Age | Year | Ref | Notes | Place |
|---------|------|-----|-----|------|-----|-------|-------|
| KELLY | Celia | dau | 5 | | | | |
| KELLY | Peggy | dau | 2 | | | deceased | |
| KELLY | Catherine | dau | 1 | | | claimant | |
| | | | | | | | |
| KELLY | Michael | head | na | 1831 | 0258546 | | Monaghan |
| KELLY | Mary | wife | na | 1831 | | | Cremorne |
| KELLY | Patrick | son | 9 | | | | Muckno |
| KELLY | James | son | 7 | | | | Tullynagrow |
| KELLY | Rose | dau | 5 | | | | |
| | | | | | | | |
| KELLY | Patrick | head | na | na | 0258546 | | Donegal |
| KELLY | Mary | wife | na | na | | | Inishowen E |
| KELLY | Ann | dau | 12 | | | 20 in 1851 | Moville Lr |
| KELLY | Ellen | dau | 11 | | | 18 in 1851 | Bredagh Glen |
| KELLY | Margaret | dau | 9 | | | 16 in 1851 | |
| KELLY | Michael | son | 7 | | | 14 in 1851 | |
| KELLY | Mary | dau | 6 | | | 15 in 1851 | |
| KELLY | Bridget | dau | 4 | | | 13 in 1851 | |
| KELLY | Patrick | son | 3m | | | claimant, 7 in 1851 | |
| KELLY | Andrew | son | 0 | | | 5 in 1851 | |
| | | | | | | | |
| KIDD | Thomas | head | 34 | 1833 | 0258547 | 42 in 1851 | Donegal |
| KIDD | Catherine | wife | 35 | 1833 | | 43 in 1851, nee GARA | Inishowen W |
| KIDD | John | son | 5 | | | not in 1851 Census | Fahan Up |
| KIDD | William | son | 2 | | | 11 in 1851 | Ballynahone |
| KIDD | Thomas | son | 0 | | | claimant, 7 in 1851 | |
| KIDD | Henry | son | 0 | | | 5 in 1851 | |
| KIDD | Eliza J. | dau | 0 | | | 2 in 1851 | |
| | | | | | | | |
| LYNCH | George | head | na | na | 0258545 | | Donegal |
| LYNCH | Ellen | wife | na | na | | | Inishowen W |
| LYNCH | Betty | dau | 15 | | | 22 in 1851 | Fahan Lr |
| LYNCH | Nancy | dau | 13 | | | 20 in 1851 | Ballynarry |
| LYNCH | Hannah | dau | 11 | | | 18 in 1851 | |
| LYNCH | James | son | 9 | | | 17 in 1851 | |
| LYNCH | Constantin | son | 5 | | | Constantine, 15 in 1851 | |
| LYNCH | Letty | dau | 3 | | | 12 in 1851 | |
| LYNCH | Edward | son | 0 | | | claimant, 10 in 1851 | |
| | | | | | | | |
| MAGEE | Richard | head | 30? | 1820 | 0258546 | | Donegal |
| MAGEE | Easter | wife | 36? | 1820 | | | Raphoe No |
| MAGEE | Nancy | dau | 17 | | | | Taughboyne |
| MAGEE | Neal | son | 16 | | | absent | Carnshanagh & |
| MAGEE | John | son | 13 | | | absent | Drummucklagh |
| MAGEE | Mary | dau | 11 | | | claimant | |
| MAGEE | Richard | son | 8 | | | absent | |
| | | | | | | | |
| MARTIN | Hugh | head | na | 1825 | 0258546 | | Donegal |
| MARTIN | Sidney | wife | na | 1825 | | | Tirhugh |
| MARTIN | Joseph | son | 13 | | | 22 in 1851 m. Hannah 1850 | Templecare |
| MARTIN | Hannah | D/L | na | | | 30 in 1851 m. 1850 | Belalt S |
| MARTIN | Hugh | son | 9 | | | claimant, 18 in 1851 | |
| MARTIN | Mary Jane | dau | 7 | | | 16 in 1851 | |
| MARTIN | Lucinda | dau | 5 | | | Lucy, 14 in 1851 | |
| | | | | | | | |
| MOLLOY | Patrick | head | na | 1836 | 0993107 | | Donegal |

| | | | | | | | |
|---|---|---|---|---|---|---|---|
| MOLLOY | Susan | wife | na | 1825 | | m. 1825/1836 | Inishowen E |
| MOLLOY | James | son | 11 | | | step son? | Moville Lr |
| MOLLOY | John | son | 1 | | | claimant, 10 in 1851 | Ballymacarthur |
| | | | | | | | |
| MONAGHAN | Felix | head | 38 | 1827 | 0993108 | m. date 1829 in 1851 Census | Donegal |
| MONAGHAN | Ellen | wife | 30 | 1827 | 0993104 | | Tirhugh |
| MONAGHAN | Rose | dau | 13 | | | 19 in 1851 | Templecarn |
| MONAGHAN | Pat | son | 11 | | | 16 in 1851 | Tamlaght |
| MONAGHAN | Ann | dau | 9 | | | 15 in 1851 | |
| MONAGHAN | William | son | 5 | | | 13 in 1851 | 1851: |
| MONAGHAN | Celia | dau | 3 | | | Cisly, 10 in 1851 | Tyrone |
| MONAGHAN | Felix | son | 0 | | | claimant, 7 in 1851 | Strabane Lr |
| MONAGHAN | John | son | 1 | | | 5 in 1851 | Urney |
| MONAGHAN | Biddy | dau | 0 | | | claimant, 2 in 1851 | Ballycolman |
| | | | | | | | |
| MULHERON | Hugh | head | na | na | 0993106 | | Donegal |
| MULHERON | Bridget | wife | na | na | | | Raphoe |
| MULHERON | Ellen | dau | 1 | | | 10 in 1851 | Donaghmore |
| MULHERON | Mary | dau | 0 | | | Cl. 7 in 1851 m. KENNEDY | Carnowen |
| MULHERON | Charles | son | 0 | | | 1 in 1851 | |
| MULHERON | S ---- | na | 3 m | | | d. 1842 | |
| MULHERON | Catherine | dau | 2 | | | d. 1847 | |
| MULHERON | Hugh | son | 5 | | | d. 1847 | |
| | | | | | | | |
| MULLOY | Edward | head | 53 | na | 0258547 | | Donegal |
| MULLOY | Annie | wife | 40 | na | | also Nancy | Boylagh |
| MULLOY | Mary | dau | 13 | | | | Lettermacaward |
| MULLOY | Nancy | dau | 12 | | | | Boyoughter |
| MULLOY | Veble | na | 9 | | | | |
| MULLOY | Manus | son | 7 | | | | |
| MULLOY | Bdgi (sic) | dau | 5 | | | | |
| | | | | | | | |
| McALEA | George | head | 21 | 1839 | 0258546 | 29 in 1851, McLEA | Donegal |
| McALEA | Mary | wife | 26 | 1839 | | 30 in 1851, nee McATEER | Raphoe |
| McALEA | James | son | 1 | | | 11 in 1851 | All Saints |
| McALEA | William | son | 1 m | | | 9 in 1851 | Ballybegly |
| McALEA | Margaret | dau | 0 | | | claimant, 7 in 1851, m. McDAID, also McCLAY? | |
| McALEA | Patrick | son | 0 | | | 4 in 1851 | |
| McALEA | Elenor | dau | 0 | | | 1 in 1851 | |
| | | | | | | | |
| McCAFFERTY | James | head | na | 1830 | 0258546 | | Donegal |
| McCAFFERTY | Mary | wife | na | 1830 | | nee DALY? per claimant not found | Tirhugh |
| McCAFFERTY | Thomas | son | 10 | | | | Templecarn |
| McCAFFERTY | William | son | 9 | | | | Belalt S |
| McCAFFERTY | Sarah | dau | 6 | | | | |
| McCAFFERTY | Francis | son | 4 | | | | |
| McCAFFERTY | Rosey | dau | 1 | | | | |
| | | | | | | | |
| McCALLION | Ann | head | na | na | 0258547 | | Donegal |
| McCALLION | Peter | son | na | na | | head in 1851 | Inishowen W |
| McCALLION | Catherine | wife | na | na | | listed in 1851 | Burt |
| McCALLION | Margaret | gr/d | 6 | | | not listed in 1851 | Bunnamayne |
| McCALLION | Anne | gr/d | 3 | | | 13 in 1851 with Peter | |
| McCALLION | Daniel | gr/s | 4 m | | | claimant, 10 in 1851, McCULLION, with Peter | |
| McCALLION | Catherine | gr/d | 0 | | | 3 in 1851 with Peter | |
| McCALLION | Peter | gr/s | 0 | | | claimant 1 in 1851 with Peter | |

| McCOLGAN | Peter | head | na | 1829 0993108 | | Donegal |
|----------|-------|------|-----|--------------|--|---------|
| McCOLGAN | Mary Ann | wife | na | 1829 | nee TONER | Inishowen W |
| McCOLGAN | Denis | son | 11 | | 21 in 1851 | Muff |
| McCOLGAN | Edward | son | 9 | | 20 in 1851 | Eskaheen |
| McCOLGAN | Sarah Ann | dau | 3 | | 12 in 1851 | |
| McCOLGAN | Elizabeth | dau | 9 | | 1st Elizabeth? d. before 1843? | |
| McCOLGAN | Elizabeth | dau | 0 | | claimant, 8 in 1851, m. DUFFY | |
| McCOLGAN | William | son | 0 | | 5 in 1851 | |
| | | | | | | |
| McCOOL | Cornelius | head | na | na 0258547 | d. 1842 | Donegal |
| McCOOL | Sarah | wife | na | na | Arthur NOGHER noted on census | Inishowen E |
| McCOOL | Michael | son | na | | 22 in 1851 | Donagh |
| McCOOL | Rose | dau | na | | 20 in 1851 | Churchland Qtrs |
| McCOOL | Hugh | son | na | | 18 in 1851 | |
| McCOOL | Pat | son | na | | 12 in 1851 | |
| McCOOL | John | son | 1 | | claimant, 10 in 1851 | |
| | | | | | | |
| McELENEY | Daniel | head | na | na 0258547 | | Donegal |
| McELENEY | Mary | wife | na | na | | Inishowen E |
| McELENEY | Grace | dau | 8 | | | Clonmany |
| McELENEY | William | son | 7 | | | Lacurrsy/Legacurry |
| McELENEY | Patrick | son | 4 | | | |
| McELENEY | Dennis | son | 2 | | | |
| McELENEY | Patt | son | na | | d. 1836 | |
| | | | | | | |
| McFEELY | Neal | head | na | na 0258547 | d. 1842 | Donegal |
| McFEELY | Ellen | wife | na | na | | Inishowen E |
| McFEELY | Mary | dau | 12 | | 20 in 1851 | Moville Up |
| McFEELY | Dan | son | 9 | | 16 in 1851 | Cabry |
| McFEELY | Margaret | dau | 7 | | 14 in 1851 | |
| McFEELY | Anne | dau | 4 | | 12 in 1851 | |
| McFEELY | Ellen | dau | 1 | | claimant, 10 in 1851, m. DEENEY | |
| | | | | | | |
| McGETTIGAN | Thomas | head | 45 | 1831 0258547 | 52 in 1851 m. date 1828 | Donegal |
| McGETTIGAN | Anne | wife | 25 | 1831 | 42 in 1851, nee PARK | Kilmacrenan |
| McGETTIGAN | William | son | 8 | | 18 in 1851 | Tullyfern |
| McGETTIGAN | Fanny | dau | 7 | | 17 in 1851 | Ballyarr Glebe |
| McGETTIGAN | James | son | 5 | | 15 in 1851 | |
| McGETTIGAN | John | son | 4 | | 13 in 1851 | |
| McGETTIGAN | Neal | son | 3 | | 11 in 1851 | |
| McGETTIGAN | Ellenor | dau | 1 | | Ellen, claimant, 10 in 1851 | |
| McGETTIGAN | Nancy | dau | 0 | | 9 in 1851 | |
| McGETTIGAN | Thomas | son | 0 | | 7 in 1851 | |
| McGETTIGAN | Charles | son | 0 | | 5 in 1851 | |
| McGETTIGAN | Margaret | dau | 0 | | 3 in 1851 | |
| McGETTIGAN | Daniel | son | 0 | | 1 in 1851 | |
| McGETTIGAN | Bernard | visit | 18 | | same surname | |
| McGETTIGAN | William | fath | 70 | na | d. 1837 | |
| | | | | | | |
| McGILLEN | James | head | 44 | 1825 0258546 | | Donegal |
| McGILLEN | Sally | wife | 35 | 1825 | | Boylagh |
| McGILLEN | Susan | dau | 14 | | | Camus |
| McGILLEN | James | son | 9 | | | Strabane |
| McGILLEN | Seragh | dau | 1 | | d. 1840 smallpox | Main St. |
| | | | | | | |
| McGINLEY | Charles | head | na | 1835 0258547 | 35 in 1851 | Donegal |
| McGINLEY | Mary | wife | na | 1835 | 31 in 1851 | Raphoe |
| McGINLEY | Margaret | dau | 2 | | 13 in 1851 | Clonleigh |
| McGINLEY | Mary | dau | 7 m | | 10 in 1851 | Millsessiagh |
| McGINLEY | Daniel | son | 0 | | 8 in 1851 | 1851: |

| | | | | | | |
|---|---|---|---|---|---|---|
| McGINLEY | Ellen | dau | 0 | | d. 1849 age 5 years | Ballindroit T |
| McGINLEY | Charles | son | 0 | | d. 1850 age 9 mo. (claimant) | |
| | | | | | | |
| McGINLY | John | head | 40 | 1825 0258547 | also McGINLAY | Donegal |
| McGINLY | Sarah | wife | 40 | 1825 | nee GALLAGHER per Cl. not fd. | Kilmacrenan |
| McGINLY | Hugh | son | 11 | | | Tullaghobegly |
| McGINLY | Magy | dau | 7 | | | Beltany Lr |
| McGINLY | Michael | son | 4 | | | |
| McGINLY | Denis | son | 1 | | age 15 months, Dinnis | |
| McGINLY | Nola | dau | 6 m | | d. 1833 | |
| McGINLY | Margaret | dau | 13 | | d. 1841 | |
| | | | | | | |
| McGLONAHEY | Samuel | head | 24 | 1833 0258547 | | Donegal |
| McGLONAHEY | Margaret | wife | 24 | 1833 | | Raphoe N |
| McGLONAHEY | Fanny | dau | 7 | | | Taughboyne |
| McGLONAHEY | Cathrine | dau | 5 | | | Listicall |
| McGLONAHEY | Sarah | dau | 2 | | | |
| McGLONAHEY | Charles | son | 1 m | | | |
| | | | | | | |
| McGLYNN | Patrick | head | na | 1826 0258547 | d. 1851? | Donegal |
| McGLYNN | Catherine | wife | na | 1826 | | Kilmacrenan |
| McGLYNN | Julia | dau | 16 | | 23 (sic) in 1851 | Conwal |
| McGLYNN | Patrick | son | 14 | | 25 in 1851 | Letterkenny Town |
| McGLYNN | Barney | son | 13 | | not listed in 1851 | Church Lane |
| McGLYNN | Edward | son | 12 | | 18 in 1851 | |
| McGLYNN | Hugh | son | 11 | | 17 in 1851 | |
| McGLYNN | Catherine | dau | 10 | | 16 in 1851 | |
| McGLYNN | Jane | dau | 6 | | 14 in 1851 | |
| McGLYNN | Joan | dau | na | | 14 in 1851 | |
| McGLYNN | Biddy | dau | 3 | | 12 in 1851 | |
| McGLYNN | Annie | dau | 3 m | | 10 in 1851 | |
| McGLYNN | Mary | dau | 0 | | claimant, 8 in 1851, m. BOYLE | |
| McGLYNN | Susie | dau | 0 | | 4 in 1851 | |
| McGLYNN | Biddy | dau | 0 | | 3 in 1851 | |
| | | | | | | |
| McLAUGHLIN | Hugh | head | na | na | 0258545 | Donegal |
| McLAUGHLIN | Sarah | wife | na | na | | Lon'derry City |
| McLAUGHLIN | Peter | son | 12 | | not in 1851 Census | 226 Bishop St. |
| McLAUGHLIN | Roseanne | dau | 10 | | 17 in 1851 | |
| McLAUGHLIN | Sarah | dau | 7 | | 13 in 1851 | |
| McLAUGHLIN | Hugh | son | 4 | | not in 1851 Census | |
| McLAUGHLIN | Daniel | son | 0 | | claimant, 8 in 1851 | |
| McLAUGHLIN | Thomas | son | 9 m | | not in 1851 Census (two children d.) | |
| | | | | | | |
| McLAUGHLIN | John | head | na | na | 0258547 | Donegal |
| McLAUGHLIN | Sarah | wife | na | na | | Inishowen E |
| McLAUGHLIN | Nancy | dau | 11 | | | Clonmany |
| McLAUGHLIN | Unity | dau | 2 | | | Cloontagh |
| McLAUGHLIN | Catherine | dau | 3 | | d. 1837 | |
| McLAUGHLIN | Mary | dau | 6 | | d. 1838 | |
| | | | | | | |
| McLOUGHLIN | William | head | 24 | 1838 0258546 | | Donegal |
| McLOUGHLIN | Margaret | wife | 24 | 1838 | nee McGINLEY per Cl. not found | Inishowen W |
| McLOUGHLIN | Elinor | dau | 2 | | | Burt |
| McLOUGHLIN | Mary | dau | 3m | | (Carrowreagh?) Carnowen | |
| | | | | | | |
| McMENAMIN | John | head | na | na | 0258547 (James) | Donegal |
| McMENAMIN | Mary Ellen | wife | na | na | | Raphoe S |
| McMENAMIN | Patrick | son | 5 | | 15 in 1851 | Donaghmore |
| McMENAMIN | Sarah | dau | 6 m | | d. 1838 | Egglybane |

| Surname | Name | Rel | Age | Year | Number | Notes | Place |
|---|---|---|---|---|---|---|---|
| McMENAMIN | John | son | 0 | | | 8 in 1851 | |
| McMENAMIN | James | son | 0 | | | (John) claimant, 6 in 1851 | |
| McMENAMIN | Michael | son | 0 | | | d. age 3 in 1842 | |
| McMENAMIN | Sarah | dau | 0 | | | d. age 6 in 1843 | |
| | | | | | | | |
| McNALLY | John | head | 38 | 1833 | 0258545 | | Monaghan |
| McNALLY | Bridget | wife | 32 | 1833 | | | Cremorne |
| McNALLY | Patrick | son | 5 | | | absent | Clontibret |
| McNALLY | Mary | dau | 2 | | | d. 1840 | Carrancreevy |
| McNALLY | Mary | dau | 4 m | | | claimant | |
| McNALLY – See | | | | | | John HAMLIN, servant | |
| | | | | | | | |
| McNIGHT | James | head | na | na | 0258546 | | Donegal |
| McNIGHT | Margaret | wife | na | na | | | Raphoe S |
| McNIGHT | Ellen | dau | 7 | | | | Donaghmore |
| McNIGHT | James | son | 5 | | | claimant | Carrickshandrum |
| McNIGHT | William | son | 2 | | | | |
| | | | | | | | |
| O'DONNELL | Neal | head | na | na | 0258547 | | Donegal |
| O'DONNELL | Mary | wife | na | na | | | Boylagh |
| O'DONNELL | Roger | son | 4 | | | 15 in 1851 | Lettermacward |
| O'DONNELL | James | son | 1 | | | 12 in 1851 | Madavagh |
| O'DONNELL | Mary | dau | 0 | | | 10 in 1851 | |
| O'DONNELL | Neal | son | 0 | | | claimant, 7 in 1851 | |
| O'DONNELL | Pat | son | 0 | | | 4 in 1851 | |
| O'DONNELL | Grace | dau | 0 | | | 2 in 1851 | |
| | | | | | | | |
| O'DONNELL | Neal | head | 50 | 1820 | 0993108 | | Donegal |
| O'DONNELL | Nancy | wife | 50 | 1820 | | | Kilmacrenan |
| O'DONNELL | Farryal (?) | son | 21 | | | | Tullaghobegley |
| O'DONNELL | Anthony | son | 17 | | | | Dore |
| O'DONNELL | Neal | son | 14 | | | | |
| O'DONNELL | Grace | dau | 8 | | | | |
| O'DONNELL | Edward | son | 6 | | | | |
| O'DONNELL | Edward | son | 15 | | | d. 1822(?) 15 mo? | |
| O'DONNELL | Daniel | son | 16 | | | d. 1838 | |
| | | | | | | | |
| O'DONNELL | Owen | head | na | na | 0258547 | | Donegal |
| O'DONNELL | Nancy | wife | na | na | | | Inishowen E |
| O'DONNELL | Sarah | dau | 8 | | | | Donagh |
| O'DONNELL | John | son | 4 m | | | | Cardoagh |
| O'DONNELL | Mary | dau | 0 | | | claimant, 7 in 1851 | |
| O'DONNELL | Teresa | dau | 1 | | | d. 1841 | |
| | | | | | | | |
| ROBINSON | Henry | head | na | 1839 | 0258547 | | Dublin |
| ROBINSON | Elizabeth | wife | na | 1839 | 0993094 | | Newcastle |
| ROBINSON | Elizabeth | dau | 9 m | | | Elizabeth Ann, 10 in 1851 | Lucan |
| ROBINSON | HenryDuke | son | 0 | | | claimant, 9 in 1851 | Lucan |
| ROBINSON | Mary Jane | dau | 0 | | | 7 in 1851 | 1851:Down, Ards Lr |
| ROBINSON | James O. | son | 0 | | | James Olliffe, 4 in 1851 | Newtownards |
| ROBINSON | William | son | 0 | | | 2 in 1851 | Loughriescouse |
| | | | | | | | |
| RODDY | John | head | 70 | na | 0258547 | | Donegal |
| RODDY | Mary | wife | 60 | na | | absent? | Inishowen W |
| RODDY | Pat | son | na | 1827 | 0993107 | 45 head in 1851, RUDDY | Fahan Up |
| RODDY | Mary | D/L | na | 1827 | | 40 in 1851 | Crislaghkeel |

-15-

| | | | | | | | |
|---|---|---|---|---|---|---|---|
| RODDY | Margery | gr/d | 11 | | | 20 in 1851 | |
| RODDY | William | gr/s | 9 | | | 18 in 1851 | |
| RODDY | Margaret | gr/d | 7 | | | 16 in 1851 | |
| RODDY | John | gr/s | 6 | | | 15 in 1851 | |
| RODDY | Patrick | gr/s | 3 | | | 13 in 1851 | |
| RODDY | Charles | gr/s | 0 | | | 10 in 1851 | |
| RODDY | Hugh | gr/s | 0 | | | 3 in 1851 | |
| RODDY | James | gr/s | 0 | | | 3 in 1851, claimant | |
| | | | | | | | |
| ROONEY | Bernard | head | na | 1831 | 0993108 | spelled Berman | Donegal |
| ROONEY | Martha | wife | na | 1831 | | | Raphoe S |
| ROONEY | Patrick | son | 9 | | | | Convoy |
| ROONEY | John | son | 6 | | | | Killynure |
| ROONEY | Denis | son | 6 | | | | |
| ROONEY | Bernard | son | 10m | | | | |
| | | | | | | | |
| ROONEY | Constantine | head | 37 | na | 0258547 | or Con, farmer | Monaghan |
| ROONEY | Catherine | wife | 36 | na | | nee McDONALD | Farney |
| ROONEY | Bryan | son | 6 | | | | Donaghmoyne |
| ROONEY | Francis | son | 6 m | | | claimant | Agheeshal |
| | | | | | | | |
| * RUSH | Sally | M/L | 73 | na | | d. 1846 (James Hegarty, 1851) | |
| | | | | | | | |
| SHEALS | John | head | 30 | 1838 | 0258547 | | Donegal |
| SHEALS | Ann | wife | 25 | 1838 | | nee COYLE | Raphoe N |
| SHEALS | Ellener | dau | 2 | | | Ellen, claimant, m. O'DONNELL | Raphoe |
| SHEALS | Margaret | dau | 3 m | | | | Ballyholey Far |
| | | | | | | | |
| SIMISON | Samuel | head | 40 | 1818 | 0258547 | m. date 1828? 45 wid in 1851 | Donegal |
| SIMISON | Mary | wife | 32 | 1818 | | d. 1849 age 40 | Raphoe |
| SIMISON | Joseph | na | 16 | | | not listed 1851 | Clonleigh |
| SIMISON | Robert | son | 9 | | | 17 in 1851 | Cunninghamstown/ |
| SIMISON | Margaret | dau | 6 | | | 13 in 1851 | Legnabraid |
| SIMISON | Thomas | son | 3 | | | 12 in 1851 | |
| SIMISON | Francis | son | 1 | | | not listed in 1851 | |
| SIMISON | Fanny | dau | 0 | | | claimant, 8 in 1851 | |
| SIMISON | Eliza Ann | dau | 0 | | | 6 in 1851 | |
| SIMISON | Mary | dau | 0 | | | d. 1849 age 3 months | |
| | | | | | | | |
| SLEVAN | James | head | na | na | 0258546 | | Donegal |
| SLEVAN | Betty | wife | na | na | | Elizabeth, nee BAXTER | Tirhugh |
| SLEVAN | James | son | 14 | | | | Kilbarron |
| SLEVAN | Rebecca | dau | 11 | | | | Ballyshannon |
| SLEVAN | Mary | dau | 8 | | | | Ballynanadd St. |
| SLEVAN – See | | | | | | Margaret HAGGERTY, mother & Rebecca BAXTER, M/L | |
| | | | | | | | |
| SOMERS | Thomas | head | na | 1832 | 0258546 | | Cavan |
| SOMERS | Jane | wife | na | 1832 | | | Clanmahon |
| SOMERS | William | son | na | | | | Ballynachugh |
| SOMERS | Mary | dau | 3 | | | | Pottle/ |
| SOMERS | Ellen | dau | 1 | | | | Pottleboy |
| SOMERS | James | son | 5 m | | | | |
| SOMERS | Thomas | son | na | | | | |
| | | | | | | | |
| SWEENEY | John | head | na | na | 0258546 | | Donegal |
| SWEENEY | Mary | wife | na | na | | | Inishowen W |
| SWEENEY | Margaret | dau | 8 | | | 17 in 1851 | Inch |

| | | | | | | |
|---|---|---|---|---|---|---|
| SWEENEY | Mary Anne | dau | 4 | | 14 in 1851 | Castlequarter |
| SWEENEY | Dan | son | 2 | | 12 in 1851 | |
| SWEENEY | Jane | dau | 0 | | 9 in 1851 | |
| SWEENEY | Sarah | dau | 0 | | claimant, 7 in 1851, m. CRAIG | |
| SWEENEY | Lizzie | dau | 0 | | 5 in 1851 | |
| SWEENEY | John | son | 0 | | 2 in 1851 | |
| SWEENEY | Mary Anne | dau | na | | d. date na | |
| | | | | | | |
| TIERNAN | John | head | 41 | 1827 0258546 | | Leitrim |
| TIERNAN | Bridget | wife | 36 | 1827 | d. 1848, age 42, nee DONGAN | Mohill |
| TIERNAN | Mary | dau | na | | d. 1838 age 9 | Cloone |
| TIERNAN | Ellen | dau | 13 | | 21 absent in 1851 | Tooman |
| TIERNAN | Bridget | dau | 11 | | 19 in 1851 | |
| TIERNAN | Margret | dau | 6 | | d. 1851 age 16 | |
| TIERNAN | Pat | son | 4 | | 14 in 1851 | |
| TIERNAN | Anne | dau | 2 | | 11 in 1851 | |
| TIERNAN | Catherine | dau | 0 | | 8 in 11 | |
| TIERNAN | Eliza | dau | 0 | | claimant, 6 in 1851, m. LYONS | |
| TIERNAN | John | son | 0 | | 4 in 1851 | |
| | | | | | | |
| TURNER | James | head | na | 1837 0258547 | in America in 1851? | Cavan |
| TURNER | Elizabeth | wife | na | 1837 | | Tullygarvey |
| TURNER | Mary | dau | 2 | | | Larah |
| TURNER | John | son | 3 m | | claimant | Moneycass Glebe |
| | | | | | | |
| WALKER | David | head | na | na 0258546 | | Donegal |
| WALKER | Betty | wife | na | na | nee KILGORE | Inishowen W |
| WALKER | Robert | son | 13 | | 22 in 1851 | Muff |
| WALKER | William | son | 10 | | 19 in 1851 | Muff |
| WALKER | Jane | dau | 7 | | 17 in 1851 | |
| WALKER | Isabella | dau | 4 | | 14 in 1851 | |
| WALKER | Adam | son | 6 m | | claimant, 10 in 1851 | |
| WALKER | Lizzie | dau | 0 | | 7 in 1851 | |
| WALKER | David | son | 0 | | 4 in 1851 | |
| WALKER | Rebecca | dau | 0 | | 6 mo in 1851 | |
| | | | | | | |
| WARNOCK | David | head | na | na 0258546 | | Donegal |
| WARNOCK | Margaret | wife | na | na | Mary Anne 1841 Census & per Cl. | Inishowen |
| WARNOCK | John | son | 8 | | claimant, na in 1851 | Moville Lr |
| WARNOCK | Robert | son | na | | 16 in 1851 | Gulladoo/Gulladuff |
| WARNOCK | David | son | na | | 14 in 1851 | |
| WARNOCK | Jane | dau | na | | 11 in 1851 | |
| WARNOCK | Mary | dau | 0 | | 9 in 1851 | |
| WARNOCK | Moses | son | 0 | | 4 in 1851 | |
| WARNOCK | James | son | 0 | | 1 in 1851 | |
| | | | | | | |
| WILSON | Robert | head | 26 | 1836 0258547 | 30 in 1851 Census | Donegal |
| WILSON | Jane | wife | 25 | 1836 | Jean? 33 in 1851, nee DOHERTY | Raphoe |
| WILSON | Mary Ann | dau | 2 | | 10 in 1851, bap Feb 17 1839 | Clonleigh |
| WILSON | James | son | 4 | | d. 1840 | Mulnaveagh |
| WILSON | Robert | son | 0 | | 8 in 1851, bap Oct 31 1841 | |
| WILSON | Elizabeth | dau | 0 | | Eliza, Cl. 6 in 1851, m. LAFFERTY 1851: | |
| WILSON | Jane | dau | 0 | | 4 in 1851, bap Sep 9 1845 | Gortgranagh |
| WILSON | James | son | 0 | | 2 in 1851, bap Sep 24 1848 | |

# APPENDIX FOR 1841 IRISH CENSUS ABSTRACTS
from Old Age Pension records held in Belfast at the Public Record Office of Northern Ireland for Republic of Ireland locations

Bernard CARVILLE 30 head m. 1838, Alice 5 wife; ABS: Thomas 18 months son. DEC: Margaret 1 dau d. 1839 (light record).
> Tullynageer, Muckno, Cremorne, Monaghan, LDS film no. 0258547

Charles HENRY 39 head m. 1835/1840, Ann 29 wife m. 1840. DEC: Elnor (nee DOUGHARTY per claimant not found) wife d. 1837.
> Malin T, Clonca, Inishowen E, Donegal, 0258547

Biddy JORDAN 50 head n.m. (widow?) with children Charles BURROWS 23, Loftus 17, Lewis 15, Teresa 13, Bess 9 (claimant m. GREEN) (children's surname Burrows, rel. na).
> Knockatober, Kilross, Tirerrill, Sligo, 0258545

James McCROSSAN 24 head m. 1840, Ann 24 wife, Fanny 4 months dau (claimant Frances 11 in 1851, parents 43 and 40 spelled Crossan).
> Cabry, Up Moville, Inishowen E, Donegal, 0258547

John SHERIDAN 56 head m. 1813, Ann 56 wife, Pat McCLINE 26 S/L m. 1839, Mary McCline (nee Sheridan) 22 dau m. 1839, Steven McCline 2 months gr son, John Sheridan 26 son, Elenor Sheridan 24 dau n.m. (m. GREEN, mother of Mary Ann Green? claimant not found), Patrick Sheridan 16 son, Margaret Sheridan 10 dau; ABS: Biddy Sheridan 20 dau, Susan Sheridan 18 dau.
> Drumhallagh, Killygarvan, Kilmacrenan, Donegal, 0258545

Elizabeth SHORT 50 head n.m., Mary McQUADE 40 niece, Anne (claimant m. GRIMLEY) 12, Mary 10, John 8, children of Mary McQuade. DEC: Catherine Short, sister of Elizabeth, d. 1838 age 60, Sarah SIMPLE 80 lodger d. 1839.
> Knockronaghan, Donagh, Trough, Monaghan, 0258545

Pady WARD 28 head m. 1837, Mary 28 wife (nee BROWN per claimant not found), John 3. DEC: Brine 4 months d. 1838.
> Adderwell (Adderwal), Inishkeel, Boylagh, Donegal, 0258547

Mary Ann WILKIE 50 head m. 1808 widow (65 m. 1811 in 1851 Census), Mary Ann Wilkie 23 dau (30 in 1851), Eliza Wilkie 20 dau (m. FORSYTHE d. 1847 age 26), James Wilkie 19 son (26 in 1851 Census), William BUCHANAN 11 nephew (listed age 20 as gr son in 1851 Census), Jane Forsythe (claimant, 8 in 1851 Census) gr dau. DEC: John Buchanan 2 nephew(?) d. 1839.
> Croaghan, Clonleigh, Raphoe N, Donegal, 0258547

Robert YOUNG 48 head m. 1817 (57 in 1851), Martha 47 wife (56 in 1851), m. date 1815 in 1851 Census, Daniel WAKEFIELD 26 S/L m. 1835 (35 in 1851), Mary A. Wakefield 26 dau m. 1835 (34 in 1851), Eliza Wakefield 30 in 1841 niece, Mary A. Young 14 in 1841 cousin, Margaret DEAN 13 in 1841 serv, Eliza A. Wakefield 7 in 1851 (claimant m. JAMES, parents Daniel and Mary A. Wakefield), Mary J. Wakefield age 3 months in 1851.
> Fogher, Tullyfern, Kilmacrenan, Donegal, 0258547

Burnt fragment of the 1841 Census of Ireland, County Cork

Burnt fragment of the 1841 Census of Ireland, County Cork

INFORMATION FROM BURNT FRAGMENTS OF THE 1841 CENSUS FOR IRELAND –
taken June 6, 1841. Locations: County <u>Cork</u>, County <u>Fermanagh</u>, County <u>Waterford</u>; for a
few listings no location could be determined. Some locations were added from a previously
transcribed list of householders found on the same film, following the fragment portion. This
is an edited composite. Locations in Northern Ireland included.

Mary BARRY 34 wife m. 1832 R, Robert 9 son R, Mary 7 dau, Alley(?) Barry 75 M/L
widow m. 1800, Alley(?) NAIL 20 S/L n.m.; ABS: Edward Barry 41 head, laborer, in Cty.----
-- (illegible). DEC: Denis Nail 61 F/L lab d. 1831(?) -------- in his leg, Catherine Nail 30 S/L
d. 1833 childbirth, Catherine Barry 1 dau d. 1835 convulsions, Edward Barry 1 son d. 1835
convulsions, Johana Barry 18 mo dau d. 1840 decline.
    No. 5 <u>Cork</u> WR ED W Carbery, Aughadown, Beg M------

Cornelius BRYAN 51(?) head, lab, wife 31, Bridget 5, Ellen 2. DEC: Luty age 1 dau, all b. in
Cork.
    <u>Cork</u>, ED W Carbery

Robert CASY 44 head m. 1820 farmer, Margret 44, William 18 son lab R, Patt 16 son lab,
Cathrine 14 dau missing school, Mary DONOUGH 13 serv missing school, Patt COLLINS 24
serv lab, Mary Casy 70 visitor m. 1816.
    No. 29 <u>Cork</u> ED W Carbery, Drinagh, Driminidy

Michael CAVERLY 31 head m. 1820, Mary 33 wife, Michael 14 son lab R b. Co Cork, John
13 son lab R b. Co Cork. DEC: dau age 6 d. 1840 stoppage in air.
    No. 5 <u>Cork</u> ED W Carbery, Aughadown

Cornelius COLLINS head 59 m. 1805(?) lab, Mary 55 wife, John 30 son n.m. lab RW, Mary
Collins 23 dau n.m. spinning yarn R, son 15 RW.
    No. 12 <u>Cork</u> WR ED W Carbery, Drinagh, Driminidy

Timothy CRAUGH head m. 1809, wife m. 1809, son 25 n.m. lab RW, dau 8 dairy maid R,
son 10(?) lab RW, son at Mr. Driscoll's school RW, dau R, a male serv 20 lab.
    Location not determined.

Pk. John CRONIN (signature Cronin, Cronan on householders' list) head m. 1825
basketmaker RW, wife m. 1825 lacemaker RW, son basketmaker R, son at Mr. Lyons' school
R, son 2, dau lacemaker R, dau 13 not at school, dau 11, dau 6, dau 4, dau 7 months.
    No. 62 <u>Waterford</u>, Coshmore & Coshbride, Lismore

Jeremiah CROWLY 27 head m. 1837 farmer RW, Mary 26 m. 1837, Mary 3 dau, Jeremiah
HENIGAN 20 serv n.m. lab, Patrick REAGAN 87 beggar m. twice. DEC: ------ Crowly 70
father farmer, ------- BRYAN 68 mother, ------- Crowly son 8 months.
    No. 4 <u>Cork</u> WR ED W Carbery, Drinagh, Curriglan (Carrigbaun or Carrigboy?)

James DALY 65 head, Jane 52, Margaret 18, James 15.
    Fermanagh, Coole, Currin, Aghnaskew Glebe (Northern Ireland location)

Timothy DALY 50 head m. 1824 lab, Margret 43 m. 1824, John 8, Timothy 5, Narry 2 (a
female).
    No. 28 <u>Cork</u>, ED W Carbery, Drinagh

William DALY 30 head, Mary 30 wife, James 1 month.
    Fermanagh, Coole, Currin, Aghnaskew Glebe

Patrick DARLY (Patt Darley on front page of census report) 40 head lab, b. Leitrim(?), ------
Darly 30(38?) brother lab n.m., b. Fermanagh(?), ------ 24 sister n.m. R b. Fermanagh(?);
ABS: ------ Darly 32 brother, army. DEC: Mary(?) Darly mother 62 consumption.
    No. 16 Waterford, Coshmore & Coshbride, Lismore

Jeremiah DEMPSY head m. 1820/1835/1841 lab, wife m. 1841. DEC: Cathrin wife d. 183-,
wife age 46 d. 184-.
    No. 25 Cork, ED W Carbery, Drinagh, Keelovong (Killaveenoge?)

Michael DONOUGH 38 head m. 1824(?) blacksmith, wife Catherine(?) 38 m. 1824, John(?)
14 son, son 12, Mary(?) female 11, Michael 9(?), son 5, Thomas 3, Johana 8 mo dau, Timothy
COLLINS Br/L 20 blacksmith n.m., Thomas HANRAHAN(?) 24 n.m. (relationship na)
blacksmith; ABS: mother age 60. DEC: John 2-1/2 son, dau age 1.
    No. 11 Cork, ED W Carbery, Drinagh

Jeremiah DONOVAN 35 head m. 1839 farmer RW, Nony 28 wife m. 1839 RW, Ellen 2 dau,
Mary 2 mo, Peter 31 brother n.m. lab RW, Thomas CONNOLY 19 male serv, Margaret
LEHAY(?) 22 female serv n.m. spinning wool, Jeremiah Donovan 10 cousin Mr. Young's
school RW.
    No. 37 Cork ED W Carbery, Drimoleague (Dromdaleague T.?)

Mathew DOWDS 65 head, occupation higlar, Mary 10, James 18.
    Fermanagh, Coole, Currin, Hermitage

John DRISCOLL 47 head m. 1824 R, Mary 35 wife m. 1827, Daniel 11 son in school R,
Margaret 9 dau in school can write, Jeremiah 6 son in school R, Ellen 4 dau, all born in Co
Cork.
    No. 28 Cork WR ED W Carbery, Aughadown, Beg

Timothy DRISCOLL head m. 1802 lab b. Co Cork, wife m. 1802 b. Co Cork, 2 persons n.m.
b. Co Cork, 2 persons listed on Form 3 as having died in the past 10 years, ages 28 and 21.
    No. 32 Cork WR ED W Carbery, Creagh, Trinisboy

------- DRISCOLL 58 head m. 1827 lab, Cathrine 53 m. 1827, Timothy TOOHY 24 step son
n.m. lab R, John Toohy 17 step son lab.
    No location determined.

------- DRISCOLL 42 head m. 1819/1827 farmer, ------ Driscoll 20 son n.m. lab, Mary 30
wife m. 1827 spinster RW, Helena 13 dau in school R, Margaret 9 in school R, Mary Anne 6
dau, John 4 son, Bridget 2 dau, Taid RYAN 16 serv lab, John HORRENTON 50 visitor n.m.
mason, Mary Anne, John, Bridget, Ryan and Horrenton born in Co Cork.
    No location determined.

Robin FARLEY 41 head, Mary 36, William 12, James 7, son age 4, two other children ages 4
and 1.
    Fermanagh, Coole, Currin, Aghnaskew Glebe

Edmond FENNEY 40 head m. 1839 lab, wife ------- KEGAN 36 m. 1839, son ------- Fenney 4 mo(?), step dau 11.

No. 15, no further data.

John FLANNIGAN (signed Flanagan) 38 head m. 1834 lab R, b. Co <u>Cork</u>, wife 29 m. 1834 b. Co Waterford, David(?) son at -------making school b. Co <u>Cork</u>, Bridget 3(?) dau b. Co Waterford, Michael(?) 2 mo son b. Co Waterford, Bridget(?) MARA 40 wid visitor, b. Co <u>Cork</u>, William(?) Mara age 1 son b. Co <u>Cork</u>.

No. 13 <u>Waterford</u>, Coshmore & Coshbride, Lismore

------- HANADAY male 63 head m. 1801 farmer, wife 63 m. 1801 spinster, son 21(?) n.m. lab RW, Mary LEARY 11(?) serv. (This surname, Hanaday, was not found on householders' list.)

Location not determined.

Patick HERLIHY head, Mary wife, 5 children: John(?), Patt(?), James(?), Mary(?) and Michael. (This surname was not found on householders' list.)

Location not determined.

Timothy KEAGON head m. 1838 farmer R, Mary 23 wife m. 1838, dau age 1, ------ GREDY 9 S/L.

No. 12 <u>Cork</u> ED W Carbery, Aughadown

Jeremiah LOYNS 42 head m. 1823 farmer, Mary 38 m. 1823, Patrick ------- 20 serv, Mary CRIMMUN(?) 38 visitor (brother's wife) wid m. 1826 begging, son 13, Johana 11 dau, son 8, Jeremiah 5 son, ------ CROWLY 60 female visitor n.m. spinning wool.

No. 10 <u>Cork</u> ED W Carbery

John LYNCH 50 head m. 1827, Catherine 40 m. 1827, son 18 lab RW, Michael 12 son missing school RW, John 10 son in school RW, Anne 7 dau in school, Ellen 4 dau.

<u>Cork</u> WD ED W Carbery, Aughadown, Paddock

Marget MAGUIRE 67 head, Mary CLERK 50 (relationship not available), Catharine MAGAHRAN 30 h serv(?), Bernard MAGAHRON 28 lab(?), Alliss Maguire 10 visitor(?).

Fermanagh, Coole, Currin, Aghnaskew Glebe

Patrick MAGUIRE 32 head m. 1826 lab, Margaret 31(?) wife m. 1826, Patrick 12 son, Michael 9 son, John 7 son, Denis 3(?), Mary 3, Margaret 2, Cathrine 1.

No. 21 <u>Cork</u> ED W Carbery, Drinagh

Bridget(?) MAHONY 50 head m. 1805 wid farmer, son 24 n.m. farmer, Catharine 27 dau n.m., Johanah 19 dau, Ellen 16 dau, Mary 13 dau, Peggy 10 dau, John 9 son. DEC: Timothy Mahony head, farmer d. 1840 ------ in bowel.

No. 23 <u>Cork</u> ED W Carbery, Aughadown, Townland Nuro------?

James MURPHY 27 head, Marget 27 wife, Marget 6, Bernard 3.

Fermanagh, Coole, Currin, Hermitage

John MURRAY 57 head, Juduth 60, Patt 30, James 23, Thomas 26, female 24, female 17.

No. 8 Fermanagh, Coole, Currin, Aghnaskew Glebe

Edward MURRY 35 head, Catherine MAGARTY 60 serv, Christopher LYNCH 14 serv lab.

Fermanagh, Coole, Currin, Aghnaskew Glebe

------- McCARTHY 35(?) head, wife 35(?), Margaret 10(?), Mary Ann 5(?) dau, John son.
(This surname was not found on householders' list.)
    Location not determined.

Michael McGRATH 47 head m. 1822 tanner, wife 41(?) m. 1822, dau 7 assistant RW, son at
Mr. Towhel's school RW, son at Mr. Towhel's school R.
    No. 5 Fermoy(?)  (This location was found on householders' list.)

Rose McGUIRE (Maguire on householders' list) 52 head, James 14, Patrick 12 (Alice
McGuire 10 crossed off.)
    Fermanagh, Coole, Currin, Aghnaskew Glebe

Mary McMAHON (McMaghon on top sheet of census record) 49 head, spinner, Mary
McDONALD 24, Marget MAGUIRE 8 (relationship na).
    Fermanagh, Coole, Currin, Hermitage (on top sheet of census record)

Peter McMAHON (spelled McMaghon on previously transcribed list) 42 head, Biddy 32
wife, Bessy 6 niece, Bernard 4 nephew.
    Fermanagh, Coole, Currin, Hermitage

James POWER 54 head, Mary 50 wife, John 21 son, Michael 14(?) son.
    No. 5 Waterford, Coshmore & Coshbride, Lismore

Bernard QUIGLEY 30 head, Cathrine 23, Mary McCERNON 50, Ann Quigley 2.
    Fermanagh, Coole, Currin, Hermitage

Mary REILEY 28 head, Anne 6, John 3, Mary 6 months, Nancy NEAL 55.  (Mary is not
listed as a widow.  James Reiley is shown as the head of the household on previous list.)
    Fermanagh, Coole, Currin, Aghnaskew Glebe

Jeremiah RYAN 39 head m. 1827 farmer, wife 38 m. 1827, son 13, Michael 10 son RW,
Mary 5 dau R, Daniel 2 son, Catherine and Ellen 2 mo(?) daughters, Ellen(?) CONNOLLY 20
(relationship illegible), Catherine MURPHY 70 widow visitor.
    No. 15 Cork, ED W Carbery, Drinagh, Carrybawn

James SHAW (name on Form 3) died age 60, George Shaw crossed off (filmed with a Form 1
fragment listing a lab RW b. Fermanagh, housekeeper who reads b. Monaghan, a person at
school b. in Fermanagh, 2 more entries of persons b. in Fermanagh; unknown if fragments
are related to Shaw.  This name was not found on the householders' list.)
    Location not determined.

John SULLIVAN 60 head m. 1820 lab, wife 40 farmer's wife, Timothy 20 n.m. lab, son 14
lab, Bridget 11 dau, Peter 7 son not at school, Margaret 3 dau.
    No. 5 Cork, ED W Carbery, Kilcrohane

------- TICHARDSON 63 head, female, widow, son 30 n.m., son 28 n.m. RW, son 25 n.m.,
dau 21 n.m. R, son 19 n.m. shoemaker RW.
    No. 13 Cork, ED W Carbery, Drinagh (location of Julian Richardson on householders'
    list)

James YOUNG 42 head m. 1834 farmer RW, wife Jane(?) 40 m. 1834, Jane 7(?) dau, Thomas Young 1 mo son, male serv 35, Jeremiah COUGHLIN 35 serv lab, Jeremiah Coughlin 17 serv lab, Bridget MAHONEY 30 serv. DEC: ------ Young 65 mother, cause of death unknown, William(?) Young 80 father, decline/age, ------ Young 67 uncle, pleurisy.
> No. 11 Cork WR ED W Carbery, Aughadown, Letter (Letterscanlan?)

Notes: The names of Cornelius Driscoll, John Hurley and John (T)owhig, which appear on the list of heads of households previously transcribed, were not found among the fragments during this transcription, however, James Shaw (Form 3 only), Patrick Herlihy and the surnames Driscoll (2 of them), Hanaday and McCarthy, without given names, were found, which were not on the list.

Patrick Darly was listed as Patt Darrley, their Robert Farley appears to read Robin Farley on the fragment, Margaret McGuire was found as Marget Maguire. There was a widow, ------ Tichardson, but the householders' list had a Julian Richardson. Mary Reiley was found as head of a household, but the householders' list reads James Reiley.

The previously transcribed list, which was transcribed before the filming in 1951, was helpful in identifying locations, but for many entries the information was either indefinite or omitted.

Transcribed from LDS film no. 0100816. Original records filmed by the Genealogical Society of Utah, May 1951. Some of the original burnt fragments, which survived the fire of 1922, are at the National Archives, Dublin, Ireland, listed in their reading room in the Pre-1901 Censuses Catalogue. Viewing and reproduction of the originals are on a limited basis due to their fragile condition, but copies may be made from their film N1837, which is also the National Library of Ireland film number.

********************

Transcript of Public Record of Ireland – Certified Copies of portions of some returns from the 1841 Census for Ireland, microfilmed copies at the National Archives, Dublin, Ireland, their M5248, transcribed from LDS film 0101767. A number of copies of additional returns were obtained directly from the National Archives and the information extracted and incorporated in this compilation:

James CARBERRY 35 head m. 1835 baker RW, Mary Anne 27 wife R, Fanny 4 dau R, all b. in Mullingar Co Westmeath.
> Record no. 2 Co Westmeath, Moyashel & Magheradernon, Mullingar, Mullingar, (Moyashell & Macheradernon)

Anne CARROLL 40 head wid m. 1825 farmer RW, Mathew 14 son Mr. Smith's school RW, Thomas 13 son Miss Dunne's school RW, James 10 son in school RW, Catharine 7 dau in school RW, Anne 6 dau, Joseph 5 son, Michael 13 son, Mary 1 dau, Luke DALY 26 nephew land surveyor RW, all born in Queens County; ABS: Judith Carroll 12 dau at Miss Dunne's school, Mary CONROY 28 serv. DEC: Judith Carroll 70 M/L farmer d. 1836 old age, Michael Carroll 40 husband farmer d. 1840 apoplexy. Thomas Carroll 70 F/L farmer d. 1840 pleurisy.
> B. 7 Queens County, Tinnahinch Barony, Kilmanman Parish, Coolaboghlan Townland (Tinnehinch Barony); (not on LDS film)

Owen CASEY 49 head m. 1818 farmer, Jane 48 wife R, Mary 5 dau, all b. Queens County.
Record no. 18 Queens County, Ballyadams, Ballyadams, Ballinclea

Patt DOODY 50 head m. 1822 publican RW, Magret (sic) 40 wife RW, Johana 10 dau RW, all b. Liberty of Limk. (sic).
Record no. 40 Co Limerick, City of Limerick, South Liberty, St. Patrick, Corbally St.

John DORAN 35 head m. 1831 lab and ploughman b. Co Kildare, Anne 32 wife R b. Dublin, Julia 9 dau b. Co Wicklow.
Record no. 9 Co Wicklow, Up Talbotstown, Rathtoole, Rathtoole

John EARLEY (Early on front sheet) 28 head n.m. dairy business RW b. Co Wicklow, Sarah 18 RW b. City of Dublin, William 16 brother RW b. City of Dublin, Wenafer BYRNE 20 serv R b. Co Wicklow, Ellen KERNEY 16 serv b. City of Dublin, all working in the dairy business. DEC: John Earley 60 father dairy d. 1835 decline, Catherine Earley 52 mother dairy d. 1839 decline.
B. 104 Co City of Dublin, St. Luke Parish, Coombe (not on LDS film)

Rev. John ELMES 35 head m. 1833 vicar of St. John's RW b. Bandon, Marian 27 wife RW b. Bandon, John Blair Elmes 5 son R, Thomas 4 son, Mary King Elmes 2 dau, Elizabeth Jane 3 months dau, Jane OAKES 16 serv RW b. Doon, Ellen GRIFFIN 22 serv R b. Tulla. (See also 1851 record.)
B. 4 Co Limerick, Irish Town Barony, St. John's Parish, John's Square, Limerick (not on LDS film)

Thomas FLANAGAN 54 head m. 1811 farmer, Honor 56 wife, Marey (sic) 17 dau lab, all b. Co Dublin.
Record no. 2 Co Dublin, Coolock, Coolock, Tolnagee (Tonlegee)

John FLYNN 43 head m. 1821 R. C. lab (front page says tutor) RW, Mary 35 wife R.C. spinner of wool, Ellen 1 dau R. C., all b. Co Leitrim.
Record B. 34 Co Leitrim, Drumnahair, Drumrilley, Tullyvacan (Drumahaire, Drumreilly; not on LDS film)

John GERAGHTY 46 head m. 1821 lab R, Mary 43 wife spinner R, Andy 3 son, all b. Co Longford.
Record no. 3 Co Longford, Moydow, Ballinmacormick, Knockabarry Pointon (Ballymacormick, Knockatarry, Poynton)

Patrick HARNETT 46 head m. 1828 farmer RW, Jules (sic) 34 wife RW, Cathorina 4 dau, all b. Co Limerick.
Record no. 32 Co Limerick, Glenquin, Killeedy, Toornafulla

Thomas IRETON 38 head m. 1827 gamekeeper R, Jane 36 wife R, Fiddealew (sic) 2 dau, all b. Co Wicklow.
Record no. 69 Co Wicklow, Shillelagh, Mullinacuff, Ballynultagh

Patrick KEANEY 38 head m. 1827 farmer RW, Catherine 35, William 3 son, all b. Co Cavan.
Record no. 12 Co Cavan, Castlerahan, Castleloughan, Castlerahan

Mary Ann KENEDY (sic) 34 head wid m. 1827 farmer R, Marsella 11 dau Mr. Hand's school R, Thomas 8 son in school, Anne 5 dau, James 4 son, Jane 2 dau, all b. Co Dublin. DEC: John 8 son d. 1838 decline, James Kenedy 48 husband farmer d. 1839 decline.

    B. 15 Co <u>Dublin</u>, Balrothery Barony, Balrothery Parish, Stephenstown Townland (not on LDS film)

Patt KENNEDY (signed Patt Kenedy) 50 head m. 1812 farmer RW, Catherine 52 wife, Jane 22 dau R, Dennis 16 son lab RW, Richard 15 son lab R, Bridget 12 dau, all b. Co Dublin; ABS: Nicholas Kennedy 26 son lab <u>in America</u>, Patt 21 son blacksmith in Co Dublin, John 24 son cutting furs in Co Dublin.

    B. 6 Co <u>Dublin</u>, Balrothery Barony, Balrothery Parish, Knock Tnld (not on LDS film)

Thomas KENNEDY 51 head m. 1814 farmer RW b. Co Dublin, Elizabeth 45 wife RW, Jane 20 dau spinning RW, John 18 son lab RW, Marcella 14 dau R, Patrick 12 son Mr. Quinn's school RW, Valentine 9 son in school R, Bridget 5 dau, Mary 2, all b. Co Dublin. DEC: Richard Kennedy 28 brother bootmaker d. 1832 decline, Anne DUNGAN 41 S/L spinner d. 1841 decline.

    B. 31 Co <u>Dublin</u>, Balrothery Barony, Lusk Parish, Balcunnin Tnld (not on LDS film)

James LYNCH 42 head m. 1820 lab, Catrin 47 wife spinner, Henery 10 son, Rosey 8 dau, all b. Co Cavan.

    B. 28 Co <u>Cavan</u>, Clonmahon Barony, Drumlumon Parish, Mullahoron Townland (Clanmahon, Drumlumman, Mullaghoran; not on LDS film)

Martin MULLANNEY (signed Martin Mullaney) 40 head m. 1826 landholder, Sally 40 wife, Thomas 6 son school, all b. Co Mayo.

    B. 13 Co <u>Mayo</u>, Gallen, Kilconduff, Laughcurragh (Lagcurragh)

Andrew MULLIN 35 head m. 1837 lab, Margret 30 wife, Edward 3, all b. Co Meath.

    Record no. 35 Co <u>Meath</u>, Skreen, Skreen, Village of Skreen

John McARDLE 30 head m. 1832 farmer, Seragh 25, Owen 4 son, all b. Co Monaghan.

    Record no. 29 Co <u>Monaghan</u>, Cremorne, Clentibret, Knockavolis

Mary McCALL 50 head wid m. 1812 RW, James 26 son n.m. lab RW, Bridget 24 dau n.m. R, Patrick 21 son n.m. lab RW, Thomas 15 son lab RW, Laurence 12 son Mr. McHugh school R, Joseph 10 son Mr. McHugh school R, Catherine 2 (sic) gr dau Mr. McHugh school , all b. Co Carlow; ABS: John McCall 18 son apprentice to grocer in Dublin. DEC: Patrick McCall 54 head of family farmer d. 1837 decline.

    Record no. 9 Co <u>Carlow</u>, Rathvilly Barony, Clonmore Parish, Killalongford Townland

Bryan McGUIRE (signed Bryne Meguire) 28 head m. 1840 lab, Elenor 21 wife, James 6 months son, all b. Co Mayo.

    Record no. 21 Co <u>Mayo</u>, Erris, Kilcommon, Dooyork

Martin McKNALLEY (signed Martin McNally) 50 head m. 1815 farmer RW b. Co Dublin, Mary 2 wife b. Dublin, Jane 2 dau b. Dublin.

    Record no. 10 Co <u>Dublin</u>, Up Cross, Tallagh, Conard (Cunard)

Hugh O'DONEL 75 wid m. 1794 farmer RW, John 37 son m. 1829 farmer RW, Maria (Maria

Teresa, per claimant) 33 D/L m. 1829 hk RW, Maria 11 gr dau Miss Moffit's school RW, Hugh 8 gr son John McGowan's school RW, John 6 gr son in school, Eugene 3 gr son (claimant), Bessy 1 gr dau, Catherine CARSON 81 sister wid m. 1784 R, Sally CLANCY 26 serv n.m., John TEAF 39 n.m. serv RW, all born Co Leitrim. DEC: Mary SWOONEY 71 cousin d. 1841 fandies.

> B. 7 Co Leitrim, Drumahaire Barony, Drumlease Parish, Moneyduff Townland (not on LDS film)

Manus O'DONNEL 80 head m. 1788 farmer RW , Bridget 76 wife spinning flax, Manus 28 son m. 1834 lab RW, Catherine 25 D/L m. 1834 spinning flax R, Bridget 5 gr dau, Edward 2 gr son, Hannah O'Donnel 11 serv herding, Edward McELWANE 14 serv herding, all b. Goldrum.

> B. 5 Co Donegal, Kilmacrenan Barony, Kilmacrenan Parish, Goldrum Townland (not on LDS film)

Patt PHILIPS 31 head m. 1833 lab, Bridget 32 wife, Nelly 5 dau, all b. Co Mayo.

> Record no. 22 Co Mayo, Costello, Kilmavee (Kilmovee), Uggove (Uggool)

Patrick ROYNANE (return signed by Patk. Ronayne) 50 head wid m. 1818 gentleman RW, Eliza 20 dau RW, Patrick 19 son RW, John 18 son RW, Sally 15 dau RW, Jane 14 dau RW, Margaret 13 dau RW, Luisa 11 dau RW, Mary Anne 10 dau RW, William 9 son RW, James 8 son R, Michael 6 son, Thomas 3 son, Mary O'BRIEN 50 n.m. governess RW, Mary LEHANE 50 wid m. 1818, Ellen CONNELL 24 n.m. child maid, Margaret QUINTON 23 n.m. dairy maid, Margaret SHEA 20 cook, Denis MURPHY 20 stable boy RW, Matthew Connell 19 inside serv RW, John LOVE 30 visitor m. (date na) gentleman RW, all born Co Cork. DEC: Mary Anne Roynane 40 wife d. 1840 accouchment, Jeoffery Connell 50 gardener d. 1834 cholera, Margaret Connell 25 h maid d. 1834 cholera.

> B. 19 Co Cork W R West Muskerry Barony, Macloneigh Parish, Inchinashinan (Inchinashingane) Townland (not on LDS film)

Racheal SMYTH 55 head wid m. 1805 RW, Johanna IRWIN 40 sister wid m. 1815 dressmaker RW, Racheal Smyth 17 dau RW, Frances Smyth 14 dau Mr. Kerr's school R, Patt Smyth 8 son school R, all born in Co Kilkenny, Mary Irwin 17 niece R b. City of Dublin; ABS: Robert Smyth 23 son slater in Kilkenny. DEC: John Smyth 66 husband slater d. 1833 cholera, Mary 10 dau d. 1833 cholera, Honour 30 dau serv d. 1840 decline. (Signature of person making and affirming return, William Freeman).

> B. 2 Co Kilkenny, Shillelogher Barony (Callan Barony?), Callan Parish, Callan Townland, Callan Newmarket Lane (not on LDS film)

Denis SWEENEY 36 head m. 1832 farmer RW, Catherine 27 wife, Mary 2 dau, all b. Co Cork.

> Record no. 5 Co Cork, Duhallow, Cullin (Cullen), Cruckaun

Peter WADE 36 head m. 1824 steward RW, Jane 36 wife, Peter 6 son school, all b. Dublin.

> Record no. 49 Co Dublin, Coolock, Grangegorman, Grangegorman Middle Townland, Fawcett Lane

Raymond WALSH 35 head m. 1829 porter to N. Bank RW b. Co Kilkenny, Bridget 35 wife RW b. Co Tipperary, Mary 9 dau b Co Tipperary.

> Record no. 44 Co Tipperary, Eliogarty Barony, Thurles Parish, T or V of Thurles

Note: More Certified Copies are available on LDS film but those with only one child, the claimant, were used for this listing only if the marriage were recent, i.e. 1837 or later, or if the location were one of those with few records available. The National Archives hold a large number of additional Certified Copies, especially for locations in the Republic, used for Old Age Pension purposes, but few have a full record of the family.

********************

Transcription of abstracts from the 1841 Census returns for COUNTY GALWAY, Loughrea Town, from a private accession held at the National Archives, their M150/2

MAIN ST.
Edward HYOR 30 bank manager (of Waterford), Margaret 21 wife (of Galway) Edward 8 mo son, Anne FEENY 32 serv, Bridget STAUNTON 21 nurse, Augustine COYNE 40 bank porter.

Laurence FAHY 46 m. 1817, Belinda 51 wife m. 1801/1817, Honoria 35, Laurence 26, Maria 20.

Stephen MADDEN 56 commissioner of affidavits, Honoria 52 wife, James Darcy 24 son, Mary Matilda 22 dau, Sarah 21 dau.

Isabella DALY 36 wife m. 1823, Peter 16 son, Mary Anne 14 dau, Matilda 13 dau, Margaret 10 dau, John 7 son; ABS: John Daly 40 husband in America, Belinda 17 dau at school in Galway.

Mary DALY 53 m. 1816/1824 dealer, Bridget 15 dau.

Michael EGAN 41 malster (sic), Clare 32 wife, Julia 9 dau, Mary 7 dau, Patrick 2 son, Honoria 1 mo dau; ABS: Pat (sic) 5 son. DEC: Julia 63 mother d.1832 cholera, Mathew 34 brother d.1832 cholera, Patrick 85 father d.1841 weakness.

BOHERCOM LANE
Mathias COIN 50 m. 1817 fisherman, Bridget 40 wife, Pat 23 son, William 14 son.

BRIDE ST.
Henry CLORAN 29 m. 1835 medical doctor (from Loughrea), Eleanor 32 wife (Dublin), Henry 3 yrs 2 mo son (Dublin), John 11 mo son (Loughrea), Thomas BYRNE 30 m. 1837 serv, Joseph FARRELL 23, Ella MORIARTY 23, Anne KELLY 19.

DUNKELLIN ST.
Thomas WALSH 49 (1st m. Jan 15, 1816, 2nd m. Sep 3, 1834), solicitor and attorney for Galway, Agnes 36 wife, Mary Frances 21 dau, Wm. John 16 son studies, Honoria 8 yrs 11 mo dau school, Ellen 5 yrs 10 mo, Agnes Eliz. 4 yrs 11 mo, Grace 3 yrs 8 mo, Charles 8 mo, Stephen MADDEN 29 Br/L gentleman at large, 7 serv and 2 nurses; ABS: Ellen 30 (Sr) in Gort, Daniel 24 son serv East India Co, Sholpore, India, Thomas 23 yrs 2 mo son attorney at 10 Lr. Mecklinburgh St., Dublin. DEC: Honoria 40 first wife d. 1832 cholera, Frances 1 yr 10 mo dau d.1841 croup.

Transcription of abstracts from the 1841 Census returns for COUNTY KILKENNY and 3 returns for COUNTY WATERFORD from the E. Walsh Kelly transcriptions held at the Genealogical Office, Dublin, Ireland, their reference GO Mss. 683-86, LDS film 0100158

COUNTY KILKENNY

Barony of Gowran, Parish of Clara, Townland of Churchclara

1. Nicholas KEEFE 43 m. 1840 farmer, Margaret 24 wife, Ann 6 months, one serv.

2. Ann KEEFE 72 m. 1789 wid farmer, Henry 50 m. 1824, Mary his wife 40, Ann 16, Bridget 14, Ellen 12, Catherine 9, Matthew 7, Mary 5, Philip 3, John 6 mo, grandchildren; John 47 son n.m., Andrew 36 son n.m., Michael 30 son n.m., Ann KEALY 32 niece n.m., three serv.

3. Nora KELLY (age na) m. 1787 wid, Mary 45, James 43, John 40, Catherine 25, Richard 23. DEC: Mark Kelly 70 (since 1831).

4. Ed HART 50 m. 1820 farmer, Catherine (KEEFE) 38 wife, Mary 17, Catherine 14, Margaret 7, James 5, eight servants; ABS: Agnes age 1 month in Kilkenny. DEC: Martin d. 1832, Ed. d. 1837, Paul d. 1838, all died young; ------ MULHALL (1st cousin) d. 1837, ------ FITZGERALD 70 cousin d. 1838.

Barony of Gowran, Parish of Clara, Townland of Clarabricken

1. Patrick HART 52 m. 1817 farmer, Johanna 48 wife, Catherine 21, Matthew 19, James 17, Patrick and Mary Teresa 15, Ellen 11, Bridget 9, Ed. 7, Mary 81 mother m. 1778, five serv; ABS: Thomas 20 apprentice in Kilkenny. DEC: Thomas 60 brother d. 1838, Johanna 3 d. 1839.

4. Mary HART 28 m. 1833 wid, Margaret 7, James 5, Mary 3, 7 serv; ABS: James(?) 3 in Kilkenny. DEC: Patrick 34 husband d. 1838.

5. Elenor HART 58 m. 1804 wid lab, Ed. 31, Michael 29, Thomas 26, Matthew 15; ABS: Patrick 17 tailor in Kilkenny. DEC: William 54 husband d. 1832.

6. Michael HART 60 m. 1808 lab, Catherine 57 wife, William 26, Michael 23, James 15, Walter 10, Matthew 5, Thomas FARRELL 27 tailor; ABS: Ed. 27 in America. DEC: Johanna 19 d. 1839.

7. Richard HART 44 m. 1825 farmer, Ellen 36 wife, James 15, Nicholas 13, Margaret 11, Johanna 9, Richard 6, Elizabeth 1, five serv. DEC: Ed. 3 mo d. 1837, Mary 3 mo d. 1838, Patrick 2 mo d. 1840.

8. Patrick HART 54 m. 1811 mason, Betty 50 wife, Ed. 20, James 9, Judith 28, Mary 26, Bridget 24, Ellen 18, Margaret 16, Catherine 14, Betty 6.

(All born in county of residence unless otherwise specified)

Barony of Gowran, Parish of Clara, Townland of Clifden

1. Patrick BLANCHFIELD 38 n.m. farmer, Mary 30 sister, Margaret CAHILL 12, Ellen Cahill 8, nieces, five serv. DEC: James 74 d. 1834.

27. Walter HART 38 m. 1829 lab, Mary 42 wife, Mary 8, Ellen 5, Elizabeth 1. DEC: Ellen, Michael, William and Edmund died young in 1831, 1832, 1833 and 1840.

Barony of Gowran, Parish of Clara, Townland of Upper Clara

2. Anthony BYRNE 37 m. 1827 farmer, Ann 36 wife, Elizabeth 12, Mary 10, Ann 8, Teresa 5, Michael 3, Anthony 6 months, Elizabeth (age na) mother m. 1797 wid, five serv.

Barony of Ida, Parish of Kilclumb, Townland of Knockbrace

6. Alice FITZGERALD 40 m. 1833 wid farmer, Johanna 8, John 6. DEC: Thomas Fitzgerald 32 B/L d. 1832, Johanna 80 M/L d. 1833, James 50 husband d. 1839.

12. Patrick FITZGERALD 40 m. 1826 farmer, Mary 36 wife, John 14, Bridget 13, Peirse 9, Kate 7, Mary 5, Walter 3, James 9 months.

15. Michael FITZGERALD 40 m. 1826 wid farmer, Johanna 15. DEC: Ellen 32 wife d. 1833, John 6 mo son d. 1833, Mary 5 dau d. 1834.

Barony of Ida, Parish of Kilcolumb, Townland of Rochestown

4. Patrick KELLY 45 m. 1824 farmer, Elenor 38 wife, no children, three serv, Bridget HENEBERY 23 and Mary Henebery 24 visitors. DEC: Mary Kelly 79 mother d. 1840.

16. Mary KELLY 58 m. 1821 wid weaver, Patrick 15 at Lady Esmond's School; ABS: John 18 clerk in New York. DEC: John 72 husband d. 1835.

19. Thomas GAHAN 43 m. 1827 farmer, Anastasia 43 wife, John 8, Anastasia 70 mother wid m. 1793, Mary GRANT 58 S/L m. 1818 wid.

35. John GAHAN 46 m. 1829 farmer, Elizabeth 30 wife, Margaret 5, Mary 3, John 1 son, Patrick 50 brother m. 1824 wid, Thomas 15 nephew, John 13, Laurence 11, Laurence 40 brother, Margaret mother 88 m. 1789 wid, two serv. DEC: Mary 32 S/L d. 1834, also three young children.

36. John GAHAN 40 m. 1825 farmer, Elenor 38 wife, Margaret 14, Richard 12, Michael 10, Mary 8, Johanna 6, Joseph 4, Catherine 22 sister, Joseph 28 brother, Bridget AYLWARD 8 niece. DEC: Richard father 80 d. 1841, William 1 son d. 1839.

E. Walsh Kelly transcription of portions of the 1841 Census records for Counties Kilkenny and Waterford

Barony of <u>Ida</u>, Parish of <u>Rathpatrick</u>, Townland of <u>Kilmurry</u>

38. Michael TOBIN 34 m. 1829, Alice 33 wife, Richard 11, Ann 9, Thomas 8, John 3, Patrick 2, Margaret STEPHENS 16 serv.

67. David GRANT 27 tailor, William 23 brother, Thomas 19 brother tailor.

77. Patrick TOBIN 70 m. 1799 farmer, Mary 68 wife, Margaret 25, Patrick 22, Ellen GORMAN 33 dau, Michael Gorman 30 S/L, William 5, Catherine 3, Mary 3, John 6 mo, their children.

78. James TOBIN 50 m. 1806 farmer, Johanna 54 wife, Anastasia 19, Mary 18, Ally 13, Ed. 26 m. 1836, Kate his wife 26, James age 4 mo, their son.

94. David GRANT 51 m. 1806/1831 farmer, Johanna 41 wife m. 1822/1831, Thomas 22, Laurence 20, Ed. 17, James 8, Mary 6, Patrick 4, William 2, Bridget 1.

95. Thomas GRANT 63 m. 1807 wid farmer, James 27, David 25, William 22, Laurence 32, Ellen (age na) his wife m. 1839, Bridget 1, Thomas 4 mo, their children, 2 serv. DEC: Bridget 56 wife d. 1835.

96. James GRANT 54 m. 1825 lab, Anastasia 46 wife, Laurence 14, Ed. 12, Patrick 10, Mary 7.

Barony of <u>Ida</u>, Parish of <u>Rathpatrick</u>, Townland of <u>Rathpatrick</u>

16. Laurence GRANT (age na) m. 1826 farmer, Judith 36 wife, Mary 14, Margaret 12, Thomas 10, Patrick 8, Ellen 6, William 4, Ed. 1, one serv.

17. Margaret GRANT 48 m. 1812 wid, Ed. 25, William 23, Ellen 21, Thomas 19, all in Co Kilkenny (sic).

18. Mary GRANT 56 m. 1801 wid, Nora 24, John 21, Mary MURRY 4 gr dau; ABS: Ellen 28, Thomas 24, Ed. 18. DEC: John Murry S/L boatman d. 1834 drowned.

19. Nat TAYLOR 42 n.m. miller, Margaret 43 sister, Mary 20 niece, Michael WHELAN serv.

20. Michael NEILL 40 m. 1833 lab, Johanna 30 wife, Margaret GRANT 27 S/L, Bridget H ------ 67 M/L m. 1801 wid. DEC: Ed. Grant F/L d. 1836.

Barony of <u>Iverk</u>, Parish of <u>Aglish</u>, Townland of <u>Aglish North</u>

1. Richard McDONALD 49 m. 1808/1825 occupation smith RW, Anastasia wife 56, Bridget 24 strawplatter, Margaret 15 in school, Richard McDonald 25 visitor smith b. Co <u>Waterford</u>.

2. Edmond FEORE (or Foire) 40 m. 1825 farmer RW, Margaret 36 wife, Bridget 14 in school, Catherine 11 in school, Mary 9 in school, Johanna 7 in school, James 4, Anastasia 3, Ann BRENNAN 60 visitor spinner, Andrew Foire 21 cousin workman, Elenor BOLAN 23 serv. DEC: James Foire 60 father farmer d. 1832 decline, Catherine 58 mother d. 1838 decline.

3. Walter FEORE 51 n.m., Mary 55 sister n.m., Margaret 53 sister n.m., William 37 brother m. 1841, Allis, brother's wife, 30, Anastasia GRACE 20 niece n.m., Judy Grace (age na) niece, Thomas (surname na) 33 n.m. lab R, Honora CARY 28 visitor lab b. City of Waterford, William MANY 8 visitor pauper b. City of Waterford, Patrick Many ditto. DEC: Richard 84 father d. 1837 decline, Anastasia 79 mother d. 1837 decline.

4. Catherine DELAHUNTY 32 wid m. 1828 farmer RW, Johanna 12, Anne 9, John 7, Margaret 3, all in school, Mary HENEBERY 20 cousin dressmaker b. Waterford, Thomas DOWLEY 36 serv, Nicholas GUINAN 26 visitor lab, Michael WALSH 60 m. 1800 serv. DEC: Patrick 36 husband farmer d. 1837 fever, Margaret 18 mo d. 1837 teething, Mary 4 d. 1837 fever.

5. Patrick PHELAN (or Whealan) 55 m. 1817 farmer RW, Margaret 48 wife, Nicholas 24 ploughman, Thomas 22 in school, Andrew 20 lab, Walter 18 lab, Peter 15, Patrick 11, Michael 8, last three in school, Catherine Phelan 38 sister n.m. flax spinner, Johanna BROADERS 29 cousin n.m. mantuamaker, David CONDON 12 visitor b. Waterford. DEC: Margaret 75 mother d. 1834, Catherine POWER 9 visitor d. 1840 measles.

6. Edward FARRELL 54 m. 1811 farmer RW, Nancy 50 wife, Bridget 19, Peter 18, Anastasia 16, Margaret 12, all in school, Patrick 50 brother farmer, Laurence O'HAREN 68 cousin serv, Thady SULLIVAN (age na) workman b. Kerry, Thomas Sullivan 19 workman b. Kerry, Bridget Sullivan 15 serv b. Kilkenny.

7. John DOWDY 27 m. 1838 farmer RW, Anastasia 26 wife, Peter 2 mo, Edmond 30 brother lab, Thomas 24 brother lab, Anastasia 64 grand aunt, Honora 23 serv, Andy 21 serv. DEC: Edmond Dowdy 80 grandfather farmer d. 1832 decline, Margaret Dowdy 49 mother d. 1838 decline.

8. Richard WALSH 36 m. 1833 (28.1.34) farmer RW, Mary 29 wife R, Mary 6, Catherine 4, Margaret 2, all in school, Johanna DOWDY 25 S/L serv, Margaret Dowdy 54 M/L m. 1810, John FEORE 36 serv, Laurence MURPHY 40 workman, Catherine BROEFIE 15 serv. DEC: Thomas Dowdy 48 F/L farmer d. 1835 fever.

9. Edward FOERE 32 m. 1834 lab, Johanna 31 wife, Thomas 5 in school, Nicholas 2, Edward DOWDY 27 cousin lab. DEC: William Dowdy 70 uncle by law lab d. 1834 decline. Mary Dowdy 60 aunt d. 1833 decline.

10. John DOWDY 60 m. 1812 lab, Mary 54 wife(?), Edward 25 n.m., Alice 18 n.m.; ABS: Perry 22 serv, Joney 20 serv, Matthew 17 serv.

Barony of Iverk, Parish of Aglish, Townland of Aglish South

1. Ellenor FEORE 40 m. 1834 lab, Mary 4, Bridget McDONALD 22 niece R, Bridget McDonald S/L (age na).

2. John WALSH 50 m. 1815 farmer RW, Mary 40 wife, Walter 17 lab, Susan 14 dressmaker.

3. Walter WALSH 60 wid m. 1800 farmer, Edmond 37 m. 1834 farmer, Mary 30 his wife, James 27, Jonay MURPHY 24 serv.

4. Walter WALSH 50 m. 1812 farmer, Alice 52 wife, Nicholas 25 lab RW, Norah 15 RW, Mary CASEY 19 serv, Mary DOWDY 27 serv.

5. Thomas WALSH 40 m. 1832 farmer RW, Honora (NICHLAUSH) 32 wife, Walter 8 in school, Richard 7, James 6, Mary 4, Margret 3 mo, Richard 32 brother shoemaker, Michael McGRATH 30 lab, Johanna Walsh 43 sister, Catherine MURPHY 20 serv; ABS: Walter Walsh 37 brother in <u>Newfoundland</u>. DEC: Walter 70 father d. 1839 decline, Mary 65 mother d. 1838 decline.

6. Walter WALSH 47 m. 1815 farmer RW, Catherine 45 wife, Edmond 23 lab, Mary 20, Alice 17, Nicholas 30 brother lab, Catherine 28 sister lab, Patrick 30 jockey.

7. Richard KEEFE 38 m. 1828 lab RW, Anastasia 37 wife, Mary 13 in school, Anastasia 11, Nelly 8, Johanna 5, Margaret 3, Catherine 1, William 30 brother lab, Mary SULLIVAN 20 serv, Michael WALSH 15 serv, Margret MAHER 19 cousin in service. DEC: Walter 60 father farmer d. 1833 fever.

8. James MACKEY (McKay on front page of census return) 31 m. 1837 lab RW, Mary 30 wife, Michael 2, Mary 1 mo.

9. Peter KELLY 63 m. 1809 lab, Johannaugh 55 wife, James 27, Catherine 14; ABS: Margaret 25 and Johannaugh 23 servants in Co Kilkenny. DEC: Michael 25 son seaman d. 1838 drowned.

10. Thomas QUINN 52 m. 1817 farmer RW, Anastasia 49 wife, James 19 lab, Mary 16 lab.

11. Thomas HANLON 40 m. 1832 farmer RW, Johanna 40 wife, Edmond 7 in school, John 5, Anastasia 2, Catherine 3 mo, Richard WALSH 23 Br/L lab, Catherine GRANT 20 serv, Nelly Walsh 28 S/L lab. DEC: Patrick Walsh 22 B/L 22 d. 1833 decay, John Walsh 20 Br/L d. 1833 decay.

12. Richard WALSH 50 m. 1820 farmer RW, Margaret 40 wife, Catherine 19, Ellenor 18, Richard 17, Mary 16, Johanna 10, William FOERE 30 serv, Martin CARROT (sic) 18 serv. DEC: William 9 son d. 1833 decline.

13. Walter WALSH 36 m. 1837 farmer RW, Mary 28 wife, Catherine 2, Patrick McDONALD 23 lab b. <u>Waterford</u>, John DUNNE 30 lab, John CARTY 30 lab, Johanna Carty 46 m. 1812 workwoman b. <u>Kerry</u>, John KEEFE 26 serv, John SUMMERS 13 serv, Walter GRANT 8 cousin, Catherine MALONE 25 serv, Judith COLLINS 16 serv b. <u>Kerry</u>, Jerry MOORE 24 workman. DEC: Catherine Walsh 60 mother d. 1833 decline, Richard 1 d. 1841 quinsey.

14. John WALSH 40 m. 1836 farmer RW, Elenor 27 wife, Walter 3, William 2, Catherine 6 mo, Edmond QUINN 20 Br/L lab, Bridget McGUIRE 50 lab, Judith GRANT 19 serv, Nelly Grant 42 m. 1818 working, Nelly Grant 4, John Quinn 17 lab, Edward Quinn 16 lab, John RYAN 40 m. 1831 lab, Richard Walsh 30 lab.

15. James MILLEA 40 m. 1831 carpenter RW, Mary 30 wife, Thomas 8, William 6, Mary 3, Alice 3 mo.

16. Michael GUINAN 70 m. 1800 lab, Elizabeth 70 wife, Nicholas 27, Laurence 23.

17. Walter WALSH 30 n.m. publican RW, Mary 24 sister, Mary 60 mother m. 1807 wid, John 29, Jeffrey 28, James 25, Edward 23, Nicholas 19, brothers n.m., Nora 40 S/L n.m.

Barony of <u>Iverk</u>, Parish of <u>Aglish</u>, Townland of <u>Portnahully</u>

1. David DELAHUNTY 48 m. 1816 farmer RW, Mary 49 wife, John 20, Ellen 18, Johanna 14, David 12, Margaret 6, Thomas TASIFSY 27 serv, James McCARTHY 15 serv, James CONNELL 14 serv, Honora WALSH 22 serv, Johanna DOWLING 17 serv, Patrick DUDY 11 serv, James BROPHY 21, Bridget Brophy 23, Bridget Brophy 22 (sic), Elizabeth Brophy 2, all visitors, Edmond KELLY 18 visitor. DEC: John 86 father farmer d. 1834 decline, Patrick CONNOLLY 18 serv lab d. 1838 decline.

2. Thomas WALSH 54 m. 1824 farmer RW, Margaret 44 wife, Anastasia 17 dau lab, Mary 10, Elinor 6, Catherine 5, Judith 3, Michael 15, Peter 12, John 7, last three in school at Mr. Quinn's, Martin BRODERS 60 n.m. workman, Michael WHELAN (age na) serv, Mary DOLAN 20 serv, Unity BRENNAN 75 M/L m.1784 wid, Mary QUIRK 22 lab, Andrew HAYES 70 m. 1813 wid lab, Mary Hayes 16 lab. DEC: Richard Walsh 6 son in school d. 1833 chincough, John Walsh 5 son d. 1832 decline, John Walsh 1 son d. 1834 decline.

3. William DOYLE 70 m. 1797 farmer RW, Mary 64 wife, William 42 m. 1826 farmer, Mary 36 his wife, Patrick 13, Edmond and James 12, Thomas 7, Richard 5, all in school, John 3, Walter 1, all grandchildren, John 22 son. DEC: Norah Doyle 6 gr dau d. 1837 quinsey.

4. Patrick WHELAN 53 m. 1808 farmer R, Bridget 50 wife, Ellen 22 lab, Edmond 20 lab; Judith 17, Catherine 11, Thomas 5 grandson, all in school, Thomas COMMINS 25 lab, Mary ELMON 25 housekeeper, Judith CORCORAN 60 visitor pedlar; ABS: Richard 14 attending school in Kilkenny. DEC: Thomas Whelan 24 son farmer d. 1837 fever.

5. John WHELAN 54 m. 1808 wid farmer RW, Ellen 27, Mary 25, Margaret 86 mother m. 1782 wid, Thomas 25 m. 1838, Margaret 24 his wife, John 1 their son.

6. John MURRAY 36 m. 1834 lab RW, Catherine 36 wife, Mary 3, Margaret 74 mother m. 1784 wid.

7. Catherine BRENNAN 30 n.m. lab, Patrick 28 brother n.m. lab.

8. John QUINN 27 m. 1837 farmer RW, Mary 30 wife, Catherine 4, Mary 2, Michael 1 son, Michael 60 father m. 1807 wid lab, Honora 20 sister lab, Anastasia 14 sister.

9. James BRENNAN 48 m. 1825 lab, Honny 39 wife, Michael 8, John 6, Mary 5, Anastasia 4, all at John Quinn's school, Margaret 2.

10. Anty KEANE 70 m. 1790 wid lab, Johanna CONNOLLY 40 dau m. 1831 wid lab, James Connolly 8, Johanna 6, Anty 4, grandchildren. DEC: Edmond Connolly 36 S/L lab d. 1837 fever.

11. Edmond DOYLE 36 m. 1834 farmer RW, Catherine 25 wife, Anastasia 6, Margaret 2, Edmond 1 mo, Edmond CONNOLLY 26 serv, John KEATING 20 serv, Nancy BREHAN 21 serv, Mary QUINN 16 cousin at Mooncoin Nunnery School, Johanna Brehan 25 lab, Walter

DUNPHY 22 visitor ship's carpenter, William BRODER 60 m. 1798 wid visitor lab; ABS: Thomas Doyle 4 son at Mr. Quinn's school..

12. Patrick DOLAN 56 m. 1820 lab RW, Mary 50 wife, Nancy 11, Margaret 10 at Mr. Quinn's school, Catherine 7, Johanna Dolan 96 M/L (sic) m. 1779 wid .

### Barony of Iverk, Parish of Rathkyran, Townland of Ballymountain

1. Robin WALSH 60 m. 1810 lab R, Anastasia 52 wife, Richard 19 lab, Walter 15, Mary HOGAN(? age na) dau m. 1838 h serv, Mary Hogan 3 mo gr dau, Margaret CROKE 21 visitor serv; ABS: Edmond 30, Anastasia 25, Michael 16, all working in Co Kilkenny. DEC: Catherine 18 dau d. 1835 decline.

2. John COLLINE (sic) 50 m.1834 lab, Anastasia 27 wife, David 6, Peter 4, John 2, Mary DOODY 60 m. 1809 M/L wid hk. DEC: Peter Doody 29 Br/L d. 1835 murdered.

3. Richard KENNY 42 m. 1826 lab R, Mary 40 wife, Martin 9, William 5, Margaret 3. DEC: Margaret dau d. 1832, Mary CROKE 80 M/L d. 1839 infirmity, William son d. 1839.

4. Thomas FEWER 65 m. 1799 wid lab R, Walter 29 n.m. lab; ABS: Michael 22 in America. DEC: Mary 60 wife d. 1839 inward pains.

5. James OSBORNE 39 m. 1833 (4.9.'33) lab RW, Ellen 40 wife, Thomas 5, Margaret GRANT 11 visitor.

6. Thomas COLLINS 40 wid m. 1825 lab, Nancy 14, James 12, William 11, Thomas 11, Allice 9, Richard 5. Dec: Mary WALLICE 80 M/L d. 1835 decline, John 2 son d. 1840 measles, Ellen 36 wife d. 1841 decline.

7. Patrick WALSH 42 m. 1822/1826 farmer R, Mary 40 wife, Richard 12 Mr. Quinn's school, Denis 10 in school, Catherine 13, Mary 12, both at Mrs. Magdelan's school, Anastasia 7, John 40 brother m. 1836, Mary 30 his wife, Michael 18 mo nephew, Bridget Walsh 27 serv, Michael QUINN 30 visitor. Dec: Bridget 18 mo dau d. 1833 quinsey.

### Barony of Iverk, Parish of Rathkyran, Townland of Rathcurby North

1. John BRIAN 70 m. 1800 farmer RW, Johanna 60 wife, Edmond 30 lab, Andrew 45 (sic) serv lab, Catherine 32 hk, Allice 28 h serv, John 25 serv lab, David 16 serv lab.

2. Dennis BRIAN 40 m. 1830 farmer RW, Honora 33 wife, Richard GRACE 30 serv lab, William STONE 20 serv lab, Patrick KERANS 60 serv cowboy, Honora VALE (or Qale) 30 h serv, Ellen WALSH 26 h serv. Dec: Mary Brian 60 aunt d. 1834 decline.

3. Mathew REDDY 30 m. 1834 lab, Mary 30 wife, Margaret 3 mo; ABS: Edmond 4 in Co Kilkenny. DEC: David GRANT 70 F/L d. 1832 decline, Margaret Grant 70 M/L d. 1838 decline.

Barony of <u>Iverk</u>, Parish of <u>Rathkyran</u>, Townland of <u>Rathcurby South</u>

1. William MORGAN 44 m. 1815 wood ranger, Mary 46 wife, Thomas 21 n.m. lab, John 19 lab, William 17 road contractor, Ellen 3 not related.

2. John LEARY 25 m. 1840 lab, Judith 30 wife, Margaret BRENNAN 57 m. 1806 visitor flax spinner. Dec: James Brennan 60 not related d. 1840 decline.

3. Edmond BRENNAN 70 m. 1799 farmer, Judy 65 wife, Patrick 35, Anty 26, Stephen 22, Walter 40 m. 1833, Biddy his wife 33, Anty 7, Edward 6, John 4, James 9 months, their children, Teresa CAHILL 18 serv. DEC: James Brennan 28 son d. 1839.

4. Patrick MULLINS 34 m. 1832 farmer, Johanna 39 wife, Patrick READY 20 serv lab b. Co <u>Tipperary</u>, Biddy GRACE 24 h serv b. Co <u>Tipperary</u>, Peggy KENNEDY 60 h serv. DEC: Peggy BRENNAN 40 S/L d. 1839.

5. Thomas PHELAN 36 m. 1833 farmer RW, Catherine 35 wife, Elinor 6, Patrick 5, Catherine 3, Bridge Phelan 25 serv, James Phelan 50 herdsman.

6. Peter DALTON 37 m. 1832 farmer R, Catherine 29 wife, Catherine 8, John 7, Mary 6, Johanna 4, Ally 2, Patrick 3 mo, Richard 34 brother, Patrick HEARNS 36 workman, Michael MORRISSEY 15 serv, Mary WALSH 21 serv. DEC: Patrick 1 mo d. 1840 decline.

7. Thomas LANDY m. 1835 farmer RW, Betty 30 wife, Mary 5, Lilly 4, James 3, Biddy 1, Mary 80 mother m. 1790 wid, Nelly 30 sister n.m., Mary 28 sister, Billy BUTLER 16 serv.

8. Thomas BRENNAN 37 m. 1831 farmer RW, Mary 30 wife, Mary 9 in school, Elinor 8, James 6, Catherine 4, Ally 3, James 75 father m. 1795 wid, Edward 20 serv, Mary 25 serv. DEC: Margaret 1 mo d. 1841 quinsey.


COUNTY WATERFORD

County <u>Waterford</u>, (<u>Decies Without Drum</u> Barony), <u>Dungarvan</u>, <u>Blackpool</u>:

21. Patrick WALSH 51 shopkeeper m. 1822, Mary 52 wife m. 1808/1822, Robert HAMILTON 32 step son, Margaret 24 step dau, Ellen 23 step dau, Marion Walsh 18 dau, Ellen RIVER (King crossed out) 9 step niece: ABS: John Hamilton 30 in <u>East Indies</u>, Bartholomew Hamilton 28 in <u>South America</u>.

71. John DOWER 55 m. 1834 merchant and brewer, b. Co Waterford, Elizabeth 40 wife b. Co <u>Cork</u>.

137. Patrick DOWER 65 m. 1797 merchant, Margaret 60 wife, James 35, Robert 25, Anne 22. DEC: Dora d. 1837.


(All persons born in county in which they are listed in the census except where noted. Locations in parentheses added by transcriber.)

THRIFT GENEALOGICAL ABSTRACTS – 1841 Irish Census, portions of Carlow, Cork, Dublin, Galway, Limerick, Mayo, Monaghan and Roscommon held at the National Archives, Dublin, Ireland, 4845-4946, 5026 and 4947-5008, 5029, LDS film 0596418 (Northern Ireland locations omitted). Spellings of townlands may differ from those of the original transcription.

## COUNTY CARLOW

CRAWFORD, Elizabeth 55 wife m. 1811 gentlewoman RW b. Co Meath, Cathrin 30 dau n.m. gentlewoman b. Co Meath, Rebecca 28 dau n.m. gentlewoman b. Co Longford, Margaret 23 dau n.m. gentlewoman b. Co Longford, Jane OAB(?) 28 serv (entry illegible); ABS: Mathew Crawford 21 son gentleman in America, Andrew Crawford 65 head gentleman in Kingstown. DEC: John W. Crawford 17 son gentleman d. 1839 consumption, Samuel E. H. Crawford 29 son gentleman d. 1840 consumption.
> (Idrone E Barony, Dunleckny or Sliguff Townland), Kilcarry St. Bagnalstown (This entry was alphabetized under Co Meath but this location is in Co Carlow.)

## COUNTY CORK

McCARTHY, Robert 38 head m. 1829 printer RW b. Co Cork, Mary 31 wife RW b. Co Kildare, John 9, William 7 and Robert 5 sons, all at St. Nicholas School R b. City of Cork, Welbore 1 son b. City of Cork, Judith CORKERY 22 serv b. Co Cork. DEC: Margaret McCarthy 1 dau d. 1839 measles.
> Co Cork, St. Nicholas Parish, City of Cork, Teiers Walk

## COUNTY DUBLIN

DERM, James, tailor (no other data).

FEA, Rev. John 72 head m. 1795 curate of St. Thomas Parish RW, Elizabeth 60 wife RW, Mary Ann 42 dau n.m. RW, Elizabeth COOKE alias Fea 38 dau wid RW, Elizabeth Cooke Jr. 12 gr dau RW, John Arthur TUDOR 8 (no further data), James SHERIDAN 28 serv RW, Sarah O'BRIEN 20 h maid RW, Mary CASSIDY 24 cook RW, all born City of Dublin. DEC: Arthur Fea 28 son surgeon d. 1839 consumption.
> Co Dublin, Parish of St. Thomas, City of Dublin, 10 Summer Hill

GUINESS, Benjamin 29 head n.m. merchant tailor RW, Mary COSTELLO 40 wid m. 1820 serv.
> Co Dublin, St. Mary Parish, Upper Ormond Quay no. 18

## COUNTY GALWAY

BRENNAN, John 45 head m. 1814 lab, Margaret 50 wife spinner, Bridget GIBLIN 18 serv.
> Co Galway, Ballymoe Barony, Kilbegnet Parish, Leaha Townland

EAGAN, John 40 head m. 1828 lab, Wenny 33 wife, Thomas 12 son Mr. Corr's school, Mick 7 son, Biddy 2, Catherine McGUIRE 19 D/L. DEC: Bryan McGuire 60 father blacksmith d. 1838 hurt, Patt Egan (sic) 6 son d. 1837 decay, Mary Egan 3 mo dau d. 1835 unknown.

Co Galway, Ballymoe Barony, Kilbegnet Parish, Curraghbog Townland

FITZMORRIS, Patt 30 head m. 1839 lab R, Ann 29 wife R, Catherine 6 mo dau, Catherine GIBLIN 50 mother wid.
Co Galway, Ballymoe Barony, Kilbegnet Parish, Leaha Townland

GIBLIN, Barthy 54 head m. 1834 wid farmer RW, Bridget 15 dau hk R, Judy 11 dau R, Patt 8 son, Oney 6 dau. DEC: Bridget Giblin 30 wife d. 1834 visitation of death.
Co Galway, Ballymoe Barony, Kilbegnet Parish, Ballynahowna Townland

GIBLIN, Daniel 70 head m. 1802 lab R, Bridget 75 wife, John 30 son n.m. lab.
Co Galway, Ballymoe Barony, Kilbegnet Parish, Bolythomas Townland

GIBLIN, James 35 head m. 1829 land steward RW b. Co Roscommon, Mary 29 wife RW b. Co Galway, Michael 10 Mr. Collins' school RW Mara 8 Mrs. Brannelly's school RW, Celia 6 in school R, Catherine 4 in school, Ann 2 in school (sic), Mick MORGAN 20 serv lab, Margaret MURRY 30 wid h serv.
Co Galway, Ballymoe Barony, Kilbegnet Parish, Creggs Townland

GIBLIN, John 54 head m. 1811 tailor, Susana 48 wife, Patt 26 son n.m. lab RW, Kitty 20 dau, Betty 10 dau R; ABS: James Giblin 24 son broguemaker in Galway. DEC: Winifred Giblin 16 dau d. 1840 pleurisy.
Co Galway, Ballymoe Barony, Kilbegnet Parish, Moneenroe Townland

GIBLIN, John 40 head m. 1835 farmer, Nelly 35 wife spinster, Mick 6, Catherine 4, Thomas 1, Mary MORGAN 46 S/L serv.
Co Galway, Ballymoe Barony, Kilbegnet Parish, Cuilnacappy Townland

GIBLIN, John 26 head n.m. lab, Mary RYAN 33 sister m. 1839 spinning, Margaret Giblin 22 sister n.m. spinning, Mick Giblin 21 brother n.m. lab R, Honour Giblin 62 mother m. 1801 spinning; ABS: Peter Giblin 34 brother lab in America.
Co Galway, Ballymoe Barony, Kilbegnet Parish, Creggauns Townland

GIBLIN, Mary 35 head m. 1831 spinning flax, Judy 7 dau, Patt 5 son, Owen RILY 25 n.m. visitor lab; ABS: Bryan Giblin husband 40 lab in America.
Co Galway, Ballymoe Barony, Kilbegnet Parish, Ballynahowna Townland

GIBLIN, Michael, Sr. 60 head m. 1837 wid lab, Mickle Jr. 17 lab, Patt 13, Edward 6. DEC: Rose Giblin 40 wife d. 1839 decay.
Co Galway, Ballymoe Barony, Kilbegnet Parish, Sonnagh Townland

GIBLIN, Mickle 32 head m. 1834 lab R, Mary 32 wife R, Thomas 5, Honor 5, Mary 6 mo.
Co Galway, Ballymoe Barony, Kilbegnet Parish, Leaha Townland

GIBLIN, Mickle 19 head n.m. lab, Peggy 60 mother m.1811 wid spinner, Catherine 20 sister n.m. DEC: Patt Giblin 60 father lab d. 1838.
Co Galway, Ballymoe Barony, Kilbegnet Parish, Moat Townland

GIBLIN, Patt 42 head m. 1832 lab RW, Bridget 33 spinner, Patt 7, James 5, Bridget RYAN 18 serv. DEC: Francis Giblin father lab d. 1837 infirmity.
Co Galway, Ballymoe Barony, Kilbegnet Parish, Leaha Townland

GIBLIN, Richard 32 head m. 1831 lab, Judy 37 wife, Margaret 10 dau, Thomas 6 son. DEC: Bridget Giblin 2 mo dau d. 1839 dropsy.

    Co Galway, Ballymoe Barony, Kilbegnet Parish, Bolythomas Townland

GIBLIN, Thomas 55 head m. 1809 wid lab, Honour 18 dau hk, Peggy Giblin 8 visitor; ABS: Patt Giblin 25 son and Catherine 20 dau in <u>America</u>. DEC: Bridget Giblin 54 wife d. 1836.

    Co Galway, Ballymoe Barony, Kilbegnet Parish, Ballynahowna Townland

JORDON, Catherine 60 head m. 1790 wid, Richard 22 son n.m. lab R, Mary GIBLIN 16 serv, Thomas NAUGHTON 10 gr son, George 8 gr son, Andrew 6 mo gr son; ABS: Edward Jordan (sic) 24 son lab in <u>England</u>. DEC: John Jordan 70 husband lab d. 1839 decay.

    Co Galway, Ballymoe Barony, Kilbegnet Parish, Garraun South Townland

KEAVENY, John 70 head m. 1801 lab, Mary 60 wife spinner, Thomas 30 son n.m. lab, Laurence 15 son lab, Edmond 14 son lab, Bridget GIBLIN 29 dau m. 1837 spinner, Mary Giblin 1 gr dau; ABS: Peter Keaveny 22 son lab in <u>America</u>, John 19 son lab in <u>America.</u>

    Co Galway, Ballymoe Barony, Kilbegnet Parish, Bolythomas Townland

LOUGHAN, Michael head 70 m. 1800 wid lab, Kitty GIBLIN 32 dau m. 1830 hk, Catrene (sic) MAHAN 16 serv; ABS: Michael Giblin 40 S/L lab in <u>America</u>. DEC: James Giblin 10 mo gr son d. 1833 a pain.

    Co Galway, Ballymoe Barony, Kilbegnet Parish, Conderry (Camderry) Townland

(Note: The first letter of the handwritten surname MEE (or NEE) was interpreted as an M but there is a possibility that this name could be NEE. The record for Patt MEE, no. 3 below, shows his deceased wife's name as NEE. The surname NEE is also found in Co Galway.)

MEE, Daniel 35 head m. 1837 lab, Mary 32 wife, Mary 14 dau Mr. Kilroy's school RW, Thomas 11, John 10, Cathren 8, Ony 6 dau, all in school.

    Co Galway, Ballymoe Barony, Kilbegnet Parish, Derrylippo Townland

MEE, Darby 26 head m. 1840 lab, Bridget 22 wife flax spinner R, Ellen DYLE 18 serv R.

    Co Galway, Ballymoe Barony, Kilbegnet Parish, Lenarevagh Townland

MEE, Edmond 60 head m. 1811 farmer, Anne 50 wife, Mary 27 spinner, Catherine 20 spinner, Patt 24 lab, Denis 22 lab, Thomas 18 lab, John 12 in school R.

    Co Galway, Ballymoe Barony, Kilbegnet Parish, Lisduff Townland

MEE, John 36 head m. 1829 lab RW, Mary 38 wife flax spinner, John 12 son RW, Martin 9, Margaret 8, Patt 7, Peter 5.

    Co Galway, Ballymoe Barony, Kilbegnet Parish, Corlachan Townland

MEE, Malick 28 head m. 1839 landholder and lab, Biddy 21 wife flax spinner, Peter 1 son.

    Co Galway, Ballymoe Barony, Kilbegnet Parish, Lenanmarla Townland.

MEE, Margaret 60 head m. 1818 wid, Bridget 22 dau n.m. spinner, James 20 son lab, John 18 son lab.

    Co Galway, Ballymoe Barony, Kilbegnet Parish, Aghalateeve Townland

MEE, Martin 36 head m. 1831 lab, Brigget (sic) 30 wife spinning wool R, John 8 son, male child 5 son, Sally 6 dau, Caterin 2 dau.
 Co Galway, Ballymoe Barony, Kilbegnet Parish, Lenarevagh Townland

MEE, Martin 35 head m. 1835 lab, Mary 30 wife, Mary Mee, Jr. 4 dau, Mary DONNELLAN 12 h serv. DEC: John Mee 37 brother lab d. 1832 dropsy, Patt Mee age 1 brother (sic) d. 1837 convulsion.
 Co Galway, Ballymoe Barony, Kilbegnet Parish, Moat Townland

MEE, Martin 48 head m. 1837 lab, Winey 38 wife flax spinner, Mary McDERMOTT 34 n.m. flax spinner (relationship na), Mary Mee 3 dau.
 Co Galway, Ballymoe Barony, Kilbegnet Parish, Sonnagh Townland

MEE, Mary 30 head m. 1834 wid spinner, John 4 son, Thomas 2 son, Bridget 16 serv (same surname). DEC: Thomas Mee 46 husband lab d. 1839 asmatic.
 Co Galway, Ballymoe Barony, Kilbegnet Parish, Moat Townland

MEE, Mary 45 head m. 1812 wid, Patt 22 son n.m. lab; ABS: Mary 16 dau serv in Galway, Honor Mee 14 dau serv in Co Roscommon.
 Co Galway, Ballymoe Barony, Kilbegnet Parish, Lenarevagh Townland

MEE, Owen 25 head m.1838 lab R, Sally 22 wife, Owen, Jr. 1 son, Marget KELLY 17 serv flax spinner.
 Co Galway, Ballymoe Barony, Kilbegnet Parish, Lenarevagh Townland

MEE, Pat 30 head m. 1835 lab, Bridget 28 wife spinner, Honor 5, Nelly 3, John 2, Mary 15 relation spinster, Betty DEVANEY 15 serv spinner.
 Co Galway, Ballymoe Barony, Kilbegnet Parish, Lenanmarla Townland

MEE, Patt 40 head m. 1827 lab, Bridget 35 wife spinster, James 13 Mr. Collins' school R, Edward 11 in school R, Catherine 6, Martin 2, Bridget 1, Mat 1 mo son, Mary 40 sister m. 1823 spinner, Bridget 26 sister m. 1830 spinster; ABS: Nail RYAN 35 B/L lab in England, James GIBLIN 44 B/L lab in England. DEC: Bridget NEE(?) 26 wife spinner d. 1833 decay, Mary Mee 40 mother d. 1834 decay.
 Co Galway, Ballymoe Barony, Kilbegnet Parish, Lenanmarla Townland

MEE, Patt 34 head m. 1836 lab, Mary 30 wife, Denis 16 brother tailor RW, Bridget 17 sister spins wool, Catherine 16 sister; ABS: Thomas Mee 26 brother lab in England. DEC: Thomas Mee 60 father lab d. 1834 consumption, Catherine 55 mother spinner d. 1835 fever, Mickle 25 brother lab d 1834 fever, Sally 20 sister spinner d. 1835 fever.
 Co Galway, Ballymoe Barony, Kilbegnet Parish, Sonnagh Townland

MEE, Patt 56 head m. 1821 wid farmer R, Mary 24 dau m. 1840, Thomas KELLY 26 m. 1840 S/L lab. DEC: Edward Mee 22 son lab d. 1836 fever, Pat 26 son lab d. 1819 (sic) decay.
 Co Galway, Ballymoe Barony, Kilbegnet Parish, Lisduff Townland

MEE, Peter 60 head m. 1827 lab, Bridget BRENNAN 60 wife, Peter Mee 30 son n.m. lab. DEC: John Mee 1 mo son (sic) d. 1832 weakness.
 Co Galway, Ballymoe Barony, Kilbegnet Parish, Derrylippo Townland

MEE, Peter 26 head m. 1835 publican RW, Catherine 23 wife attends shop RW, Martin

GATELY 22 serv lab RW b. Co Roscommon, Sally SMYTH 22 h serv.
Co Galway, Ballymoe Barony, Kilbegnet Parish, Creggs Townland

MEE, Thomas 19 head n.m. lab RW, Honour 44 mother m. 1805 wid spinning yarn, Mary J.
18 sister R, Honor Mee 5 gr dau, John Mee 29 visitor lab, James GOLY 13 serv lab. DEC:
Owen Mee 45 father lab d. 1840 decay.
Co Galway, Ballymoe Barony, Kilbegnet Parish, Lenarevagh Townland

MULLIN, Onor 64 head m. 1800 wid landholder, Bernard 32 son n.m. lab, James 28 son n.m.
lab RW, Catherine MEE 8 gr dau, Thomas McDONNELL 7 gr son in school. DEC: Lacky
Mullin 67 father yeoman d. 1839 pains.
Co Galway, Ballymoe Barony, Kilbegnet Parish, Lisduff Townland

MULRY (Mullery), John 28 head m. 1836 tailor, Peggy 26 wife, Bryan 5, Biddy 3, Thomas
MEA 60 m. 1796 F/L lab.
Co Galway, Ballymoe Barony, Kilbegnet Parish, Derrylippo Townland

McGUIRE, Bryan 33 head m. 1829 lab, Bridget 27 wife spinner, Michael 10, Bridget 8,
Margaret 5, Thomas 2.
Co Galway, Ballymoe Barony, Kilbegnet Parish, Fairfield Townland

McGUIRE, Conner 38 head m. 1826 lab, Honora 33 wife, Catherine 14 dau in school R, Patt
12 in school R, Mary 9 R, Michael 7 R, John 5, John McGuire 22 cousin lab.
Co Galway, Ballymoe Barony, Kilbegnet Parish, Fairfield Townland

McGUIRE, John 37 head m. 1829 smith R, Honora 32 wife, Mary 11 Mr. Corr's school R,
Bridget 6 in school, Patt 4, Conner 18 mo, Michael McGuire 18 apprentice smith RW, Peggy
LALLY 70 lodger wid m. 1801 popper (sic); ABS: Conner McGuire 25 brother blacksmith in
America, Thomas McGuire 22 brother blacksmith in England. DEC: Bernard McGuire 8 son
d. 1840 consumption.
Co Galway, Ballymoe Barony, Kilbegnet Parish, Curraghbog Townland

McGUIRE, Luke 32 head m. 1837 lab, Catherine 27 wife spinner, Michael 2, John 78 father
wid m. 1798 lab. DEC: Margaret McGuire 77 mother spinner d. 1837 decay.
Co Galway, Ballymoe Barony, Kilbegnet Parish, Fairfield Townland

McGUIRE, Margaret 30 m. 1835 R, Martin 5 son, Bernard 3 son, Bridget 18 mo dau, Judy
HEATH 16 serv; ABS: Patrick McGuire 30(?) husband blacksmith probably in America.
Co Galway, Ballymoe Barony, Kilbegnet Parish, Aghalateeve Townland

McKAGUE, Edward 29 head m. 1835 lab, Catherine 25 wife, Mary 5 dau, Margaret 3 dau,
James IGO 24 serv n.m. lab, Bridget GIBLIN 25 n.m. h serv, Mickle McGARRY 10 serv lab.
DEC: Honora McKague 6 dau d. 1841 smallpox.
Co Galway, Ballymoe Barony, Kilbegnet Parish, Funshin Townland

NEARY, Peter(?) 25 head n.m. tailor, Onny Neary 20 (relationship na) hk R, Denis MEE 14
apprentice R. DEC: Hugh Neary 60 father lab d. 1838 decay.
Co Galway, Ballymoe Barony, Kilbegnet Parish, Aghalateeve Townland

COUNTY LIMERICK

FARR, Henry 20 head m. 1840 civil asst. Ordnance Survey Ireland RW b. Co Tyrone, Jane 33 wife RW b. Co Mayo, Mary Ann 4 mo dau b. Co Limerick.
    Co Limerick, City of Limerick, Upper Myles Lane

FEORE, John 44 head m. 1815 farmer RW, Honora 46 wife RW, Martin 23 n.m. schoolmaster RW, Honora 21 RW, Laurence 20 RW, Catherine 18 RW, John 16 RW, Alice 15 RW, Margaret 13 R, Mary 11 R, Thomas 9 R, Johanna 7 R, Michael 5 R. DEC: Henery McDONAGH 8 mother's cousin, visitor d. 1833 smallpox, Catherine Feore mother and visitor d. 1837 fever.
    Co Limerick, Lib Kilmallock Barony, Sts. Peter & Paul Parish, Graiganster Townland

FEORE, John 50 head m. 1827 farmer RW, Mary 40 R, Thomas 13 at Mr. Gordan's school RW, Peggy 11 in school RW, Edmond 9 in school R, Mary 4 in school, Bridget 2. DEC: Garth Feore 8 son d. 1826 convulsions.
    Co Limerick, Barony Kilmallock Liberties, Sts. Peter & Paul Parish, Cullamus Tnld

FEORE, Martin 60 head farmer RW, Catherine 52 wife RW, Mary 22 RW, Thomas 20 RW, John 18 RW, Mary SULLIVAN 58 sister flax spinner, Bartholomew TOOMY 24 visitor n.m. lab. DEC: Debora Feore 9 dau d. 1838 decline.
    Co Limerick, Barony Kilmallock Liberties, Sts. Peter & Paul Parish, Cullamus Tnld

FOER (sic), Patrick 32 head m. 1839 lab RW, Norah 25 wife. DEC: Ann Foer 3 mo dau d. 1840 convulsions.
    Co Limerick, City of Limerick, Welshes Lane

FRAHER, David 32 head m. 1827 wid lab RW, Honora 13 dau hk, Margret 9, Anne 5, Catherine 3. DEC: Catherine CANNANE 38 wife d. 1833 in labor, Anne Fraher 60 mother d. 1835 decline, Mary Fraher 32 wife d. 1840 decline.
    Co Limerick, Barony Kilmallock Liberties, Sts. Peter & Paul Parish, Deebert Tnld

FRAHER, Mary 30 head m. 1827 begging, Mary 8 dau, Catherine 3 dau. DEC: John Fraher 40 husband lab d. 1837.
    Co Limerick, Barony Kilmallock Liberties, Sts. Peter & Paul Parish, Deebert Tnld

PHAYER, William 26 head m. 1837 coachmaker RW b. Co Limerick, Ellen 22 wife RW b. City of Limerick, Richard 3, Elizabeth 1, Richard 18 brother coachmaker RW, Thomas 16 brother coachmaker RW, Grace LYONS 16 serv, Johana GILBERT 26 serv RW all b. City of Limerick.
    Co Limerick, City of Limerick, St. Michael Parish, Shannon St.


COUNTY MAYO

CAREY, Daniel 61 head m. 1818 farmer, Mary 45, John 21 son farming, Barbara 17 sewing and knitting, Martin 16 farming, Patrick 9 at chapel school, Michael 7 in school, Mary Ann 5 in school, Peter McGINTY 34 lodger sadler n.m., all b. Co Mayo. DEC: Hugh DEVER 80 F/L farmer d. 1840, Ellen Carey 6 dau 1835 chincough, Margaret 5 dau d. 1836 chincough.
    Co Mayo, Burrishoole Barony, Burrishoole Parish, Newport

COUNTY MEATH – see CRAWFORD under COUNTY CARLOW

## COUNTY MONAGHAN

NORRIS, Margaret 60 head m. 1802 wid Presbyterian R b. Co Monaghan, Alex 35 son n.m. carter RW, John 33 son m. 1836 publican RW, Thomas 29 son m. 1831 farmer RW b. Co Cavan, Mary Ann Norris 24 dau n.m. RW; ABS: William Johnston Norris 28 son in the army, Cape of Good Hope, Robert Norris 21 son constabulary in Red Hill, Co Cavan. DEC: Margarett Eliza Norris 19 dau mantuamaker d. 1838 fever.
  Co Monaghan, Trough Barony, Donagh Parish, Corracrin Townland

NORRIS, John 36 head . 1830 publican Presbyterian RW, Mary 35 wife RW, Mary Ann in school spells, Mary HACKETT 24 serv n.m. R, Mary RENICK(?) 70 M/L Presbyterian.
  Co Monaghan, Trough Barony, Donagh Parish, Carriagans Townland

NORRIS, Jane 67 head m. 1797 wid sewing R, Mary Ann WALL 17 gr dau RW.
  Co Monaghan, Trough Barony, Donagh Parish, Derryhallagh Townland

## COUNTY ROSCOMMON

BRIUN, Mat 56 head n.m. lab RW, Patt GIBLIN 12 visitor.
  Co Roscommon, Athlone Barony, Fuerty Parish, Aghagad Townland

GIBLIN, Honor 35 head m. 1826 wid huckster, Anne 10 dau in school; ABS: John 12 son in school. DEC: William 40 husband lab d. 1833 pleurisy, Honor 3 dau d. 1837 severe cold.
  Co Roscommon, Athlone Barony, Fuerty Parish, Clooneenbaun Tnld, Rockfield V

GIBLIN, John 40 head m. 1831 farmer RW, Mary 30 wife, Michael 9 son in school, Patrick 7 in school, Maria 5, Anne 2, Thomas KENNY 70 m. 1800 visitor lab RW; ABS: Mary MULLIGAN 61 M/L.
  Co Roscommon, Athlone Barony, Fuerty Parish, Clooneenbaun Townland

GIBLIN, Michle 42 head m. 1820 farmer RW, Catherine 32, Anne 19, Catherine 15, Mary 13 Mrs. Verdon's school RW, Margret 11 in school RW, Winny 9 in school RW, Eliza 7 in school R, Michle 5, Celia 3, James NAUGHTON 22 serv lab, Peggy CAIN 30 h serv, Anne COYLE 14 h serv; ABS: James Giblin 17 son at school in Derry.
  Co Roscommon, Athlone Barony, Fuerty Parish, Aghagower Townland

GIBLIN, Owen 50 head m. 1810 lab, Onny or Ann 42, Patt 21, Sally 18 R, Thomas 15 lab.
  Co Roscommon, Athlone Barony, Fuerty Parish, Creemully Townland

GIBLIN, Thady 50 head n.m. farming RW, Patrick 13 son lab.
  Co Roscommon, Athlone Barony, Fuerty Parish, Clooneenbaun Tnld, Rockfield V

GIBLIN, Thomas 60 head n.m. lab, John Giblin 24 nephew lab R. DEC: Bridget Giblin 70 mother (date na) infirmity.
  Co Roscommon, Athlone Barony, Fuerty Parish, Creemully Tnld, Creemully V

GIBLIN, Timothy 44 head n.m. lab, Michael 36 brother n.m. lab RW, Margaret 70 mother m. 1790 wid.

Co Roscommon, Athlone Barony, Fuerty Parish, Clooneenbaun Tnld, Rockfield V

GIBLIN, Timothy 32 head m. 1830 gentleman RW, Rose 39 (29?) RW, Mickle 9 in school RW, Margret 8 in school RW, Maria 6 in school R, Timothy 4, Annie 2, James 4 mo, Loughlin CONNOR 21 serv lab RW, Bridget ROONEY 15 h serv RW, Jane KELLEY 11 h serv R. DEC: Michle Giblin 73 head, land steward d. 1833 consumption.
    Co Roscommon, Athlone Barony, Fuerty Parish, Muff Townland

GIBLIN, William 41 head m. 1824 RW, Mary 35 wife RW, Timothy 17 in school RW, Michael 10 in school RW, Margrett 7 in school RW, Patt 7 in school RW, Mary 5 in school R, Charles 3 William 2. DEC: Charles 9 mo son d. 1832 smallpox, William 4 son d. 1835 smallpox.
    Co Roscommon, Athlone Barony, Fuerty Parish, Muff Townland

HIGGINS, Bernard 35 head m. 1824 farmer RW, Mary 32, Maria 15 R, Eliza 8 in school, Bedelia 5, Anne 2; ABS: Catherine 10 dau in Co Galway, Maggie 12 dau in Roscommon.
    Co Roscommon, Ballintober Barony, Roscommon Parish, Ardkeel Townland

HIGGINS, James 25 head m. 1838 steward RW, Susan 24 wife RW, Eliza 2 dau, Ellen FITZGERALD 26 n.m. h serv R.
    Co Roscommon, Ballintober Barony, Roscommon Parish, Lisnamult Townland

HIGGINS, John 34 head m. 1833 farmer RW, Mary 32 RW, John 62 father wid m. 1806 lab RW, Bridget 15 sister R, Ann 7 dau in school, Patt 6 son in school, Joseph 4 son in school R.
    Co Roscommon, Ballintober South Barony, Roscommon Parish, Ballybride Townland

HIGGINS, Luke 60 head m. 1836 farmer RW, Catherine 56 RW, Eliza 19 dau RW, Anne 15 dau RW, Bedilia FAHEY 22 m. 1840 dau RW. DEC: Margaret 22 dau d. 1834 consumption.
    Co Roscommon, Ballintober South Barony, Roscommon Parish, Lisnamult Townland

HIGGINS, Martin 30 head m. 1828 lab, Ann 40 wife, John 12, Henry 10, Bernard 8, Patt 6, Cathrine 3, Elizabeth 1.
    Co Roscommon, Ballintober South Barony, Kilteeran Parish, Newtown Townland

HIGGINS, Mary 60 head n.m. begging.
    Co Roscommon, Ballintober Barony, Roscommon Parish, Ballypheasan Townland

HIGGINS, Pat 37 head m. 1826 farmer, Jane 36 wife lab, Bridget 13, Mary 11, Anne 8, Thomas 5, Catherine 3.
    Co Roscommon, Ballintober South Barony, Roscommon Parish, Ardkeel Townland

HIGGINS, Patt 25 head m. 1841 lab, Mary 21 wife.
    Co Roscommon, Ballintober South Barony, Roscommon Parish, Ballinagard Tnld

HIGGINS, Thady 38 head m. 1821 weaver R, Bridget 45 R, John 18 lab, Thomas 15 lab, Timothy 11.
    Co Roscommon, Ballintober South Barony, Roscommon Parish, Stonepark Townland

HIGGINS, Thomas 29 sub-constable n.m. RW b. Co Galway.
    Town of Roscommon, constabulary occupying Ordnance Barracks at Roscommon

HIGGINS, Thomas 45 head wid m. 1817 farmer RW, Patt 20 son lab RW, Bridget 19 R, Timothy 18 lab R, Bernard 16 lab RW, Maria 14 R, James 12 lab, Ellen 8 in school R, Luke 6 in school; ABS: John 22 son lab in <u>America</u>. DEC: Catherine TUCKER 40 wife d. 1836.
  Co Roscommon, Ballintober Barony, Roscommon Parish, Ardkeel Townland

HIGGINS, William 34 head m. 1831 lab R, Mary 25 R, Maria 7, Patt 5, Thomas 3, Michael 8 mo. DEC: Bridget 2 dau d. 1833 decay.
  Co Roscommon, Ballintober Barony, Roscommon Parish, Ballypheasan Townland

MANNION, Lacky 58 head m. 1814 farmer, Bridget 54 wife knitting, John 24 son n.m. lab, Michael 16 son lab RW, Jane QUIGLEY 38 cousin m. 1833 serv; ABS: Patrick 26 son lab in <u>America</u>. DEC: Mary 12 dau d. 1833 measles.
  Co Roscommon, Ballintober Barony, Fuerty Parish, Cooly Townland

QUIGLEY, Michael 50 head m. 1826 lab, Mary 40 wife, son 11, Thomas(?) 9, Mary 7, Margrate 5, Cathrine 2.
  Co Roscommon, Ballintober South Barony, Kilteeran Parish, Newtown Townland

QUIGLEY, Patt 48 head m. 1813 farmer and publican RW, Matilda 51 wife RW, Kitty 20 industry RW, William 17 lab RW, James 11 in school, Matilda BARRETT 3 gr dau.
  Co Roscommon, (Athlone Barony, Fuerty Parish) Village of Fuerty

QUIGLEY, Patt 52 head m. 1822 lab, Peggy 50 wife spins wool, Bridget 17, Mary 16, Michael 14, Patt 11. DEC: Honoria 1 dau d. 183- (illegible, off page) cause unknown.
  Co Roscommon, Ballintober Barony South, Kilteeran Parish, Newtown Townland

QUIGLY, Mary 23 head n.m., Catherine BANAGHAN 3 dau, Bridget Quigley (sic) 20 sister m. 1840, Margaret Quigley 17 sister, Mary MULVEY 31 n.m. visitor, Anne Mulvey 25 visitor, Maria LEHANY 19 visitor, Mary McDONNELL 6 visitor, Patrick FARRELL 14 mo visitor. DEC: Bridget Quigly 40 mother d. 1839 decay, Michael 18 brother lab d. 1836 suddenly.
  Co Roscommon, Ballintober South Barony, Roscommon Parish, Ballypheasan Tnld

RATICAN (Ratigan), Michael 40 head m. 1841 lab, Mary 38 wife spins linen, Bridget GIBLIN 30 S/L n.m. spinner.
  Co Roscommon, Athlone Barony, Fuerty Parish, Aghagower Townland

********************

1841 Census record from the <u>Wilson family transcription</u> held at PRONI in Belfast, Republic of Ireland location:

BERRY, Smith M. 53 head m. 1818 wid farmer, Thomas Francis Berry 21 son miller n.m., Isabella A. Berry 20 dau, Allen Noble Berry 17 son, Marlboro Parsons Berry 15 son, 4 female and 2 male serv.
  Kings County, Eglish Barony, Eglish Parish, Eglish Townland

Aylward, Bridget, 29

Banaghan, Catherine, 44
Barrett, Matilda, 44
Barry, Alley, 19
Barry, Catherine, 19
Barry, Edward, 19
Barry, Johana, 19
Barry, Mary, 19
Barry, Robert, 19
Berry, Allen Noble, 44
Berry, Isabella A., 44
Berry, Smith M., 44
Berry, Thomas Francis, 44
Berry, Marlboro Parsons, 44
Blanchfield, James, 29
Blanchfield, Mary, 29
Blanchfield, Patrick, 29
Bolan, Elenor, 30
Brehan, Johanna, 33
Brehan, Nancy, 33
Brennan, Ally, 35
Brennan, Anastasia, 33
Brennan, Ann, 30
Brennan, Anty, 35
Brennan, Biddy, 35
Brennan, Bridget, 39
Brennan, Catherine, 33, 35
Brennan, Edmond, 35
Brennan, Edward, 35
Brennan, Elinor, 35
Brennan, Honny, 33
Brennan, James, 33, 34, 35
Brennan, John, 33, 35, 36
Brennan, Judy, 35
Brennan, Margaret, 33, 35, 36
Brennan, Mary, 33, 35
Brennan, Michael, 33
Brennan, Patrick, 33, 35
Brennan, Peggy, 35
Brennan, Stephen, 35
Brennan, Thomas, 35
Brennan, Unity, 33
Brennan, Walter, 35
Brian, Allice, 34
Brian, Andrew, 34
Brian, Catherine, 34
Brian, David, 34
Brian, Dennis, 34
Brian, Edmond, 34
Brian, Honora, 34
Brian, Johanna, 34
Brian, John, 34
Brian, Mary, 34
Broaders, Johanna, 31

Broder, William, 34
Broders, Martin, 33
Broefie, Catherine, 31
Brophy, Bridget, 33
Brophy, Elizabeth, 33
Brophy, James, 33
Bryan, Bridget, 19
Bryan, Cornelius, 19
Bryan, Ellen, 19
Bryan, Luty, 19
Buchanan, John, 18
Buchanan, William, 18
Burrows, Bess, 18
Burrows, Charles, 18
Burrows, Lewis, 18
Burrows, Loftus, 18
Burrows, Teresa, 18
Butler, Billy, 35
Byrne, Ann, 29
Byrne, Anthony, 29
Byrne, Elizabeth, 29
Byrne, Mary, 29
Byrne, Michael, 29
Byrne, Teresa, 29
Byrne, Thomas, 27
Byrne, Wenafer, 24

Cahill, Ellen, 29
Cahill, Margaret, 29
Cahill, Teresa, 35
Cain, Peggy, 42
Cannane, Catherine, 41
Carberry, Fanny, 23
Carberry, James, 23
Carberry, Mary Anne, 23
Carey, Barbara, 41
Carey, Daniel, 41
Carey, Ellen, 41
Carey, John, 41
Carey, Margaret, 41
Carey, Martin, 41
Carey, Mary, 41
Carey, Mary Ann, 41
Carey, Michael, 41
Carey, Patrick, 41
Carroll, Anne, 23
Carroll, Catharine, 23
Carroll, James, 23
Carroll, Joseph, 23
Carroll, Judith, 23
Carroll, Mary, 23
Carroll, Mathew, 23
Carroll, Michael, 23
Carroll, Thomas, 23
Carrot, Martin, 32

Carson, Catherine, 26
Carty, Johanna, 32
Carty, John, 32
Carville, Alice, 18
Carville, Bernard, 18
Carville, Margaret, 18
Carville, Thomas, 18
Cary, Honora, 31
Casey, Jane 24
Casey, Mary, 24, 32
Casey, Owen, 24
Cassidy, Mary, 36
Casy, Cathrine, 19
Casy, Margret, 19
Casy, Mary, 19
Casy, Patt, 19
Casy, Robert, 19
Casy, William, 19
Caverly, John, 19
Caverly, Mary, 19
Caverly, Michael, 19
Clancy, Sally, 26
Clerk, Mary, 21
Cloran, Eleanor, 27
Cloran, Henry, 27
Cloran, John, 27
Coin, Bridget, 27
Coin, Mathias, 27
Coin, Pat, 27
Coin, William, 27
Colline, Anastasia, 34
Colline, David, 34
Colline, John, 34
Colline, Peter, 34
Collins, Allice, 34
Collins, Cornelius, 19
Collins, Ellen, 34
Collins, James, 34
Collins, John, 19, 34
Collins, Judith, 32
Collins, Mary, 19
Collins, Nancy, 34
Collins, Patt, 19
Collins, Richard, 34
Collins, Thomas, 34
Collins, Timothy, 20
Collins, William, 34
Commins, Thomas, 33
Condon, David, 31
Connell, Ellen, 26
Connell, James, 33
Connell, Jeoffery, 26
Connell, Margaret, 26
Connell, Matthew, 26
Connolly, Anty, 33
Connolly, Edmond, 33

Connolly, Ellen, 22
Connolly, James, 33
Connolly, Johanna, 33
Connolly, Patrick, 33
Connoly, Thomas, 20
Connor, Loughlin, 43
Conroy, Mary, 23
Cooke, Elizabeth, 36
Corcoran, Judith, 33
Corkery, Judith, 36
Costello, Mary, 36
Coughlin, Jeremiah, 23
Coyle, Anne, 42
Coyne, Augustine, 27
Craugh, Timothy, 19
Crawford, Andrew, 36
Crawford, Cathrin, 36
Crawford, Elizabeth, 36
Crawford, John W., 36
Crawford, Margaret, 36
Crawford, Mathew, 36
Crawford, Rebecca, 36
Crawford, Samuel E. H., 36
Crimmun, Mary, 21
Croke, Margaret, 34
Croke, Mary, 34
Cronin, Patrick John, 19
Crowly, Jeremiah, 19
Crowly, Mary, 19

Dalton, Ally, 35
Dalton, Catherine, 35
Dalton, Johanna, 35
Dalton, John, 35
Dalton, Mary, 35
Dalton, Patrick, 35
Dalton, Peter, 35
Dalton, Richard, 35
Daly, Belinda, 27
Daly, Bridget, 27
Daly, Isabella, 27
Daly, James, 19, 20
Daly, Jane, 19
Daly, John, 19, 27
Daly, Luke, 23
Daly, Margaret, 19, 27
Daly, Mary, 20, 27
Daly, Mary Anne, 27
Daly, Matilda, 27
Daly, Narry, 19
Daly, Peter, 27
Daly, Timothy, 19
Daly, William, 20
Darly, Mary, 20
Darly, Patrick, 20
Dean, Margaret, 18
Delahunty, Anne, 31
Delahunty, Catherine, 31

Delahunty, David, 33
Delahunty, Ellen, 33
Delahunty, Johanna, 31, 33
Delahunty, John, 31, 33
Delahunty, Margaret, 31, 33
Delahunty, Mary, 31, 33
Delahunty, Patrick 31
Dempsy, Cathrin, 20
Dempsy, Jeremiah, 20
Derm, James, 36
Devaney, Betty, 39
Dever, Hugh, 41
Dolan, Catherine, 34
Dolan, Johanna, 34
Dolan, Margaret, 34
Dolan, Mary, 33, 34
Dolan, Nancy, 34
Dolan, Patrick, 34
Donnellan, Mary, 39
Donough, Catherine, 20
Donough, Johana, 20
Donough, John, 20
Donough, Mary, 19, 20
Donough, Michael, 20
Donough, Thomas, 20
Donovan, Ellen, 20
Donovan, Jeremiah, 20
Donovan, Mary, 20
Donovan, Nony, 20
Donovan, Peter, 20
Doody, Johana, 24
Doody, Magret (sic), 24
Doody, Mary, 34
Doody, Patt, 24
Doody, Peter, 34
Doran, Anne, 24
Doran, John, 24
Doran, Julia, 24
Dowds, James, 20
Dowds, Mary, 20
Dowds, Mathew, 20
Dowdy, Alice, 31
Dowdy, Anastasia, 31
Dowdy, Andy, 31
Dowdy, Edmond, 31
Dowdy, Edward, 31
Dowdy, Honora, 31
Dowdy, Johanna, 31
Dowdy, John, 31
Dowdy, Joney, 31
Dowdy, Margaret, 31
Dowdy, Mary 31, 32
Dowdy, Matthew, 31
Dowdy, Perry, 31
Dowdy, Peter, 31
Dowdy, Thomas, 31
Dowdy, William 31
Dower, Anne, 35
Dower, Dora, 35

Dower, Elizabeth, 35
Dower, James, 35
Dower, John, 35
Dower, Margaret, 35
Dower, Patrick, 35
Dower, Robert, 35
Dowley, Thomas, 31
Dowling, Johanna, 33
Doyle, Anastasia, 33
Doyle, Catherine, 33
Doyle, Edmond, 33
Doyle, James, 33
Doyle, John, 33
Doyle, Margaret, 33
Doyle, Mary, 33
Doyle, Norah, 33
Doyle, Patrick, 33
Doyle, Richard, 33
Doyle, Thomas, 33
Doyle, Walter, 33
Doyle, William, 33
Driscoll, Bridget, 20
Driscoll, Cathrine, 20
Driscoll, Daniel, 20
Driscoll, Ellen, 20
Driscoll, Helena, 20
Driscoll, Jeremiah, 20
Driscoll, John, 20
Driscoll, Margaret, 20
Driscoll, Mary, 20
Driscoll, Mary Anne, 20
Driscoll, Timothy, 20
Dudy, Patrick, 33
Dungan, Anne, 25
Dunne, John, 32
Dunphy, Walter, 33
Dyle, Ellen 38

Eagan, Biddy, 36
Eagan, John, 36
Eagan, Mick, 36
Eagan, Thomas, 36
Eagan, Wenny, 36
Earley, Catherine, 24
Earley, John, 24
Earley, Sarah, 24
Earley, William, 24
Egan, Clare, 27
Egan, Honoria, 27
Egan, Julia, 27
Egan, Mary, 27, 36
Egan, Mathew, 27
Egan, Michael, 27
Egan, Patrick/Patt, 27, 36
Elmes, Elizabeth Jane, 24
Elmes, John Blair, 24
Elmes, John, Rev., 24
Elmes, Marian, 24

Elmes, Mary King, 24
Elmes, Thomas, 24
Elmon, Mary, 33

Fahey, Bedilia, 43
Fahy, Belinda, 27
Fahy, Honoria, 27
Fahy, Laurence, 27
Fahy, Maria, 27
Farley, James, 20
Farley, Mary, 20
Farley, Robin, 20
Farley, William, 20
Farr, Henry, 41
Farr, Jane, 41
Farr, Mary Ann, 41
Farrell, Anastasia, 31
Farrell, Bridget, 31
Farrell, Edward, 31
Farrell, Joseph, 27
Farrell, Margaret, 31
Farrell, Nancy, 31
Farrell, Patrick, 31, 44
Farrell, Peter, 31
Farrell, Thomas, 28
Fea, Arthur, 36
Fea, Elizabeth, 36
Fea, John, Rev., 36
Fea, Mary Ann, 36
Feeny, Anne, 27
Fenney, Edmond, 20
Feore, Alice, Allis, 31, 41
Feore, Anastasia, 30, 31
Feore, Andrew, 30
Feore, Bridget, 30, 41
Feore, Catherine, 30, 41
Feore, Debora, 41
Feore, Edmond, 30, 41
Feore, Ellenor, 31
Feore, Garth, 41
Feore, Honora, 41
Feore, James, 30
Feore, Johanna, 30, 41
Feore, John, 31, 41
Feore, Laurence, 41
Feore, Margaret, 30, 31, 41
Feore, Martin, 41
Feore, Mary, 30, 31, 41
Feore, Michael, 41
Feore, Peggy, 41
Feore, Richard, 31
Feore, Thomas, 41
Feore, Walter, 31
Feore, William, 31
Fewer, Mary, 34
Fewer, Michael, 34
Fewer, Thomas, 34
Fewer, Walter, 34

Fitzgerald, Alice, 29
Fitzgerald, Bridget, 29
Fitzgerald, Ellen, 29, 43
Fitzgerald, James, 29
Fitzgerald, Johanna, 29
Fitzgerald, John, 29
Fitzgerald, Kate, 29
Fitzgerald, Mary, 29
Fitzgerald, Michael, 29
Fitzgerald, Patrick, 29
Fitzgerald, Peirse, 29
Fitzgerald, Thomas, 29
Fitzgerald, Walter, 29
Fitzmorris, Ann, 37
Fitzmorris, Catherine, 37
Fitzmorris, Patt, 37
Flanagan, Honor, 24
Flanagan, Marey, 24
Flanagan, Thomas, 24
Flannigan, Bridget, 21
Flannigan, David, 21
Flannigan, John, 21
Flannigan, Michael, 21
Flynn, Ellen, 24
Flynn, John, 24
Flynn, Mary, 24
Foer, Ann, 41
Foer, Norah, 41
Foer, Patrick, 41
Foere, Edward, 31
Foere, Johanna, 31
Foere, Nicholas, 31
Foere, Thomas, 31
Foere, William, 32
Forsythe, Jane, 18
Fraher, Anne, 41
Fraher, Catherine, 41
Fraher, David, 41
Fraher, Honora, 41
Fraher, John, 41
Fraher, Margret, 41
Fraher, Mary, 41

Gahan, Anastasia, 29
Gahan, Catherine, 29
Gahan, Elenor, 29
Gahan, Elizabeth, 29
Gahan, Johanna, 29
Gahan, John, 29
Gahan, Joseph, 29
Gahan, Laurence, 29
Gahan, Margaret, 29
Gahan, Mary, 29
Gahan, Michael, 29
Gahan, Patrick, 29
Gahan, Richard, 29
Gahan, Thomas, 29
Gahan, William, 29

Gately, Martin, 39, 40
Geraghty, Andy, 24
Geraghty, John, 24
Geraghty, Mary, 24
Giblin, Ann/Anne, 37, 42
Giblin, Annie, 43
Giblin, Barthy, 37
Giblin, Betty, 37
Giblin, Bridget, 36, 37, 38,
        40, 42, 44
Giblin, Bryan, 37
Giblin, Catherine, 37, 38, 42
Giblin, Celia, 37, 42
Giblin, Charles, 43
Giblin, Daniel, 37
Giblin, Edward, 37
Giblin, Eliza, 42
Giblin, Francis, 37
Giblin, Honor/Honour, 37, 38,
        42
Giblin, James, 37, 38, 39, 42,
        43
Giblin, John, 37, 42
Giblin, Judy, 37, 38
Giblin, Kitty, 37, 38
Giblin, Mara, 37
Giblin, Margaret, 37, 38, 42,
        43
Giblin, Maria, 37
Giblin, Mary, 37, 38, 42, 43
Giblin, Michael, 37, 38, 42, 43
Giblin, Michle, 42, 43
Giblin, Mick, 37
Giblin, Mickle, 37, 42, 43
Giblin, Mickle, Jr., 37
Giblin, Nelly, 37
Giblin, Oney/Onny, 37, 42
Giblin, Owen, 42
Giblin, Patrick, 42
Giblin, Patt, 37, 38, 42, 43
Giblin, Peggy, 37, 38
Giblin, Peter, 37
Giblin, Richard, 38
Giblin, Rose, 37, 43
Giblin, Sally, 42
Giblin, Susana, 37
Giblin, Thady, 42
Giblin, Thomas, 37, 38, 42
Giblin, Timothy, 42, 43
Giblin, William, 42, 43
Giblin, Winifred, 37
Giblin, Winny, 42
Gilbert, Johana, 41
Goly, James, 40
Gorman, Catherine, 30
Gorman, Ellen, 30
Gorman, John, 30
Gorman, Mary, 30
Gorman, Michael, 30

Gorman, William, 30
Grace, Anastasia, 31
Grace, Biddy, 35
Grace, Judy, 31
Grace, Richard, 34
Grant, Anastasia, 30
Grant, Bridget, 30
Grant, Catherine, 32
Grant, David, 30, 34
Grant, Ed/Ed., 30
Grant, Ellen, 30
Grant, James, 30
Grant, Johanna, 30
Grant, John, 30
Grant, Judith, 30, 32
Grant, Laurence, 30
Grant, Margaret, 30, 34
Grant, Mary, 29, 30
Grant, Nelly, 32
Grant, Nora, 30
Grant, Patrick, 30
Grant, Thomas, 30
Grant, Walter, 32
Grant, William, 30
Griffin, Ellen, 24
Guinan, Elizabeth, 32
Guinan, Laurence, 32
Guinan, Michael, 32
Guinan, Nicholas, 31, 32
Guiness, Benjamin, 36

Hackett, Mary, 42
Hamilton, Bartholomew, 35
Hamilton, Ellen, 35
Hamilton, John, 35
Hamilton, Margaret, 35
Hamilton, Robert, 35
Hanlon, Anastasia, 32
Hanlon, Catherine, 32
Hanlon, Edmond, 32
Hanlon, Johanna, 32
Hanlon, John, 32
Hanlon, Thomas, 32
Hanrahan, Thomas, 20
Harnett, Cathorina, 24
Harnett, Jules, 24
Harnett, Patrick, 24
Hart, Agnes, 28
Hart, Betty, 28
Hart, Bridget, 28
Hart, Catherine, 28
Hart, Ed/Ed., 28
Hart, Edmund, 29
Hart, Elenor, 28
Hart, Elizabeth 28, 29
Hart, Ellen, 28, 29
Hart, James, 28
Hart, Johanna, 28

Hart, Judith, 28
Hart, Margaret, 28
Hart, Martin, 28
Hart, Mary, 28, 29
Hart, Mary Teresa, 28
Hart, Matthew, 28
Hart, Michael, 28, 29
Hart, Nicholas, 28
Hart, Patrick, 28
Hart, Paul, 28
Hart, Richard, 28
Hart, Thomas, 28
Hart, Walter, 28, 29
Hart, William, 28, 29
Hayes, Andrew, 33
Hayes, Mary, 33
Hearns, Patrick, 35
Heath, Judy, 40
Henebery, Bridget, 29
Henebery, Mary, 29, 31
Henigan, Jeremiah, 19
Henry, Ann, 18
Henry, Charles, 18
Henry, Elnor, 18
Herlihy, James, 21
Herlihy, John, 21
Herlihy, Mary, 21
Herlihy, Michael, 21
Herlihy, Patrick/Patt, 21
Higgins, Ann/Anne, 43
Higgins, Bedelia, 43
Higgins, Bernard, 43, 44
Higgins, Bridget, 43, 44
Higgins, Catherine, 43
Higgins, Eliza, 43
Higgins, Elizabeth, 43
Higgins, Ellen, 43, 44
Higgins, Henry, 43
Higgins, James, 43, 44
Higgins, Jane, 43
Higgins, John, 43, 44
Higgins, Joseph, 43
Higgins, Luke, 43, 44
Higgins, Maggie, 43
Higgins, Margaret, 43
Higgins, Maria, 43, 44
Higgins, Martin, 43
Higgins, Mary, 43, 44
Higgins, Michael, 43, 44
Higgins, Pat/Patt, 43, 44
Higgins, Susan, 43
Higgins, Thady, 43
Higgins, Thomas, 43, 44
Higgins, Timothy, 43, 44
Higgins, William, 43, 44
Hogan, Mary, 34
Horrenton, John, 20
Hyor, Edward, 27
Hyor, Margaret, 27

Igo, James, 40
Ireton, Fiddealew, 24
Ireton, Jane, 24
Ireton, Thomas, 24
Irwin, Johanna, 26
Irwin, Mary, 26

Jordan, Biddy, 18
Jordon, Catherine, 38
Jordon, Edward, 38
Jordon, John, 38
Jordon, Richard, 38

Keagon, Mary, 21
Keagon, Timothy, 21
Kealy, Ann, 28
Keane, Anty, 33
Keaney, Catherine, 24
Keaney, Patrick, 24
Keaney, William, 24
Keating, John, 33
Keaveny, Edmond, 38
Keaveny, John, 38
Keaveny, Laurence, 38
Keaveny, Mary, 38
Keaveny, Peter, 38
Keaveny, Thomas, 38
Keefe, Anastasia, 32
Keefe, Andrew, 28
Keefe, Ann, 28
Keefe, Bridget, 28
Keefe, Catherine, 28, 32
Keefe, Ellen, 28
Keefe, Henry, 28
Keefe, Johanna, 32
Keefe, John, 28, 32
Keefe, Margaret, 28, 32
Keefe, Mary, 28, 32
Keefe, Matthew, 28
Keefe, Michael, 28
Keefe, Nelly, 32
Keefe, Nicholas, 28
Keefe, Philip, 28
Keefe, Richard, 32
Keefe, Walter, 32
Keefe, William, 32
Kelley, Jane, 43
Kelly, Anne, 27
Kelly, Catherine, 28, 32
Kelly, Edmond, 33
Kelly, Elenor, 29
Kelly, James, 28, 32
Kelly, Johannaugh, 32
Kelly, John, 28, 29
Kelly, Margaret, 32, 39
Kelly, Mark, 28
Kelly, Mary, 28, 29

Kelly, Michael, 32
Kelly, Nora, 28
Kelly, Patrick, 29
Kelly, Peter, 32
Kelly, Richard, 28
Kelly, Thomas, 39
Kenedy, Anne, 25
Kenedy, James, 25
Kenedy, Jane, 25
Kenedy, John, 25
Kenedy, Marsella, 25
Kenedy, Mary Ann, 25
Kenedy, Thomas, 25
Kennedy, Bridget, 25
Kennedy, Catherine, 25
Kennedy, Dennis, 25
Kennedy, Elizabeth, 25
Kennedy, Jane, 25
Kennedy, John, 25
Kennedy, Marcella, 25
Kennedy, Mary, 25
Kennedy, Nicholas, 25
Kennedy, Patrick/Patt, 25
Kennedy, Peggy, 35
Kennedy, Richard, 25
Kennedy, Thomas, 25
Kennedy, Valentine, 25
Kenny, Margaret, 34
Kenny, Martin, 34
Kenny, Mary, 34
Kenny, Richard, 34
Kenny, Thomas, 42
Kenny, William, 34
Kerans, Patrick, 34
Kerney, Ellen, 24

Lally, Peggy, 40
Landy, Betty, 35
Landy, Biddy, 35
Landy, James, 35
Landy, Lilly, 35
Landy, Mary, 35
Landy, Nelly, 35
Landy, Thomas, 35
Leary, John, 35
Leary, Judith, 35
Leary, Mary, 21
Lehane, Mary, 26
Lehany, Maria, 44
Lehay, Margaret, 20
Loughan, Michael, 38
Love, John, 26
Loyns, Jeremiah, 21
Loyns, Johana, 21
Loyns, Mary, 21
Lynch, Anne, 21
Lynch, Catherine, 21, 25
Lynch, Christopher, 21

Lynch, Ellen, 21
Lynch, Henery, 25
Lynch, James, 25
Lynch, John, 21
Lynch, Michael, 21
Lynch, Rosey, 25
Lyons, Grace, 41


Mackey, James, 32
Mackey, Mary, 32
Mackey, Michael, 32
Madden, Honoria, 27
Madden, James Darcy, 27
Madden, Mary Matilda, 27
Madden, Sarah, 27
Madden, Stephen, 27
Magahran, Catharine, 21
Magahron, Bernard, 21
Magarty, Catherine, 21
Maguire, Alliss, 21
Maguire, Cathrine, 21
Maguire, Denis, 21
Maguire, John, 21
Maguire, Margaret, 21, 22
Maguire, Mary, 21
Maguire, Michael, 21
Maguire, Patrick, 21
Mahan, Catherine, 38
Maher, Margret, 32
Mahoney, Bridget, 23
Mahony, Bridget, 21
Mahony, Catharine, 21
Mahony, Ellen, 21
Mahony, Johanah, 21
Mahony, John, 21
Mahony, Mary, 21
Mahony, Peggy, 21
Mahony, Timothy, 21
Malone, Catherine, 32
Mannion, Bridget, 44
Mannion, John, 44
Mannion, Lacky, 44
Mannion, Mary, 44
Mannion, Michael, 44
Mannion, Patrick, 44
Many, Patrick, 31
Many, William, 31
Mara, Bridget, 21
Mara, William, 21
Mea (sic), Thomas, 40
Mee, Anne, 38
Mee, Biddy/Bridget, 38, 39
Mee, Catherine, 38, 39, 40
Mee, Daniel, 38
Mee, Darby, 38
Mee, Denis, 38, 39, 40
Mee, Edmond, 38
Mee, Edward, 39

Mee, Honor/Honour, 39, 40
Mee, James, 38, 39
Mee, John, 38, 39, 40
Mee, Malick, 38
Mee, Margaret, 38
Mee, Martin, 38, 39
Mee, Mary, 38, 39
Mee, Mary J., 40
Mee, Mat, 39
Mee, Mickle, 39
Mee, Nelly, 39
Mee, Ony, 38
Mee, Owen, 39, 40
Mee, Owen, Jr., 39
Mee, Pat/Patt, 38, 39
Mee, Peter, 38, 39
Mee, Sally, 39
Mee, Thomas, 38, 39, 40
Mee, Winey, 39
Millea, Alice, 32
Millea, James, 32
Millea, Mary, 32
Millea, Thomas, 32
Millea, William, 32
Moore, Jerry, 32
Morgan, Ellen, 35
Morgan, John, 35
Morgan, Mary, 35, 37
Morgan, Mick, 37
Morgan, Thomas, 35
Morgan, William, 35
Moriarty, Ella, 27
Morrissey, Michael, 35
Mullaney, Martin, 25
Mullanney, Sally, 25
Mullanney, Thomas, 25
Mulligan, Mary, 42
Mullin, Andrew, 25
Mullin, Bernard, 40
Mullin, Edward, 25
Mullin, James, 40
Mullin, Lacky, 40
Mullin, Margret, 25
Mullin, Onor, 40
Mullins, Johanna, 35
Mullins, Patrick, 35
Mulry, Biddy, 40
Mulry, Bryan, 40
Mulry, John, 40
Mulry, Peggy, 40
Mulvey, Anne, 44
Mulvey, Mary, 44
Murphy, Bernard, 21
Murphy, Catherine, 22, 32
Murphy, Denis, 26
Murphy, James, 21
Murphy, Jonay, 31
Murphy, Laurence, 31
Murphy, Marget, 21

Murray, Catherine, 33
Murray, James, 21
Murray, John, 21, 33
Murray, Juduth, 21
Murray, Margaret, 33
Murray, Mary, 33
Murray, Patt, 21
Murray, Thomas, 21
Murry, Edward, 21
Murry, John, 30
Murry, Margaret, 37
Murry, Mary, 30


McArdle, John, 25
McArdle, Owen, 25
McArdle, Seragh 25
McCall, Bridget, 25
McCall, Catherine, 25
McCall, James, 25
McCall, John, 25
McCall, Joseph, 25
McCall, Laurence, 25
McCall, Mary, 25
McCall, Patrick, 25
McCall, Thomas, 25
McCarthy, James, 33
McCarthy, John, 22, 36
McCarthy, Margaret, 22, 36
McCarthy, Mary, 36
McCarthy, Mary Ann, 22
McCarthy, Robert, 36
McCarthy, Welbore, 36
McCarthy, William, 36
McCernon, Mary, 22
McCline, Mary, 18
McCline, Pat, 18
McCline, Steven, 18
McCrossan, Ann, 18
McCrossan, Fanny, 18
McCrossan, James, 18
McDermott, Mary, 39
McDonagh, Henery, 41
McDonald, Anastasia, 30
McDonald, Bridget, 30, 31
McDonald, Margaret, 30
McDonald, Mary, 22
McDonald, Patrick, 32
McDonald, Richard, 30
McDonnell, Mary, 44
McDonnell, Thomas, 40
McElwane, Edward, 26
McGarry, Mickle, 40
McGinty, Peter, 41
McGrath, Michael, 22, 32
McGuire, Alice, 22
McGuire, Bernard, 40
McGuire, Bridget, 32, 40
McGuire, Bryan, 25, 36, 40

McGuire, Catherine, 36, 40
McGuire, Conner, 40
McGuire, Elenor, 25
McGuire, Honora, 40
McGuire, James, 22, 25
McGuire, John, 40
McGuire, Luke, 40
McGuire, Margaret, 40
McGuire, Martin, 40
McGuire, Mary, 40
McGuire, Michael, 40
McGuire, Patt/Patrick, 22, 40
McGuire, Rose, 22
McGuire, Thomas, 40
McKague, Catherine, 40
McKague, Edward, 40
McKague, Honora, 40
McKague, Margaret, 40
McKague, Mary, 40
McKnalley, Jane, 25
McKnalley, Martin, 25
McKnalley, Mary, 25
McMahon, Bernard, 22
McMahon, Bessy, 22
McMahon, Biddy, 22
McMahon, Mary, 22
McMahon, Peter, 22
McQuade, Anne, 18
McQuade, John, 18
McQuade, Mary, 18


Nail, Alley, 19
Nail, Catherine, 19
Nail, Denis, 19
Naughton, Andrew, 38
Naughton, George, 38
Naughton, James, 42
Naughton, Thomas, 38
Neal, Nancy, 22
Neary, Hugh, 40
Neary, Onny, 40
Neary, Peter, 40
Nee (sic), Bridget, 39
Nee – see Mee
Neill, Johanna, 30
Neill, Michael, 30
Norris, Alex, 42
Norris, Jane, 42
Norris, John, 42
Norris, Margaret, 42
Norris, Margrett Eliza, 42
Norris, Mary, 42
Norris, Mary Ann, 42
Norris, Robert, 42
Norris, Thomas, 42
Norris, William Johnston, 42

O'Brien, Mary, 26
O'Brien, Sarah, 36
O'Donel, Bessy, 26
O'Donel, Eugene, 26
O'Donel, Hugh, 25, 26
O'Donel, John, 25, 26
O'Donel, Maria, 25, 26
O'Donnel, Bridget, 26
O'Donnel, Catherine, 26
O'Donnel, Edward, 26
O'Donnel, Hannah, 26
O'Donnel, Manus, 26
O'Haren, Laurence, 31


Oab, Jane, 36
Oakes, Jane, 24
Osborne, Ellen, 34
Osborne, James, 34
Osborne, Thomas, 34


Phayer, Elizabeth, 41
Phayer, Ellen, 41
Phayer, Richard, 41
Phayer, Thomas, 41
Phayer, William 41
Phelan, Andrew, 31
Phelan, Bridget, 35
Phelan, Catherine, 31, 35
Phelan, Elinor, 35
Phelan, James, 35
Phelan, Margaret, 31
Phelan, Michael, 31
Phelan, Nicholas, 31
Phelan, Patrick, 31, 35
Phelan, Peter, 31
Phelan, Thomas, 31, 35
Phelan, Walter, 31
Philips, Bridget, 26
Philips, Nelly, 26
Philips, Patt, 26
Power, Catherine, 31
Power, James, 22
Power, John, 22
Power, Mary, 22
Power, Michael, 22


Quigley, Ann, 22
Quigley, Bernard, 22
Quigley/Quigly, Bridget, 44
Quigley, Cathrine, 22, 44
Quigley, Honoria, 44
Quigley, James, 44
Quigley, Jane, 44
Quigley, Kitty, 44
Quigley/Quigly, Margt., 44
Quigley/Quigly, Mary, 44

Quigley, Matilda, 44
Quigley/Quigly, Michael, 44
Quigley, Patt, 44
Quigley, Peggy, 44
Quigley, Thomas, 44
Quigley, William, 44
Quinn, Anastasia, 32, 33
Quinn, Catherine, 33
Quinn, Edmond, 32
Quinn, Edward, 32
Quinn, Honora, 33
Quinn, James 32
Quinn, John, 32, 33
Quinn, Mary, 32, 33
Quinn, Michael, 33, 34
Quinn, Thomas, 32
Quinton, Margaret, 26
Quirk, Mary, 33

Ratican, Mary, 44
Ratican, Michael, 44
Ready, Patrick, 35
Reagan, Patrick, 19
Reddy, Edmond, 34
Reddy, Margaret, 34
Reddy, Mary, 34
Reddy, Mathew, 34
Reiley, Anne, 22
Reiley, James, 22
Reiley, John, 22
Reiley, Mary, 22
Renick, Mary, 42
Rily, Owen, 37
River, Ellen, 35
Rooney, Bridget, 43
Roynane, Eliza, 26
Roynane, James, 26
Roynane, Jane, 26
Roynane, John, 26
Roynane, Luisa, 26
Roynane, Margaret, 26
Roynane, Mary Anne, 26
Roynane, Michael, 26
Roynane, Patrick, 26
Roynane, Sally, 26
Roynane, Thomas, 26
Roynane, William, 26
Ryan, Bridget, 37
Ryan, Catherine, 22
Ryan, Daniel, 22
Ryan, Ellen, 22
Ryan, Jeremiah, 22
Ryan, John, 32
Ryan, Mary, 22, 37
Ryan, Michael, 22
Ryan, Nail, 39
Ryan, Taid, 20

Shaw, George, 22
Shaw, James, 22
Shea, Margaret, 26
Sheridan, Ann, 18
Sheridan, Biddy, 18
Sheridan, Elenor, 18
Sheridan, James, 36
Sheridan, John, 18
Sheridan, Margaret, 18
Sheridan, Patrick, 18
Sheridan, Susan, 18
Short, Catherine, 18
Short, Elizabeth, 18
Simple, Sarah, 18
Smyth, Frances, 26
Smyth, Honour, 26
Smyth, John, 26
Smyth, Mary, 26
Smyth, Patt, 26
Smyth, Racheal, 26
Smyth, Robert, 26
Smyth, Sally, 40
Staunton, Bridget, 27
Stephens, Margaret, 30
Stone, William 34
Sullivan, Bridget, 22, 31
Sullivan, John, 22
Sullivan, Margaret, 22
Sullivan, Mary, 32, 41
Sullivan, Peter, 22
Sullivan, Thady, 31
Sullivan, Thomas, 31
Sullivan, Timothy, 22
Summers, John, 32
Sweeney, Catherine, 26
Sweeney, Denis, 26
Sweeney, Mary, 26
Swooney, Mary, 26

Tasifsy, Thomas, 33
Taylor, Margaret, 30
Taylor, Mary, 30
Taylor, Nat., 30
Teaf, John, 26
Tichardson, widow, 22
Tobin, Alice/Ally, 30
Tobin, Anastasia, 30
Tobin, Ann, 30
Tobin, Ed., 30
Tobin, James, 30
Tobin, Johanna, 30
Tobin, John, 30
Tobin, Kate, 30
Tobin, Margaret, 30
Tobin, Mary, 30
Tobin, Michael, 30
Tobin, Patrick, 30
Tobin, Richard, 30

Tobin, Thomas, 30
Toohy, John, 20
Toohy, Timothy, 20
Toomy, Bartholomew, 41
Tucker, Catherine, 44
Tudor, John Arthur, 36

Vale, Honora, 34

Wade, Jane, 26
Wade, Peter, 26
Wakefield, Daniel, 18
Wakefield, Eliza, 18
Wakefield, Eliza A., 18
Wakefield, Mary A., 18
Wakefield, Mary J., 18
Wall, Mary Ann, 42
Wallice, Mary, 34
Walsh, Agnes, 27
Walsh, Agnes Elizabeth 27
Walsh, Alice, 32
Walsh, Anastasia, 33, 34
Walsh, Bridget, 26, 34
Walsh, Catherine, 31, 32, 33,
          34
Walsh, Charles, 27
Walsh, Daniel, 27
Walsh, Denis, 34
Walsh, Edmond, 31, 34
Walsh, Edward, 33
Walsh, Ellenor/Elinor, 32, 33
Walsh, Ellen 27, 34
Walsh, Frances, 27
Walsh, Grace, 27
Walsh, Honora, 32, 33
Walsh, Honoria, 27
Walsh, James, 31, 32, 33
Walsh, Jeffrey, 33
Walsh, Johanna, 32
Walsh, John, 31, 32, 33
Walsh, Judith, 33
Walsh, Margaret, 31, 32, 33
Walsh, Marion, 35
Walsh, Mary, 26, 31, 32, 33,
          34, 35
Walsh, Mary Frances, 27
Walsh, Michael, 31, 32, 33, 34
Walsh, Nelly, 32
Walsh, Nicholas, 32, 33
Walsh, Nora, 32, 33
Walsh, Patrick, 31, 32, 34, 35
Walsh, Peter, 33
Walsh, Raymond, 26
Walsh, Richard, 31, 32, 33, 34
Walsh, Robin, 34
Walsh, Susan, 31
Walsh, Thomas, 27, 32, 33

Walsh, Walter, 31, 32, 33, 34
Walsh, William, 32
Walsh, William John, 27
Ward, Brine, 18
Ward, John, 18
Ward, Mary, 18
Ward, Pady, 18
Whelan, Bridget, 33
Whelan, Catherine, 33
Whelan, Edmond, 33
Whelan, Ellen, 33

Whelan, John, 33
Whelan, Judith, 33
Whelan, Margaret, 33
Whelan, Mary, 33
Whelan, Michael, 30, 33
Whelan, Patrick, 33
Whelan, Richard, 33
Whelan, Thomas, 33
Wilkie, Eliza, 18
Wilkie, James, 18
Wilkie, Mary Anne, 18

Young, James, 23
Young, Jane, 23
Young, Martha, 18
Young, Mary A., 18
Young, Robert, 18
Young, Thomas, 23
Young, William, 23

Married Name Cross-Index – 1841 Census
Republic of Ireland Locations

Anderson, Catherine dau nee Jack

Baxter, Betty wife m. Slevan
Boyle, Mary dau nee mcGlynn
Brennan, Bridget wife m. Peter Mee (p. 39)

Cannane, Catherine wife m. Fraher (p. 41)
Connolly, Johanna dau nee Keane (p. 33)
Cooke, Elizabeth dau/wid nee Fea (p. 36)
Coyle, Ann wife m. Sheals
Craig, Sarah dau nee Sweeney
Croke, Mary wife m. Kenny (p. 34)

Davis, Nancy wife m. Jack/Jackson
Deeney, Ellen dau nee McFeely
Doherty, Ann wife m. Cavanagh
Doherty, Jane wife m. Wilson
Dongan, Bridget wife m. Tiernan
Duffy, Elizabeth dau nee McColgan

Forsythe, Eliza dau nee Colgan
Forsythe, Eliza dau nee Wilkie (A)

Gara, Catherine wife m. Kidd
Gorman, Ellen dau nee Tobin (p. 30)
Grant, Mary wife m. Rddy (p. 34)
Green, Bess dau nee Burrows (Jordan) A
Greer, Jane dau nee Doherty
Gribbven, Mary wife m. Kearney
Grimley, Anne dau nee McQuade (Short) A
Guy, Elizabeth wife m. Dean

Hildebrand, Sarah wife m. Bland
Hogan, Mary dau nee Walsh (p. 34)

Illen, Sally wife m. Anderson

James, Eliza A. gr/dau nee Wakefield (Young) A
Johnston, Jane dau nee Cooke

Keefe, Catherine wife m. Ed Hart (p. 28)
Kennedy, Mary dau nee Mulheron
Kilgore, Betty wife m. Walker
Kinnear, Nancy dau nee Hegarty

Lafferty, Elizabeth dau nee Wilson
Lucas, Catherine wife m. Bourke
Lyons, Eliza dau nee Tiernan

Malcomson, Eliza dau nee Brice
Mee, Mary wife m. Kelly (p. 39)
Mulligan, Anne dau nee Cassidy

McAleer, Mary wife m. McAlea
McCline, Mary dau nee Sheridan (A)
McCrory, Eleanor dau nee Haughey
McDaid, Margaret dau nee Callaghan
McDaid, Margaret dau nee McAlea/McClay
McDonald, Catherine wife m. Rooney
McElwee, Elener dau nee Gillaspy
McQuade, Anne gr/niece m. Grimley (Short) A
McSorley, Bridget dau nee Bonner

Nichlaush, Honora wife m. Thos. Walsh (p. 32)
Nixon, Mary wife m. Colgan

O'Donnell, Ellener dau nee Sheals

Park, Anne wife m. McGettigan
Patton, Margaret wife m. Bradly

Scanlan, Mary dau nee Coyle

Toner, Mary Ann wife m. McColgan
Tucker, Catherine wife m. Thos Higgins (p. 44)

Wakefield, Mary A. dau nee Young (A)
Wallice, Nancy wife m. Collins (p. 34)

Note: (A) or A indicates location in Appendix

# PART TWO

1851 Irish Census Abstracts from Old Age Pension records – Republic of Ireland locations

Miscellaneous 1851 Irish Census Abstracts

The following are records of families found in the 1851 Census (not found in 1841). See 1841/1851 combined records and Appendix for additional records.

| Surname | Given | Rel | Age | Marr | Film | Remarks | Location |
|---|---|---|---|---|---|---|---|
| ARMOUR | Alexander | head | na | 1842 | 0258547 | | Donegal |
| ARMOUR | Rose | wife | na | 1842 | | | Inishowen W |
| ARMOUR | Nancy | dau | 8 | | | | Fahan Lr |
| ARMOUR | Thomas | son | 6 | | | | Adaravan |
| ARMOUR | George | son | 4 | | | | |
| ARMOUR | Bella | dau | 1 | | | Isabella claimant | |
| ARMOUR | | | | | | | |
| | | | | | | | |
| AVEA | John | head | na | na | 0258547 | | Monaghan |
| AVEA | Anna Maria | wife | na | na | | | Monaghan |
| AVEA | Sarah | dau | 3 | | | | Kilmore |
| AVEA | Margaret | dau | 1 | | | claimant, m. McCLELLAND | Armagheroy |
| AVEA | William | son | 3 w | | | | |
| | | | | | | | |
| BAIRD | Francis | head | na | 1839 | 0258547 | | Monaghan |
| BAIRD | Martha | wife | na | 1839 | | nee CRAWFORD per Cl. not fd. | Dartree |
| BAIRD | Catherine | dau | 11 | | | | Clones Lr |
| BAIRD | Daky | dau | 9 | | | | Poundhill |
| BAIRD | Jane | dau | 6 | | | | |
| BAIRD | Margret | dau | 3 | | | | |
| | | | | | | | |
| BALDRICK | George | head | na | na | 0258547 | | Donegal |
| BALDRICK | Margaret | wife | na | na | | | Inishowen W |
| BALDRICK | Bridget | dau | 5 | | | claimant | Desertegny |
| BALDRICK | Sarah | dau | 3 | | | | Ballyannon |
| BALDRICK | John | son | 2 m | | | d. 1844 | |
| | | | | | | | |
| BALDRICK | Thomas | head | na | 1831 | 0258546 | | Donegal |
| BALDRICK | Letitia | wife | na | 1831 | | | Inishowen W |
| BALDRICK | Eliza | dau | 18 | | | | Fahan Lr |
| BALDRICK | James | son | 14 | | | | Ardaravan |
| BALDRICK | George | son | 12 | | | | |
| BALDRICK | John | son | 10 | | | | |
| BALDRICK | Thomas | son | 9 | | | | |
| BALDRICK | Mary A. | dau | 4 | | | Mary Ann, claimant, m. CRAIGS | |
| BALDRICK | Andrew | son | na | | | d. date na | |
| BALDRICK | Letitia | dau | na | | | d. date na | |
| | | | | | | | |
| BARR | Andy | head | 25 | 1842 | 0258547 | Andrew | Donegal |
| BARR | Jane | wife | 30 | 1842 | | | Raphoe S |
| BARR | Nancy | dau | 8 | | | Annie, claimant | Urney |
| BARR | Ellen | dau | 8 | | | | Coolyshin |
| BARR | Eliza | dau | 7 | | | | |
| BARR | Andy | son | 1 | | | | |
| | | | | | | | |
| BARRON | Norah | head | na | na | 0258546 | wid, Hannah per claimant not found | Donegal |
| BARRON | Bridget | dau | 15 | | | | Tirhugh |
| BARRON | Catherine | dau | 11 | | | | Templecarn |
| BARRON | John | son | 9 | | | John? | Lettercran |
| BARRON | Gus | son | 7 | | | Gus? | |

| BARRON | John | husb na | na | | d. 1843 | |
|--------|------|---------|-----|---|---------|---|

| BATES | James | head na | 1845 0258547 | | Donegal |
|-------|-------|---------|--------------|---|---------|
| BATES | Sarah | wife na | 1845 | | Raphoe S |
| BATES | William | son 5 | | | Urney |
| BATES | James | son 4 | | claimant | Alt Up |
| BATES | Beckey | dau 1 | | | |

| BOGAL | Thomas | head 45 | na 0258547 | | Donegal |
|-------|--------|---------|------------|---|---------|
| BOGAL | Eliza | wife 33 | na | | Raphoe S |
| BOGAL | James | son 14 | | | Urney |
| BOGAL | John | son 12 | | | Gortnagrace |
| BOGAL | Maryan | dau 10 | | | |

| BONER | James | head 40 | 1834 0258547 | claimant spells BONAR | Donegal |
|-------|--------|---------|--------------|------------------------|---------|
| BONER | Mary | wife 41 | 1834 | claimant says Matilda | Raphoe N |
| BONER. | William | son 16 | | | Urney |
| BONER | Letitia | dau 14 | | | Alt |
| BONER | Mary | dau 11 | | | |
| BONER | Robert | son 9 | | | |
| BONER | Margaret | dau 6 | | claimant, m. CAMPBELL | |
| BONER | Eliza | dau 4 | | | |
| BONER | Matilda | dau 9 m | | | |

| BOUGLE | Andrew | head 40 | 1831 0258547 | | Donegal |
|--------|-----------|---------|--------------|---|---------|
| BOUGLE | Catherine | wife 40 | 1831 | | Raphoe S |
| BOUGLE | Matilda | dau 12 | | | Donaghmore |
| BOUGLE | William | son 10 | | | Gornamuck |
| BOUGLE | Andrew | son 7 | | claimant, spells BOGLE | |
| BOUGLE | Catherine | dau 2 | | | |

| BOYLE | Cornelius | head na | 1841 0258547 | | Donegal |
|-------|-----------|---------|--------------|---|---------|
| BOYLE | Julia | wife na | 1841 | | Inishowen W |
| BOYLE | William | son 9 | | | Muff |
| BOYLE | Rose | dau 7 | | claimant, m. McLAUGHLIN | Derryvane |
| BOYLE | Sarah | dau 4 | | | |
| BOYLE | Cornelius | son 2 | | | |

| * BOYLE | Eleanor | lodg 60 | 1808 0258547 | See H. McCLOSKEY | |
|---------|---------|---------|--------------|------------------|---|

| BRADLEY | Margaret | head na | na 0258546 | wid of Michael? | Donegal |
|---------|----------|---------|------------|-----------------|---------|
| BRADLEY | William | son 28 | | | Raphoe |
| BRADLEY | Mary | dau 25 | | | Convoy |
| BRADLEY | Anne | dau 21 | | | Lettermore |
| BRADLEY | Michael | son 13 | | | |

| BRADLEY | Nenion | head na | 1847 0258546 | (Nenion sic) | Donegal |
|---------|--------|---------|--------------|--------------|---------|
| BRADLEY | Fanny | wife na | 1847 | | Raphoe N |
| BRADLEY | Jane | dau 2 | | | Raymoghy |
| BRADLEY | Sarah | dau 2 m | | claimant, m. KILGORE | Dunduffsfort |

| BRANNAN | James | head 60 | 1825 0258547 | | Donegal |
|---------|----------|---------|--------------|---|---------|
| BRANNAN | Jane | wife 58 | 1825 | nee DONNELL | Raphoe N |
| BRANNAN | Mary | dau 20 | | | Clonleigh |
| BRANNAN | Margaret | dau 19 | | absent | Glenfad |
| BRANNAN | Richard | son 18 | | absent | |
| BRANNAN | William | son 17 | | claimant, spells BRENNAN | |
| BRANNAN | Jane | dau 14 | | | |
| BRANNAN | Nancy | dau 10 | | | |
| BRANNAN | James | son 7 | | | |

| | | | | | | |
|---|---|---|---|---|---|---|
| BRANNAN | Robert | son | 5 | | | |
| BRANNAN | Catherine | dau | 3 | | | |
| | | | | | | |
| BREESON | Pat | head | 25 | 1847 0258546 | | Donegal |
| BREESON | Mary | wife | 28 | 1847 | | Raphoe S |
| BREESON | Pat | son | 3 | | | Urney |
| BREESON | James | son | 9 m | | claimant, spells BRYSON | Gortnagrace |
| | | | | | | |
| BRENNAN | John | head | na | 1846 0258547 | R.I.C. | Cavan |
| BRENNAN | Catherine | wife | na | 1846 | nee CAHILL | Loughtee Up |
| BRENNAN | Daniel | son | 4 | | | Larah |
| BRENNAN | Bridget | dau | 2 | | | Stradone Town |
| BRENNAN | Annie | dau | 1 | | claimant | |
| | | | | | | |
| BROWN | Robert | head | 40 | 1830 0258547 | | Donegal |
| BROWN | Martha | wife | 37 | 1830 | nee LITTLE per claimant not found | Inishowen E |
| BROWN | Matty | dau | 20 | | in America | Moville Up |
| BROWN | Ann | dau | 18 | | in America | Ballyargus |
| BROWN | Mary | dau | 12 | | | |
| BROWN | Francis | son | 6 | | | |
| BROWN | John | son | 4 | | | |
| BROWN | John | son | 2 | | d. 1844 | |
| | | | | | | |
| BUTLER | William | head | na | na | 0258547 | Donegal |
| BUTLER | Mary | wife | na | na | | Inishowen E |
| BUTLER | Mary | dau | 19 | | | Moville U |
| BUTLER | Sarah | dau | 17 | | | Cabry |
| BUTLER | John | son | 14 | | | |
| BUTLER | William | son | 12 | | | |
| BUTLER | Ann | dau | 8 | | | |
| BUTLER | George | son | 6 | | | |
| BUTLER | Elizabeth | dau | 2 | | claimant, m. QUINN | |
| | | | | | | |
| BYRNE | Maurice | head | na | 1846 0258547 | | Donegal |
| BYRNE | Bridget | wife | na | 1846 | | Banagh |
| BYRNE | Bridget | dau | 4 | | claimant, m. TAYLOR | Kilcar |
| BYRNE | James | son | 2 | | | Kilcar |
| | | | | | | |
| BYRNE | Owen | head | 40 | 1836 0258547 | | Donegal |
| BYRNE | Annie | wife | 32 | 1836 | nee DOHERTY | Banagh |
| BYRNE | Denis | son | 13 | | | Kilcar |
| BYRNE | Mary | dau | 11 | | | Bogagh Glebe |
| BYRNE | Ann | dau | 9 | | | |
| BYRNE | Peter | son | 7 | | | |
| BYRNE | Biddy | dau | 5 | | claimant, m. McMENAMIN | |
| BYRNE | Alice | dau | 2 | | | |
| BYRNE | Margaret | dau | 3 m | | | |
| | | | | | | |
| CAIRNS | John | head | na | 1833 0258547 | | Donegal |
| CAIRNS | Margaret | wife | na | 1833 | | Raphoe N |
| CAIRNS | James | son | 15 | | | Raymoghy |
| CAIRNS | Margaret | dau | 12 | | | Killyverry |
| CAIRNS | John | son | 10 | | | |
| CAIRNS | Sarah | dau | 8 | | | |
| CAIRNS | Thomas | son | 5 | | claimant, or CARNS | |
| CAIRNS | Mary | dau | 18m | | | |
| | | | | | | |
| CALLAGHAN | John | head | na | na | 0258547 | Donegal |

| CALLAGHAN | Fanny | wife | na | na | | | Inishowen E |
|-----------|-------|------|----|----|--|--|-------------|
| CALLAGHAN | John | son | 4 | | | | Culdaff |
| CALLAGHAN | Edward | son | 2 | | | | Oort |
| CALLAGHAN | Mary | dau | 1 | | claimant | | |
| | | | | | | | |
| CAMPBELL | Patrick | head | 55 | 1839 | 0258547 | CAMPBLE, m. 1829?/1840 | Donegal |
| CAMPBELL | Magy | wife | 30 | 1840 | | nee GALLAGHER | Boylagh |
| CAMPBELL | John | son | 19 | | | absent | Inishkeel |
| CAMPBELL | Magy | dau | 18 | | | | Lughveen |
| CAMPBELL | Biddy | dau | 17 | | | d. 1851 | |
| CAMPBELL | Rose | dau | 12 | | | | |
| CAMPBELL | Ann | dau | 8 | | | | |
| CAMPBELL | Mary | dau | 7 | | | claimant, m. CULLEN | |
| CAMPBELL | James | son | 5 | | | | |
| | | | | | | | |
| CANNON | Thomas | head | na | na | 0258547 | | Mayo |
| CANNON | Mary | wife | na | na | | nee KELLY | Burrishoole |
| CANNON | Charles | son | 4 | | | | Burrishoole |
| CANNON | Anne | dau | 2 | | | claimant, m. MURPHY | Newport |
| CANNON – See | | | | | | Catherine KELLY, S/L | Main St. |
| | | | | | | | |
| CARLAND | William | head | 50 | 1823 | 0258547 | | Donegal |
| CARLAND | Betty | wife | 45 | 1823 | | Elizabeth | Raphoe N |
| CARLAND | John | son | 27 | | | | Clonleigh |
| CARLAND | William | son | 24 | | | | Mulnagung |
| CARLAND | Charles | son | 21 | | | | |
| CARLAND | Margaret | dau | 16 | | | | |
| CARLAND | Hannah | dau | 14 | | | | |
| CARLAND | Mary | dau | 11 | | | | |
| CARLAND | Thomas | son | 7 | | | Cl. spells CARLIN/CAROLAN | |
| CARLAND | Catherine | dau | 11 | | | d. 1843 | |
| | | | | | | | |
| CARR | Patrick | head | na | 1837 | 0258546 | also KERR | Monaghan |
| CARR | Mary | wife | na | 1837 | | | Trough |
| CARR | Mick | son | 19 | | | | Douagh |
| CARR | Patrick | son | 16 | | | | Emyvale Town |
| CARR | Ann | dau | 15 | | | | |
| CARR | Catherine | dau | 15 | | | | |
| CARR | Mary | dau | 12 | | | | |
| CARR | Hannah | dau | 9 | | | | |
| CARR | Margaret | dau | 4 | | | claimant, m. MURTAGH | |
| | | | | | | | |
| CATTERSON | Michael | head | 45 | 1822 | 0258547 | | Donegal |
| CATTERSON | Mary | wife | 43 | 1822 | | nee McNULLY | Raphoe |
| CATTERSON | Ellen | dau | 19 | | | | Donaghmore |
| CATTERSON | Margaret | dau | 14 | | | | Ballybun |
| CATTERSON | Pat | son | 13 | | | | |
| CATTERSON | Susan | dau | 10 | | | | |
| CATTERSON | Thomas | son | 8 | | | claimant | |
| | | | | | | | |
| CAVANAGH | Hugh | head | na | 1840 | 0258547 | | Donegal |
| CAVANAGH | Mary | wife | na | 1840 | | | Inishowen W |
| CAVANAGH | Philip | son | 10 | | | | Muff |
| CAVANAGH | Patrick | son | 7 | | | claimant | Derryvane |
| | | | | | | | |
| CLARKE | James | head | 47 | 1833 | 0258547 | | Donegal |
| CLARKE | Jane | wife | 44 | 1833 | | | Raphoe N |
| CLARKE | George | son | 17 | | | | Clonleigh |
| CLARKE | Catherine | dau | 15 | | | | Ballynabreen |
| CLARKE | Isabella | dau | 13 | | | | |

| CLARKE | Grace | dau | 7 | | | claimant, m. DOHERTY | |
|---|---|---|---|---|---|---|---|
| CLARKE | Mary | dau | 5 | | | | |
| CLARKE | Joseph | son | 18m | | | | |
| | | | | | | | |
| CLONOUGHAN | Charles | head | 35 | 1835 | 0258547 | CONAGHAN per claimant | Donegal |
| CLONOUGHAN | Mary | wife | 35 | 1835 | | | Raphoe N |
| CLONOUGHAN | Mary | dau | 13 | | | | Clonleigh |
| CLONOUGHAN | Ann | dau | 13 | | | | Springhill |
| CLONOUGHAN | Bridget | dau | 8 | | | | |
| CLONOUGHAN | Sarah | dau | 5 | | | claimant, m. HUSTON | |
| CLONOUGHAN | Charles | son | 4 m | | | | |
| | | | | | | | |
| COLL | Charles | head | na | na | 0258546 | | Donegal |
| COLL | Isabella | wife | na | na | | | Kilmacrenan |
| COLL | Margaret | dau | 19 | | | | Aughnish |
| COLL | William | son | 18 | | | | Rathmelton |
| COLL | Dan | son | 16 | | | | |
| COLL | Catherine | dau | 14 | | | | |
| COLL | Sarah | dau | 11 | | | | |
| COLL | Charles | son | 9 | | | | |
| COLL | Isabella | dau | 7 | | | | |
| COLL | George | son | 4 | | | claimant | |
| | | | | | | | |
| COLLINS | James | head | na | na | 0258547 | | Donegal |
| COLLINS | Ellen | wife | na | na | | | Inishowen E |
| COLLINS | Philip | son | 30 | | | | Moville Lr |
| COLLINS | Michael | son | 26 | | | | Carrickmaquigley |
| COLLINS | William | son | 24 | | | | |
| COLLINS | Nancy | dau | 16 | | | | |
| COLLINS | Patrick | son | 12 | | | claimant | |
| | | | | | | | |
| CONAGHAN | Charles | head | na | na | 0258547 | | Donegal |
| CONAGHAN | Bridget | wife | na | na | | | Kilmacrenan |
| CONAGHAN | Fanny | dau | 19 | | | | Gartan |
| CONAGHAN | Mary | dau | 8 | | | | Lossett |
| CONAGHAN | Michael | son | 6 | | | | |
| CONAGHAN | Neal | son | 3 | | | claimant | |
| CONAGHAN | Phil | son | 1 | | | | |
| | | | | | | | |
| * CONNOLLY | Bridget | serv | 18 | | 0258547 | with Edward TREANOR | |
| | | | | | | | |
| CONNOLLY | Felix | head | na | 1848 | 0258547 | | Monaghan |
| CONNOLLY | Mary | wife | na | 1848 | | | Monaghan |
| CONNOLLY | Mary Ann | dau | 2 | | | claimant, m. WOODS | Tedavnet |
| CONNOLLY | Michael | son | 6 m | | | | Killygavna |
| | | | | | | | |
| COOKE | John | head | na | na | 0258547 | | Donegal |
| COOKE | Catherine | wife | na | na | | | Raphoe N |
| COOKE | Mary Ann | dau | 12 | | | | All Saints |
| COOKE | Kitty | dau | 10 | | | | Monglass |
| COOKE | Stephen | son | 7 | | | | |
| COOKE | Sarah | dau | 2 | | | claimant, m. DEVLIN | |
| COOKE | William | son | 1 | | | d. 1847 | |
| | | | | | | | |
| COULTER | Charles | head | na | na | 0258546 | | Donegal |
| COULTER | Anne | wife | na | na | | | Tirhugh |
| COULTER | Catherine | dau | 9 | | | claimant, m. GALLAGHER | Templecarn |
| COULTER | Neal | son | 7 | | | | Tullylark |
| COULTER | John | son | 6 | | | | |
| COULTER | William | son | 3 | | | | |

| COULTER | Anne | dau | 1 | | | | |
|---------|------|-----|---|---|---|---|---|
| * COYLE | Catherine | gr/d | 12 | | 0258547 | with J. DONNELL, Cl.? m. MAGUIRE | |
| | | | | | | | |
| COYLE | James | head na | | na | 0258547 | | Donegal |
| COYLE | Margaret | wife na | | na | | | Raphoe N |
| COYLE | Lizzie | dau | 7 | | | claimant | All Saints |
| COYLE | Catherine | dau | 5 | | | | Cornacamble |
| COYLE | Mary | dau | 3 | | | | |
| COYLE | James | son | 5 w | | | age 5 weeks | |
| | | | | | | | |
| COYLE | Owen | head | 34 | | 1839 0258547 | | Donegal |
| COYLE | Kitty | wife | 34 | 1839 | | Kate, nee CAROLAN | Inishowen W |
| COYLE | Manus | son | 11 | | | | Burt |
| COYLE | Henry | son | 9 | | | | Bunnamayne |
| COYLE | Ellen | dau | 6 | | | | |
| COYLE | Denis | son | 3 | | | claimant | |
| COYLE | Catherine | dau | 1 | | | | |
| COYLE | Mary | dau | 1 | | | d. 1849 | |
| | | | | | | | |
| COYLE | Pat | head na | | | 1832 0258547 | | Donegal |
| COYLE | Margaret | wife na | | 1832 | | nee McCAFFERTY | Raphoe N |
| COYLE | John | son | 11 | | | | All Saints |
| COYLE | Dorcas | dau | 8 m | | | claimant | Castruse |
| | | | | | | | |
| COYLE | William | head na | | na | 0258547 | | Donegal |
| COYLE | Ellen | wife na | | na | | nee DOHERTY per Cl. not found | Raphoe N |
| COYLE | Anne | dau | 12 | | | | Taughboyne |
| COYLE | James | son | 10 | | | | Ardagh |
| COYLE | Ellen | dau | 6 | | | | |
| COYLE | Rose | dau | 3 | | | | |
| COYLE | William | son | 2 m | | | d. 1843 | |
| | | | | | | | |
| CRAWFORD | Mary | head | 50 | na | 0993107 | | Donegal |
| CRAWFORD | Margaret | dau | 21 | | | | Banagh |
| CRAWFORD | Catherine | dau | 18 | | | | Killmard |
| CRAWFORD | Andy | son | 16 | | | | Eddrim Glebe |
| CRAWFORD | Matt | son | 14 | | | | |
| | | | | | | | |
| CREANOR | Bernard | head na | | | 1828 0258547 | | Donegal |
| CREANOR | Margaret | wife na | | 1828 | | nee McSWEENEY per Cl. not fd. | Raphoe N |
| CREANOR | John | son | 18 | | | | Clonleigh |
| CREANOR | Sarah | dau | 16 | | | | Boylagh |
| CREANOR | Margaret | dau | 14 | | | Margaret LOGUE claimant? | |
| CREANOR | Eleanor | dau | 12 | | | | |
| CREANOR | Bernard | son | 12 | | | | |
| CREANOR | Catherine | dau | 8 | | | | |
| CREANOR | Edward | son | 6 | | | | |
| CREANOR | Susan | dau | 16 | | | d. 1844 | |
| CREANOR | Catherine | dau | 17 | | | d. 1846 | |
| | | | | | | | |
| CREANOR | James | head na | | | 1831 0258547 | (See TOURISH in Appendix) | Donegal |
| CREANOR | Hannah | wife na | | 1831 | | | Raphoe N |
| CREANOR | Margaret | dau | 16 | | | | Clonleigh |
| CREANOR | George | son | 6 | | | | Mulnaveagh |
| CREANOR | Mary Anne | dau | 4 | | | claimant, m. BROWN | |
| | | | | | | | |
| CRESSWELL | Joseph | head na | | na | 0258547 | | Donegal |
| CRESSWELL | Martha | wife na | | na | | nee STEVENSON | Inishowen W |
| CRESSWELL | Eliza Mary | dau | 10 | | | claimant | Burt |

| CRESSWELL | James | son | 5 | | | | Carrowreagh |
| CRESSWELL | Jane Ann | dau | 2 | | | | |

| CROSSAN | Catherine | head | 60 | 1810 0258547 | | wid | Donegal |
| CROSSAN | Thomas | son | 35 | 1839 | | | Raphoe N |
| CROSSAN | Margaret | dau | 27 | n.m. | | | Clonleigh |
| CROSSAN | Hugh | son | 25 | n.m. | | | Roughan |
| CROSSAN | Ann | dau | 20 | n.m. | | | |

| CROSSAN | James | head | na | 1846 0258547 | | | Donegal |
| CROSSAN | Margaret | wife | na | 1846 | | | Kilmacrenan |
| CROSSAN | Lizzie | dau | 3 | | | | Aghanunshin |
| CROSSAN | James | son | 2 | | claimant | | Loughagannon |

| CROSSAN | William | head | 25 | na | 0258547 | listed as grandson | Donegal |
| CROSSAN | Mary | wife | 28 | na | | | Kilmacrenan |
| CROSSAN | William | son | 7 | | | | Aghanunshin |
| CROSSAN | James | son | 6 | | | | Loughagannon |
| CROSSAN | Mary Ann | dau | 4 | | | | |
| CROSSAN | Margaret | dau | 2 | | | | |
| CROSSAN | John | son | 6 m | | | | |
| CROSSAN | William | gr/f | na | 1801 | | | |
| CROSSAN | Margaret | gr/m | na | 1801 | | | |

| CROSSAN | William | head | na | na | 0258547 | | Donegal |
| CROSSAN | Roseann | wife | na | na | | | Kilmacrenan |
| CROSSAN | James | son | 16 | | | | Aghanunshin |
| CROSSAN | Henry | son | 12 | | | | Loughagannon |
| CROSSAN | Mary | dau | 8 | | | | |
| CROSSAN | Catherine | dau | 5 | | | | |
| CROSSAN | William | son | 2 | | | | |

| CROSSEN | Margaret | head | 70 | 1800 0258547 | | wid | Donegal |
| CROSSEN | Phil | son | 40 | 1847 | | | Raphoe N |
| CROSSEN | Rebekah | dau | 26 | n.m. | | | Clonleigh |
| CROSSEN | Roseanna | dau | 23 | n.m. | | | Roughan |
| CROSSEN | Thomas | gr/s | 3 | | claimant, spells CROSSAN | | |

| CRUMLISH | John | head | 51 | 1837 0258547 | | | Donegal |
| CRUMLISH | Mary | wife | 30 | 1837 | | | Inishowen E |
| CRUMLISH | Bridget | dau | 8 | | | | Moville Lr |
| CRUMLISH | James | son | 6 | | claimant | | Mossyglen |
| CRUMLISH | John | son | 4 | | | | |
| CRUMLISH | Patrick | son | 21m | | | | |
| CRUMLISH | Mary | dau | 2 | | d. 1846, dau of husband | | |
| CRUMLISH – See | | | | | Bridget McLAUGHLIN, visitor | | |

| CURRAN | Edward | head | na | na | 0258547 | | Donegal |
| CURRAN | Mary | wife | na | na | | | Kilmacrenan |
| CURRAN | Rose | dau | 20 | | | | Tullaghobegly |
| CURRAN | Manus | son | 18 | | | | Meenaclady |
| CURRAN | Ned | son | 16 | | | | |
| CURRAN | Daniel | son | 14 | | | | |
| CURRAN | Paddy | son | 11 | | | | |
| CURRAN | Mary | dau | 8 | | | | |

| CURRAN | Ned | head | 56 | 1838 0258547 | Custom Record, Edward per Cl. | | Donegal |
| CURRAN | Nelly | wife | 55 | 1838 | | | Kilmacrenan |
| CURRAN | Manus | son | 30 | 1850 | | | Tullaghobegly |
| CURRAN | Julia | dau | 30 | | D/L? | | Meenaclady |

| CURRAN | Hannah | dau | 27 | 1847 | | |
|--------|--------|-----|----|----|----|----|
| CURRAN | John | son | 24 | | in America | |
| CURRAN | James | son | 20 | | | |
| CURRAN | Ned | son | 17 | | | |
| CURRAN | Michael | son | 14 | | | |
| CURRAN | Fanny | dau | 8 | | claimant | |
| CURRAN | Nelly | dau | 3 m | | gr/dau? | |
| CURRAN | Dennis | gr/s | 3 | | | |
| | | | | | | |
| DAY | Thomas | head | 61 | na  0258547 | wid | Donegal |
| DAY | Henry | son | 22 | n.m. | | Tirhugh |
| DAY | Thomas | son | 20 | | | Templecarn |
| DAY | Margret | dau | 17 | | claimant | Aghnahoo Glebe |
| DAY | Mary | dau | 13 | | | |
| DAY | Jane | na | 38 | | d. 1841 | |
| DAY  - See | | | | | Jane SUMMERVILLE, gr/dau | |
| | | | | | | |
| DEENEY | Patrick | head | 42 | 1841 0258547 | | Donegal |
| DEENEY | Sarah | wife | na | | per claimant | Inishowen W |
| DEENEY | James | son | 9 | | | Fahan Up |
| DEENEY | Suley | dau | 7 | | claimant Cecilia? m. McDOWELL | Tievebane |
| DEENEY | Daniel | son | 5 | | | |
| DEENEY | Patrick | son | 3 | | | |
| DEENEY | Catherine | dau | 18 m | | | |
| DEENEY | John | son | 1 m | | | |
| | | | | | | |
| DELANY | James | head | 38 | 1842 0258547 | | Donegal |
| DELANY | Mary | wife | 29 | 1842 | nee BRYSON | Raphoe S |
| DELANY | Mary | dau | 8 | | | Stranorlar |
| DELANY | James | son | 6 | | claimant, spells DELANEY | Ballybofey Town |
| DELANY | Charles | son | 3 | | | |
| DELANY | John | son | 3 m | | | |
| | | | | | | |
| DERMOD | George | head | 42 | 1835 0258547 | | Donegal |
| DERMOD | Catherine | wife | 40 | 1835 | | Raphoe N |
| DERMOD | Bernard | son | 15 | | | Clonleigh |
| DERMOD | Anne | dau | 13 | | | Springhill |
| DERMOD | George | son | 10 | | claimant, spells McDERMOTT | |
| DERMOD | Edward | son | 7 | | | |
| DERMOD | Mary | dau | 4 | | | |
| | | | | | | |
| DEVER | Anthony | head | 40 | 1838 0258547 | | Donegal |
| DEVER | Susan | wife | 30 | 1838 | nee HOUSTON | Kilmacrenan |
| DEVER | Anthony | son | 10 | | | Conwall |
| DEVER | Connell | son | 7 | | | Ballaghderg |
| DEVER | Ellen | dau | 2 | | claimant, m. McCARRON | |
| DEVER | James | son | 1 | | d. 1849 | |
| DEVER | Eleanor | moth | 60 | | d. 1840 | |
| | | | | | | |
| DEVLIN | Daniel | head | na | na  0258547 | | Donegal |
| DEVLIN | Sally | wife | na | na | | Inishowen E |
| DEVLIN | Kah | dau | 17 | | (given name sic) | Clonmany |
| DEVLIN | Peggy | dau | 14 | | | Tullagh |
| DEVLIN | Daniel | son | 10 | | | |
| DEVLIN | Biddy | dau | 8 | | | |
| DEVLIN | Rose | dau | 6 | | | |
| DEVLIN | Ann | dau | 4 | | claimant | |

| DOHERTY | Cornelius | head | na | 1845 0258547 | | Donegal |
|---------|-----------|------|----|----|----|---------|
| DOHERTY | Sarah | wife | na | 1845 | | Inishowen W |
| DOHERTY | Bridget | dau | 5 | | | Fahan Lr |
| DOHERTY | George | son | 2 | | claimant | Illies |
| | | | | | | |
| DOHERTY | Daniel | head | na | 1842 0258547 | | Donegal |
| DOHERTY | Bridget | wife | na | 1842 | | Raphoe |
| DOHERTY | Ann Jane | dau | 5 | | | Stranorlar |
| DOHERTY | Michael | son | 4 | | | Cregan |
| DOHERTY | George | son | 2 | | claimant | |
| | | | | | | |
| DOHERTY | Edward | head | na | na | 0258547 | Donegal |
| DOHERTY | Betty | wife | na | na | nee LYNCH | Inishowen E |
| DOHERTY | William | son | 14 | | | Fahan Lr |
| DOHERTY | Hannah | dau | 9 | | | Ardaravan |
| DOHERTY | Margaret | dau | 7 | | | |
| DOHERTY | Sarah | dau | 4 | | | |
| DOHERTY | Edward | son | 1 | | claimant | |
| | | | | | | |
| DOHERTY | Edward | head | na | 1835 0258547 | | Donegal |
| DOHERTY | Rose | wife | na | 1835 | | Inishowen W |
| DOHERTY | John | son | 15 | | | Fahan Lr |
| DOHERTY | Ellen | dau | 13 | | | Tullyarvan |
| DOHERTY | Anne | dau | 11 | | | |
| DOHERTY | Mary | dau | 7 | | | |
| DOHERTY | Margaret | dau | 4 | | | |
| DOHERTY | Rose | dau | 2 m | | | |
| DOHERTY | Mary | dau | 1 m | | d. 1843 | |
| | | | | | | |
| DOHERTY | James | head | na | na | 0258547 | Donegal |
| DOHERTY | Sarah | wife | na | na | | Inishowen W |
| DOHERTY | Edward | son | 10 | | | Fahan Up |
| DOHERTY | John | son | 8 | | | Crislaghmore |
| DOHERTY | Hugh | son | 4 | | claimant | |
| | | | | | | |
| DOHERTY | John | head | na | 1827 0258547 | | Donegal |
| DOHERTY | Catherine | wife | na | 1827 | | Inishowen W |
| DOHERTY | Owen | son | 23 | | | Desertegny |
| DOHERTY | Michael | son | 18 | | | Tonduff |
| DOHERTY | Hugh | son | 14 | | | |
| DOHERTY | Rose | dau | 12 | | | |
| DOHERTY | James | son | 10 | | | |
| DOHERTY | Edward | son | 8 | | | |
| DOHERTY | John | son | 6 | | claimant | |
| DOHERTY | Hannah | dau | 17 | | d. 1850 | |
| | | | | | | |
| DOHERTY | John | head | 52 | 1825 0258547 | | Donegal |
| DOHERTY | Ellen | wife | 48 | 1825 | | Raphoe S |
| DOHERTY | James | son | 19 | | | Urney |
| DOHERTY | Hy | son | 15 | | (Hy checked) | Calhame |
| DOHERTY | Barney | son | 13 | | | |
| DOHERTY | Mary | dau | 7 | | claimant | |
| DOHERTY | Patt | son | 7 | | absent | |
| DOHERTY | John | son | 16 | | d. 1848 | |
| DOHERTY | Hugh | son | 8 | | d. 1849 | |
| | | | | | | |
| DOHERTY | John | head | 45 | 1840 0258547 | | Donegal |
| DOHERTY | Mary | wife | 28 | 1840 | | Inishowen W |
| DOHERTY | Margaret | dau | 6 | | claimant | Fahan Up |
| DOHERTY | Michael | son | 4 | | | Letter |

| | | | | | | |
|---|---|---|---|---|---|---|
| DOHERTY | Hugh | son | 2 | | | |
| | | | | | | |
| DOHERTY | Paddy | head | 50 | 1833 0258547 | | Donegal |
| DOHERTY | Catherine | wife | 50 | 1833 | | Inishowen E |
| DOHERTY | Michael | son | 16 | | | Culdaff |
| DOHERTY | James | son | 14 | | | Muff |
| DOHERTY | Ann | dau | 12 | | | |
| DOHERTY | Mary | dau | 10 | | | |
| DOHERTY | Charles | son | 8 | | | |
| DOHERTY | Ellen | dau | 4 | | | |
| | | | | | | |
| DOHERTY | William | head | na | na 0258547 | | Donegal |
| DOHERTY | Margaret | wife | na | na | | Kilmacrenan |
| DOHERTY | Philip | son | 10 | | | Killygarvan |
| DOHERTY | William | son | 8 | | | Oughterlin |
| DOHERTY | Grace | dau | 6 | | claimant, m. MITCHELL | |
| DOHERTY | Margaret | dau | 4 | | | |
| | | | | | | |
| DONNELL | James | head | 90 | 1811 0258547 | | Donegal |
| DONNELL | Salay | wife | 74 | 1811 | | Raphoe S |
| DONNELL | Edward | son | 34 | | | Convoy |
| DONNELL | James | son | 32 | | | Lissinore |
| DONNELL – See | | | | | Catherine COYLE, gr/dau | |
| | | | | | | |
| DOUGLAS | John | head | 76 | 1794 0993107 | | Monaghan |
| DOUGLAS | Martha | gr/d | 19 | | | Cremorne |
| DOUGLAS | Elisa | gr/d | 18 | | | Muchno |
| DOUGLAS | William | gr/s | 11 | | claimant? | Tullyvanus |
| DOUGLAS | Martha | wife | 76 | | d. 1851 | |
| | | | | | | |
| DOYLE | James | head | na | 1836 0258547 | | Dublin |
| DOYLE | Mary | wife | na | 1836 | | Castleknock |
| DOYLE | Ellen | dau | 14 | | | Palmerston |
| DOYLE | Elizabeth | dau | 11 | | | Chapelizod |
| DOYLE | Laurence | son | 2 | | | |
| | | | | | | |
| DUFFY | Hugh | head | na | 1845 0258547 | | Donegal |
| DUFFY | Ellen | wife | na | 1845 | nee McFADDEN | Kilmacrenan |
| DUFFY | Paddy | son | 8 | | | Clondahorky |
| DUFFY | Sarah | dau | 5 | | claimant, m. McGRANAHAN | Kildarragh |
| DUFFY | Peggy | dau | 1 | | | |
| DUFFY | Gracy | dau | 1 m | | | |
| | | | | | | |
| * DUNLEAVY | Esther | M/L | 70 | na 0258547 | d. 1850, mother? listed with Ellen QUINN | |
| | | | | | | |
| | | | | | | |
| EARLY | Patrick | head | 22 | 1847 0258547 | | Donegal |
| EARLY | Biddy | wife | 23 | 1847 | | Raphoe N |
| EARLY | John | son | 3 | | claimant | Clonleigh |
| EARLY | Thomas | son | 9 d | | age 9 days in 1851 Census | Lifford Town |
| | | | | | | |
| EWING | John | head | 45 | 1838 0258547 | m. 1838/1845 | Donegal |
| EWING | Betty | wife | 29 | 1845 | claimant says Margaret, nee COOK | Inishowen W |
| EWING | Mary Ann | dau | 14 | | claimant | Fahan Lr |
| EWING | Robert | son | 12 | | | Police Dist. |
| EWING | John | son | 10 | | | of Buncrana |
| EWING | Rebecca | dau | 8 | | | Meenagory |
| EWING | Samuel | son | 5 | | | |

| | | | | | | | |
|---|---|---|---|---|---|---|---|
| FARRELL | Mary | head | na | na | 0258547 | wid | Donegal |
| FARRELL | John | son | 19 | | | claimant | Inishowen |
| FARRELL | Owen | son | 17 | | | Oin | Clonmany |
| FARRELL | Bridget | dau | 15 | | | | Lenan |
| FARRELL | Michael | son | 12 | | | | |
| FARRELL | William | husb | na | | | d. 1849 | |
| | | | | | | | |
| FARREN | Patrick | head | na | na | 0993107 | | Donegal |
| FARREN | Nancy | wife | na | na | | | Inishowen E |
| FARREN | Hugh | son | 12 | | | | Moville Lr |
| FARREN | Mary | dau | 10 | | | | Ballymagaraghy |
| FARREN | Margaret | dau | 8 | | | claimant | |
| FARREN | John | son | 6 | | | | |
| FARREN | Catherine | dau | 1 | | | | |
| | | | | | | | |
| FAULKNER | Neal | head | na | na | 0258547 | | Donegal |
| FAULKNER | Margaret | wife | na | na | | | Inishowen E |
| FAULKNER | Biddy | dau | 17 | | | | Culdaff |
| FAULKNER | Patrick | son | 15 | | | | Moneydarragh |
| FAULKNER | James | son | 14 | | | | |
| FAULKNER | George | son | 11 | | | | |
| | | | | | | | |
| FERREN | John | head | na | na | 0258546 | | Donegal |
| FERREN | Jane | wife | na | na | | | Raphoe S |
| FERREN | James | son | 20 | | | | Donaghmore |
| FERREN | John | son | 13 | | | | Carn |
| FERREN | Fanny | dau | 6 | | | claimant, m. STEELE | |
| FERREN | Margaret | dau | 3 | | | | |
| | | | | | | | |
| FERRISS | Daniel | head | na | 1840 | 0258547 | | Donegal |
| FERRISS | Giley | wife | na | 1840 | | nee COYLE per claimant not found | Inishowen W |
| FERRISS | Mary | dau | 10 | | | | Burt |
| FERRISS | Daniel | son | 8 | | | | Bunnamayne |
| FERRISS | Cathrin | dau | 3 | | | | |
| FERRISS | Henry | son | 2 | | | | |
| FERRISS | James | son | 1 | | | | |
| | | | | | | | |
| FERRY | Manus | head | 38 | 1845 | 0258547 | | Donegal |
| FERRY | Biddy | wife | 27 | 1845 | | | Kilmacrenan |
| FERRY | Grace | dau | 5 | | | claimant | Tullaghobegly |
| FERRY | Micky | son | 3 | | | | Brinlack |
| FERRY | Mary | dau | 1 | | | | |
| FERRY | Michael | son | 3 | | | deceased, no date | |
| | | | | | | | |
| FIELDS | John | head | na | 1847 | 0993107 | | Donegal |
| FIELDS | Grace | wife | na | 1847 | | | Raphoe N |
| FIELDS | Patrick | son | 2 | | | claimant | Clonleigh |
| FIELDS | Catherine | dau | 6 m | | | | Rossgeir |
| | | | | | | | |
| FINEGAN | Patrick | head | 46 | 1838 | 0258547 | | Monaghan |
| FINEGAN | Mary | wife | 45 | 1838 | | Margaret per claimant | Farney |
| FINEGAN | Pat | son | 5 | | | claimant? | Donaghmoyne |
| FINEGAN | Anne | dau | 4 | | | | Drumaconvern |
| | | | | | | | |
| FLEMING | Andrew | head | 41 | 1835 | 0258547 | | Donegal |
| FLEMING | Matilda | wife | 41 | 1835 | | | Raphoe N |
| FLEMING | Mary Ann | dau | 15 | | | | Donaghmore |
| FLEMING | Matt | son | 13 | | | | Ballybun |
| FLEMING | James | son | 10 | | | | |
| FLEMING | Catherine | dau | 7 | | | claimant | |

| FLEMING | Liza | dau 4 | | | | |
|---|---|---|---|---|---|---|
| FLEMING | Allis | dau 4 | | | | |
| FLEMING | Sarah | dau 1 | | | | |
| | | | | | | |
| FLOOD | Patrick | head 48 | 1825 0258547 | | | Donegal |
| FLOOD | Catherine | wife 42 | 1825 | | | Raphoe |
| FLOOD | Edward | son 20 | | absent | | Donaghmore |
| FLOOD | Catherine | dau 19 | | | | Gortfad |
| FLOOD | James | son 8 | | claimant? | | |
| FLOOD | Charles | son 6 | | | | |
| FLOOD | Barny | son 5 | | | | |
| FLOOD | Margaret | dau 2 | | | | |
| | | | | | | |
| FLOOD | Patrick | head 25 | 1846 0258547 | | | Donegal |
| FLOOD | Catherine | wife 33 | 1846 | | | Raphoe |
| FLOOD | Sarah | dau 4 | | | | Donaghmore |
| FLOOD | James | son 1 | | claimant? | | Gortfad |
| | | | | | | |
| FREIL | John | head na | 1838 0258547 | | | Donegal |
| FREIL | Susan | wife na | 1838 | nee McGONAGLE | | Inishowen W |
| FREIL | Essie | dau 13 | | | | Burt |
| FREIL | Denis | son 11 | | | | Mulleny |
| FREIL | John | son 9 | | | | |
| FREIL | Susanna | dau 7 | | claimant, m. MERRYAN | | |
| FREIL | Margaret | dau 5 | | | | |
| | | | | | | |
| FREIL | Paddy | head na | na 0258547 | | | Donegal |
| FREIL | Mary | wife na | na | | | Kilmacrenan |
| FREIL | Bridget | dau 15 | | | | Kilmacrenan |
| FREIL | Charles | son 13 | | | | Clonkilly Beg |
| FREIL | Kate | dau 9 | | | | |
| FREIL | Mary | dau 7 | | claimant | | |
| FREIL | John | son 2 | | | | |
| | | | | | | |
| FURREN | Patrick | head na | na 0258547 | | | Donegal |
| FURREN | Nancy | wife na | na | | | Inishowen |
| FURREN | Hugh | son 12 | | | | Moville Lr |
| FURREN | Mary | dau 10 | | | | Ballymagaraghy |
| FURREN | Margaret | dau 8 | | claimant | | |
| FURREN | John | son 6 | | | | |
| FURREN | Catherine | dau 1 | | | | |
| | | | | | | |
| | | | | | | |
| GALLAGHER | Daniel | head na | na 0258547 | | | Donegal |
| GALLAGHER | Unity | wife na | na | | | Kilmacrenan |
| GALLAGHER | Edward | son 21 | | | | Gartan |
| GALLAGHER | James | son 18 | | | | Meenawilligan |
| GALLAGHER | Daniel | son 17 | | | | |
| GALLAGHER | Susan | dau 13 | | | | |
| GALLAGHER | Fanny | dau 11 | | | | |
| GALLAGHER | Unity | dau 7 | | | | |
| GALLAGHER | Ellen | dau 5 | | | | |
| GALLAGHER | Mary | dau 1 | | claimant | | |
| | | | | | | |
| GALLAGHER | Edward | head 50 | 1841 0258547 | | | Donegal |
| GALLAGHER | Hanna | wife 30 | 1841 | | | Boylagh |
| GALLAGHER | Mary | dau 7 | | | | Templecrone |
| GALLAGHER | Hanna | dau 6 | | | | Meenderrynasloe |
| GALLAGHER | Margaret | dau 4 | | | | |

| GALLAGHER | Catherine | dau | 2 | | | | |
|-----------|-----------|-----|---|---|---|---|---|
| GALLAGHER | Catherine | dau | 9 m | | | d. 1843 | |
| | | | | | | | |
| GALLAGHER | James | head | 44 | na | 0258547 | | Donegal |
| GALLAGHER | Mary | wife | 44 | na | | | Kilmacrenan |
| GALLAGHER | Mary | dau | 15 | | | | Killygarvan |
| GALLAGHER | John | son | 12 | | | | Rathmullan |
| GALLAGHER | Patrick | son | 10 | | | | |
| GALLAGHER | William | son | 6 | | | | |
| | | | | | | | |
| GALLAGHER | Patrick | head | na | 1834 | 0258547 | | Donegal |
| GALLAGHER | Mary | wife | na | 1834 | | | Raphoe S |
| GALLAGHER | John | son | 16 | | | | Donaghmore |
| GALLAGHER | Charles | son | 11 | | | | Meenlougher |
| GALLAGHER | Pat | son | 8 | | | | |
| GALLAGHER | Francis | son | 6 | | | | |
| GALLAGHER | William | son | 4 | | | claimant | |
| GALLAGHER | Catherine | dau | 1 | | | | |
| | | | | | | | |
| GAVAGAN | Hugh | head | na | na | 0258547 | | Donegal |
| GAVAGAN | Mary | wife | na | na | | | Tirhugh |
| GAVAGAN | John | son | 19 | | | | Kilbarron |
| GAVAGAN | Hugh | son | 19 | | | | Creevy |
| GAVAGAN | James | son | 14 | | | | |
| GAVAGAN | Mary | dau | 12 | | | | |
| GAVAGAN | Maggie | dau | 10 | | | | |
| GAVAGAN | Bernard | son | 8 | | | | |
| GAVAGAN | Patrick | son | 5 | | | | |
| GAVAGAN | Bessie | dau | 3 | | | Elizabeth Cl., spells GAFFIDEN | |
| GAVAGAN | Bridget | dau | 7 m | | | | |
| | | | | | | | |
| * GILES | Julia | na | 15 | | 0258547 | with Daniel McCLOSKEY | |
| | | | | | | | |
| GILLECE | Edward | head | na | 1821 | 0258547 | | Cavan |
| GILLECE | Mary | wife | na | 1821 | | | Tullyhaw |
| GILLECE | Mary | dau | 18 | | | | Killinagh |
| GILLECE | James | son | 16 | | | | Lanliss |
| GILLECE | Catherin | dau | 9 | | | | |
| GILLECE | Bidy | dau | 7 | | | | |
| GILLECE | Ellen | dau | 5 | | | | |
| | | | | | | | |
| GILLESPIE | Dick | head | na | 1841 | 0258547 | | Donegal |
| GILLESPIE | Rose | wife | na | 1841 | | | Inishowen E |
| GILLESPIE | Ana | dau | 9 | | | | Moville Lr |
| GILLESPIE | Rose | dau | 6 | | | | Carrowhugh |
| GILLESPIE | Barney | son | 4 | | | | |
| GILLESPIE | John | son | 1 | | | claimant | |
| | | | | | | | |
| GILLESPIE | Robert | head | na | 1835 | 0258546 | | Donegal |
| GILLESPIE | Ellen | wife | na | 1835 | | | Inishowen W |
| GILLESPIE | John | son | 16 | | | | Burt |
| GILLESPIE | Mary | dau | 11 | | | | Gortcormacan |
| GILLESPIE | Margaret | dau | 8 | | | | |
| GILLESPIE | Robert | son | 5 | | | | |
| GILLESPIE | Hugh | son | 3 | | | | |
| GILLESPIE | Marjory | dau | 8 m | | | claimant, m. MORAN | |
| | | | | | | | |
| GLACKIN | James | head | na | 1842 | 0258547 | | Donegal |
| GLACKIN | Martha | wife | na | 1842 | | | Raphoe S |
| GLACKIN | Charles | son | 7 | | | claimant | Conwal |

| GLACKIN | Betty | dau | 5 | | | claimant, m. LEICH | Letterleague |
| GLACKIN | Martha | dau | 2 | | | | |
| | | | | | | | |
| GORMAN | James | head | na | 1830 | 0993106 | | Sligo |
| GORMAN | Bridget | wife | na | 1830 | | nee FITZMORRIS | Leyny |
| GORMAN | Patt | son | 20 | | | | Killoran |
| GORMAN | Michael | son | 18 | | | | Carrownagleragh |
| GORMAN | Margaret | dau | 16 | | | | |
| GORMAN | Teresa | dau | 14 | | | | 1841: |
| GORMAN | Ellen | dau | 12 | | | | Carrownacligh |
| GORMAN | Richard | son | 7 | | | claimant | |
| GORMAN | Saragh | dau | 5 | | | | |
| GORMAN | James | son | 3 | | | | |
| GORMAN | Mary | dau | 1 | | | | |
| | | | | | | | |
| GORMLEY | Patrick | head | 50 | 1835 | 0258547 | | Donegal |
| GORMLEY | Sally | wife | 38 | 1835 | | | Raphoe S |
| GORMLEY | Edward | son | 13 | | | | Donaghmore |
| GORMLEY | Eliza | dau | 11 | | | | Stranamuck |
| GORMLEY | Catherine | dau | 11 | | | d. 1847 | |
| GORMLEY | John | son | 6 | | | d. 1849 | |
| GORMLEY | Margaret | dau | 4 | | | d. 1849 | |
| GORMLEY | Rebecca | dau | 10m | | | d. 1849 | |
| | | | | | | | |
| GREEN | William | head | na | na | 0258546 | | Donegal |
| GREEN | Ellen | wife | na | na | | | Inishowen E |
| GREEN | Mary | dau | 8 | | | | Inch |
| GREEN | John | son | 5 | | | claimant | Ballynakilly |
| GREEN | Patrick | son | 3 | | | | |
| | | | | | | | |
| GREEN | William | head | na | na | 0258547 | | Donegal |
| GREEN | Margaret | wife | na | na | | | Kilmacrenan |
| GREEN | William | son | 18 | | | | Killygarran |
| GREEN | Patrick | son | 16 | | | | Lurganboy |
| GREEN | John | son | 14 | | | | |
| GREEN | Susan | dau | 12 | | | | |
| GREEN | Denis | son | 10 | | | | |
| GREEN | Mary | dau | 8 | | | claimant, m. COLLINS | |
| GREEN | Daniel | son | 6 | | | | |
| GREEN | Hugh | son | 4 | | | | |
| | | | | | | | |
| GREGG | James | head | na | 1836 | 0258547 | (m. date?) | Donegal |
| GREGG | Martha | wife | na | 1836 | | | Raphoe N |
| GREGG | James | son | 19 | | | | Raphoe |
| GREGG | Mary | dau | 17 | | | | Raphoe Town |
| GREGG | Annie | dau | 14 | | | | |
| GREGG | William | son | 12 | | | | |
| GREGG | Eliza | dau | 9 | | | | |
| GREGG | John | son | 2 | | | | |
| GREGG | Robert | son | 22 | | | deceased | |
| GREGG | John | son | 3 | | | deceased | |
| GREGG | Thomas | son | 1 | | | deceased, Thomas? | |
| | | | | | | | |
| GUFFAGAN | Patrick | head | 42 | na | 0258547 | | Donegal |
| GUFFAGAN | Nancy | wife | 34 | na | | | Banagh |
| GUFFAGAN | Condy | son | 12 | | | | Inishkeel |
| GUFFAGAN | John | son | 9 | | | | Scaddaman |
| GUFFAGAN | Andrew | son | 6 | | | | |
| GUFFAGAN | Thomas | son | 4 | | | claimant, spells GIFFAGAN | |
| GUFFAGAN | Patrick | son | 1 | | | | |

| GUFFAGAN | John | brot 35 | | | | | |
|---|---|---|---|---|---|---|---|

| HANLON | Sandy | head na | na | 0993107 | Alexander per claimant not found | Donegal |
|---|---|---|---|---|---|---|
| HANLON | Jane | wife na | na | | | Boylagh |
| HANLON | William | son 3 | | | | Templecrone |
| HANLON | Catherine | dau 1 | | | | Meenabollagan |

| HANNA | John | head na | 1828 | 0993107 | | Donegal |
|---|---|---|---|---|---|---|
| HANNA | Izabella | wife na | 1828 | | | Tirhugh |
| HANNA | George | son 12 | | | | Donegal |
| HANNA | Betsey | dau 8 | | | | Keeldrum |
| HANNA | Stephen | son 6 | | | claimant | |
| HANNA | Izabella | dau 4 | | | | |
| HANNA | Susannah | dau 1 | | | | |

| HARKIN | John | head 50 | na | 0258547 | | Donegal |
|---|---|---|---|---|---|---|
| HARKIN | Margret | wife 48 | na | | | Inishowen E |
| HARKIN | Charles | son 17 | | | | Culdaff |
| HARKIN | Mary | dau 15 | | | | Muff |
| HARKIN | John | son 12 | | | | |
| HARKIN | Patrick | son 10 | | | | |
| HARKIN | James | son 8 | | | claimant | |

| HARKIN | Patrick | head na | 1837 | 0258546 | | Donegal |
|---|---|---|---|---|---|---|
| HARKIN | Nancy | wife na | 1837 | | | Inishowen E |
| HARKIN | Anne | dau 13 | | | | Moville |
| HARKIN | Rose | dau 11 | | | | Meenbaltin Up |
| HARKIN | Margaret | dau 9 | | | | |
| HARKIN | Patrick | son 7 | | | | |
| HARKIN | Catherine | dau 5 | | | | |
| HARKIN | Daniel | son 1 | | | claimant, a Daniel d. infant | |

| HAUGHEY | Patrick | head na | na | 0258547 | | Donegal |
|---|---|---|---|---|---|---|
| HAUGHEY | Anne | wife na | na | | | Banagh |
| HAUGHEY | Con | son 8 | | | | Inver |
| HAUGHEY | Pat | son 6 | | | | Knockagar |
| HAUGHEY | Margaret | dau 6 m | | | claimant | |

| HEALY | James | head na | na | 0258546 | | Donegal |
|---|---|---|---|---|---|---|
| HEALY | Nancy | wife na | na | | | Tirhugh |
| HEALY | John | son 9 | | | | Templecrone |
| HEALY | Mary | dau 7 | | | claimant (gr/f Henry) | Meenderrynasloe |
| HEALY | Rose | dau 5 | | | | |
| HEALY | Annie | dau 1 | | | | |

| HEAVER | John | head 36 | 1841 | 0258547 | | Sligo |
|---|---|---|---|---|---|---|
| HEAVER | Bridget | wife 26 | 1841 | | | Tirerill |
| HEAVER | Bridget | dau 8 | | | also Bessie, claimant m. ADAIR | Aghanagh |
| HEAVER | Mary | dau 2 | | | | Carrowkeel |

| HEGARTY | James | head na | 1815 | 0258547 | | Donegal |
|---|---|---|---|---|---|---|
| HEGARTY | Anne | wife na | 1815 | | | Raphoe N |
| HEGARTY | John | son 28 | 1851 | | | Leck |
| HEGARTY | Sarah | D/L 21 | 1851 | | nee CLIFFORD | Cullion |
| HEGARTY | William | son 24 | | | in America | |
| HEGARTY | Margaret | dau 22 | | | in America | |
| HEGARTY | Susan | dau 18 | | | claimant | |
| HEGARTY | Eliza | dau 16 | | | | |

| Surname | Given | Rel | Age | Year | Film | Notes | Place |
|---|---|---|---|---|---|---|---|
| HEGARTY | Ellen | dau | 11 | | | | |
| HEGARTY – See | | | | | | Margaret McCAFFERTY, gr/dau | |
| | | | | | | | |
| HODGE | Thomas | head na | na | | 0258546 | | Donegal |
| HODGE | Margery | wife na | na | | | | Inishowen W |
| HODGE | Joseph | son | 9 | | | claimant | Inch |
| HODGE | Jane | dau | 6 | | | | Baylet |
| HODGE | Margaret | dau | 3 | | | | |
| HODGE | Catherine | dau | 3m | | | | |
| | | | | | | | |
| HOGAN | Patrick | head na | na | | 0258547 | | Mayo |
| HOGAN | Julia | wife na | na | | | nee LARDNER | Murrisk |
| HOGAN | Ellen Mary | dau | 10 | | | | Oughaval |
| HOGAN | Julia | dau | 6 | | | claimant, m. BROWN | Westport |
| HOGAN | Nancy | dau | 5 | | | | High St. |
| HOGAN | John | son | 2 | | | | |
| HOGAN | Carolin | dau | 4 m | | | | |
| | | | | | | | |
| HOLLAND | Simon | head na | | 1848 | 0258547 | | Monaghan |
| HOLLAND | Nellie | wife na | | 1848 | | | Farney |
| HOLLAND | Ann | dau | 3 | | | claimant | Magheross |
| HOLLAND | Thomas | son | 9 m | | | | Latinalbarry |
| | | | | | | | |
| HUGHES | Michael | head na | | 1839 | 0258547 | | Monaghan |
| HUGHES | Catherine | wife na | | 1839 | | nee MALLON | Cremorne |
| HUGHES | Mary | dau | 9 | | | | Clontibret |
| HUGHES | Ellen | dau | 7 | | | claimant, m. WARREN | Drumgallan |
| HUGHES | Patrick | son | 4 | | | | |
| HUGHES | Catherine | dau | 2 | | | | |
| | | | | | | | |
| | | | | | | | |
| KEARNEY | John | head na | na | | 0258546 | | Donegal |
| KEARNEY | Sally | wife na | na | | | | Inishowen W |
| KEARNEY | Betty | dau | 5 | | | or Lizzie, claimant, m. CARLIN | Fahan Lr |
| KEARNEY | Daniel | son | 3 | | | | Tullydush Lr |
| | | | | | | | |
| * KELLY | Catherine | S/L na | na | | 0258547 | with B/L Thomas CANNON | |
| | | | | | | | |
| KELLY | Daniel | head na | na | | 0258547 | | Donegal |
| KELLY | Biddy | wife na | na | | | nee DUFFY per claimant not found | Raphoe N |
| KELLY | Francis | son | 14 | | | | Raymoghy |
| KELLY | Grace | dau | 12 | | | | Drumoghill |
| KELLY | John | son | 10 | | | 1 in 1841 | |
| KELLY | Dominick | son | 8 | | | | |
| KELLY | Robert | son | 6 | | | | |
| KELLY | Daniel | son | 4 | | | | |
| KELLY | Rose | dau | 1 | | | | |
| | | | | | | | |
| KELLY | Thomas | head | 40 | na | 0258547 | absent | Donegal |
| KELLY | Anne | wife | 26 | na | | absent, nee JOHNSTON | Inishowen W |
| KELLY | Eliza | dau | 3 | | | claimant, m. DOHERTY | Fahan Lr |
| KELLY | Jane Anne | dau | 2 | | | | Buncrana Town |
| KELLY | James | brot | 50 | 1841 | | | Main St. |
| KELLY | Jane | niec | 12 | | | | |
| | | | | | | | |
| KENEDY | James | head | 40 | 1835 | 0258547 | | Donegal |
| KENEDY | Margaret | wife | 34 | 1835 | | | Raphoe N |
| KENEDY | Sarah | dau | 14 | | | | Clonleigh |
| KENEDY | Kate | dau | 12 | | | | Ballindroit Town |

| KENEDY | Arthur | son | 10 | | | | |
|--------|--------|-----|-----|-----|-----|-----|-----|
| KENEDY | Anne | dau | 4 | | | Nancy, claimant, m. McCROSSAN | |
| KENEDY | Matty | dau | 1 | | | | |
| KENEDY | James | son | 4 h | | | d. 1843, age 4 hours | |
| KENEDY | John | son | 1 d | | | d. 1846, age 1 day | |
| | | | | | | | |
| KENNEDY | Hugh | head | 45 | 1828 | 0258547 | | Donegal |
| KENNEDY | Ellen | wife | 47 | 1828 | | nee MELVIN | Raphoe |
| KENNEDY | Gilbert | son | 17 | | | | Clonleigh |
| KENNEDY | James | son | 14 | | | | Ballindroit Town |
| KENNEDY | Anne | dau | 12 | | | claimant | |
| KENNEDY | Ellen | dau | 8 | | | | |
| KENNEDY | Margaret | dau | 4 | | | | |
| | | | | | | | |
| KINCAID | Andrew | head | 56 | 1830 | 0258546 | | Donegal |
| KINCAID | Jane | wife | 52 | 1830 | | nee RUSSELL | Raphoe S |
| KINCAID | Joseph | son | 21 | | | | Urney |
| KINCAID | Elinor | dau | 19 | | | | Fearn |
| KINCAID | Samuel | son | 16 | | | | |
| KINCAID | Matilda | dau | 9 | | | Matilda Jane, Cl. m. MOOREHEAD | |
| KINCAID | Eliza | dau | 10 m | | | d. 1847 | |
| | | | | | | | |
| KINCAID | Quanton | head | na | na | 0258547 | KINKEAD census spelling | Donegal |
| KINCAID | Jane | wife | na | na | | Jenny | Inishowen W |
| KINCAID | William | son | 13 | | | | Muff |
| KINCAID | Mary Jane | dau | 9 | | | | Ture |
| KINCAID | Eliza | dau | 7 | | | | |
| KINCAID | Rebecca | dau | 5 | | | | |
| KINCAID | James | son | 2 | | | | |
| | | | | | | | |
| | | | | | | | |
| LECKEY | Robert | head | 82 | 1810 | 0258547 | | Donegal |
| LECKEY | Oliver | son | 48 | 1845 | | | Raphoe N |
| LECKEY | Susan | D/L | 32 | 1845 | | | Donaghmore |
| LECKEY | Robert | gr/s | 7 | | | claimant, listed as nephew | Gortnamuck |
| LECKEY | John G. | gr/s | 5 | | | listed as nephew in census | |
| LECKEY | Hester | gr/d | 1 | | | listed as niece | |
| | | | | | | | |
| LENNON | Patrick | head | na | na | 0993107 | | Donegal |
| LENNON | Mary | wife | na | na | | nee McGRATH per claimant | Raphoe N |
| LENNON | Patrick | son | 21 | | | | Clonleigh |
| LENNON | John | son | 18 | | | absent | Churchtown |
| LENNON | Sam | son | 14 | | | | |
| LENNON | James | son | 12 | | | | |
| LENNON | William | son | 10 | | | | |
| LENNON | Thomas | son | 8 | | | | |
| LENNON | Joseph | son | 4 | | | | |
| LENNON | Mary | dau | 1 | | | claimant Mary McGRATH? | |
| | | | | | | | |
| * LOGUE | Fanny | gr/d | 5 | | 0258547 | claimant m. HUTTON, see Hugh McGRORTY | |
| | | | | | | | |
| LOGUE | Thomas | head | na | na | 0258546 | | Donegal |
| LOGUE | Ann | wife | na | na | | | Raphoe N |
| LOGUE | Mary | dau | 14 | | | | Clonleigh |
| LOGUE | Thomas | son | 10 | | | | Porthall |
| LOGUE | James | son | 7 | | | | |
| LOGUE | Margaret | dau | 4 | | | | |
| LOGUE | Anne | dau | 2 | | | | |

| | | | | | | |
|---|---|---|---|---|---|---|
| LOUGHREY | John | head 37 | 1845 0258547 | | | Donegal |
| LOUGHREY | Mary | wife 29 | 1845 | | | Raphoe N |
| LOUGHREY | Hanah | dau 5 | | | | Raphoe |
| LOUGHREY | Sarah | dau 2 | | | | Roosky Up |
| LOUGHREY | John | son 1 m | | | | |
| | | | | | | |
| LOUGHREY | John | head 35 | 1842 | | | Donegal |
| LOUGHREY | Mary | wife 31 | 1842 | | | Raphoe N |
| LOUGHREY | James | son 8 | | | | Raphoe |
| LOUGHREY | Edward | son 7 | | | | Roosky Up |
| LOUGHREY | Ellen | dau 6 | | claimant | | |
| LOUGHREY | Charles | son 3 | | | | |
| LOUGHREY | Patrick | son 1 | | | | |
| | | | | | | |
| LOUGHREY | William | head 28 | 1849 0258547 | | | Donegal |
| LOUGHREY | Margaret | wife 30 | 1849 | | | Raphoe N |
| LOUGHREY | Margaret | dau 1 | | | | Clonleigh |
| LOUGHREY | John | son 3 m | | claimant | | Lifford Common |
| LOUGHREY | Sarah | moth 60 | 1821 | wid | | |
| LOUGHREY | David | brot 35 | | | | |
| LOUGHREY | Hugh | brot 16 | | | | |
| LOUGHREY | William | cous 9 | | same surname | | |
| | | | | | | |
| LYNCH | Ellen | head 57 | na 0258546 | wid | | Donegal |
| LYNCH | Mary | dau 27 | | claimant, m. GALLAGHER? | | Inishowen W |
| LYNCH | John | son 18 | | | | Muff |
| LYNCH | Patt | husb 67 | | d. 1848 | | Carnamoyle |
| | | | | | | |
| LYNCH | Thomas | head 50 | 1825 0258547 | | | Donegal |
| LYNCH | Magey | wife 50 | 1825 | nee McCOOL per Cl. not found | | Raphoe N |
| LYNCH | Mary | dau 19 | | | | Killea |
| LYNCH | James | son 17 | | absent | | Glasmullan |
| LYNCH | Thomas | son 14 | | | | |
| | | | | | | |
| LYNCH | William | head 41 | 1832 0258546 | | | Donegal |
| LYNCH | Ellen | wife 47 | 1832 | | | Inishowen W |
| LYNCH | Sarah | dau 19 | | absent | | Muff |
| LYNCH | Martha | dau 18 | | | | Ture |
| LYNCH | Rebecca | dau 10 | | | | |
| LYNCH | Fanny | dau 5 | | d. 1844 | | |
| LYNCH | Robert | son 2 | | d. 1849 | | |
| | | | | | | |
| LYTTON | Mathew | head na | 1842 0258547 | | | Dublin |
| LYTTON | Jane | wife na | 1842 | nee HEFFRON | | Coolock |
| LYTTON | Margaret | dau 5 | | | | Santry T, Tnld & |
| LYTTON | Charles | son 3 | | | | Parish |
| LYTTON | Mary | dau 1 | | claimant, m. MURPHY | | Main Rd. |
| LYTTON | Michael | son 20 m | | d. 1845 | | |
| | | | | | | |
| | | | | | | |
| MAGEE | Edward | head 49 | 1833 0258546 | 1851 Census spelling | | Donegal |
| MAGEE | Cathrine | wife 43 | 1833 | nee McBARN | | Tirhugh |
| MAGEE | James | son 16 | | | | Templecarn |
| MAGEE | Alles | dau 14 | | | | Tievemore |
| MAGEE | Ellen | dau 12 | | | | |
| MAGEE | Eliza | dau 10 | | | | |
| MAGEE | Pat | son 8 | | Patrick, claimant, McGEE | | |
| MAGEE | Mary | dau 4 | | | | |

| | | | | | | | |
|---|---|---|---|---|---|---|---|
| MAGUIRE | Terence | head | na | na | 0258547 | | Leitrim |
| MAGUIRE | Bridget | wife | na | na | | | Rosclogher |
| MAGUIRE | Denis | son | 9 | | | | Rossinver |
| MAGUIRE | John | son | 7 | | | | Gornaderrary |
| MAGUIRE | Charles | son | 5 | | | | |
| MAGUIRE | Michael | son | 3 | | | | |
| MAGUIRE | Catherine | dau | 1 | | | | |
| MAGUIRE | Mary | dau | 1 | | | d. 1841 | |
| | | | | | | | |
| MAHON | George | head | 42 | 1834 | 0258546 | | Donegal |
| MAHON | Margaret | wife | 41 | 1834 | | nee GIVEN | Raphoe N |
| MAHON | Mary Jane | dau | 14 | | | | Raymoghy |
| MAHON | George | son | 12 | | | | Killyverry |
| MAHON | Margaret | dau | 8 | | | claimant, m. WILSON | |
| MAHON | Martha | dau | 6 | | | | |
| MAHON | John | son | 2 | | | | |
| | | | | | | | |
| MEENAN | Thomas | head | na | 1846 | 0258546 | | Donegal |
| MEENAN | Margaret | wife | na | 1846 | | | Kilmacrenan |
| MEENAN | William | son | 5 | | | claimant | Tullyfern |
| MEENAN | Mary | dau | 3 | | | | Gortin |
| MEENAN | Catherine | dau | 1 | | | | |
| | | | | | | | |
| MOLLOY | Edward | head | 56 | 1820 | 0258547 | m. 1820/1834/1840 | Donegal |
| MOLLOY | Giles | wife | 56 | 1815 | | m. 1815/1840 | Boylagh |
| MOLLOY | Francis | son | 30 | | | | Lettermacaward |
| MOLLOY | Owen | son | 22 | | | | Meenacarn |
| MOLLOY | Bryan | son | 20 | | | | |
| MOLLOY | Nora | dau | 19 | | | | |
| MOLLOY | Mary | dau | 16 | | | | |
| MOLLOY | Connell | son | 15 | | | | |
| | | | | | | | |
| MONAGHAN | Catherine | head | na | na | 0258547 | | Donegal |
| MONAGHAN | Hugh | son | 16 | | | | Raphoe S |
| MONAGHAN | Sarah | dau | 14 | | | | Donaghmore |
| MONAGHAN | Mary | dau | 12 | | | | Belalt |
| MONAGHAN | Margaret | dau | 10 | | | | |
| MONAGHAN | Catherine | dau | 8 | | | | |
| MONAGHAN | Annie | dau | 4 | | | claimant, m. GALLAGHER | |
| MONAGHAN | John | husb | na | | | d. 1849 | |
| | | | | | | | |
| MONTGOMERY | Robert | head | 38 | 1835 | 0258547 | | Donegal |
| MONTGOMERY | Jane | wife | 34 | 1835 | | | Inishowen W |
| MONTGOMERY | William | son | 13 | | | | Muff |
| MONTGOMERY | Nancy | dau | 7 | | | | Aught |
| MONTGOMERY | Elizabeth | dau | 5 | | | | |
| MONTGOMERY | Rebecca | dau | 5 | | | d. 1842 | |
| MONTGOMERY | Samuel | fath | 55 | | | d. 1845 | |
| MONTGOMERY | Thomas | son | 5 | | | d. 1846 | |
| | | | | | | | |
| MORAN | Michael | head | na | na | 0258547 | | Wicklow |
| MORAN | Bridget | wife | na | na | | | Shillelagh |
| MORAN | Elizabeth | dau | 16 | | | | Carnew |
| MORAN | Ann | dau | 14 | | | | Hillbrook |
| MORAN | Myles | son | 12 | | | | |
| MORAN | Martha | dau | 10 | | | | |
| MORAN | James | son | 8 | | | | |
| MORAN | Frances | dau | 6 | | | | |
| MORAN | John | son | 3 | | | | |
| MORAN | Catherine | dau | 1 | | | claimant | |

| | | | | | | | |
|---|---|---|---|---|---|---|---|
| MULREANY | Charles | head | 26 | 1848 | 0258547 | | Mayo |
| MULREANY | Margaret | wife | 22 | 1848 | | | Tirawley |
| MULREANY | Ellen | dau | 2 | | | claimant, 2 yrs 7 months | Kilmoremoy |
| MULREANY | Elena | dau | 1 | | | 1 year 5 months | Ballina |
| | | | | | | | 21 Bridge St. |
| | | | | | | | |
| McADAMS | Daniel | head | na | na | 0258547 | | Donegal |
| McADAMS | Eliza | wife | na | na | | | Inishowen W |
| McADAMS | Margaret | dau | 18 | | | | Fahan Up |
| McADAMS | Dan | son | 16 | | | | Tievebane |
| McADAMS | William | son | 14 | | | | |
| McADAMS | Hannah | dau | 8 | | | | |
| McADAMS | Andy | son | 5 | | | | |
| McADAMS | John | son | 2 | | | claimant | |
| | | | | | | | |
| McATEER | John | head | na | 1833 | 0258546 | | Donegal |
| McATEER | Eliza | wife | na | 1833 | | | Inishowen W |
| McATEER | Patrick | son | 17 | | | | Inch |
| McATEER | John | son | 9 | | | | Ballynakilly |
| McATEER | Sarah | dau | 5 | | | | |
| McATEER | Mary | dau | 2 | | | | |
| McATEER | James | son | 7 | | | d. 1846 | |
| | | | | | | | |
| McBARRON | Patrick | head | na | na | 0258547 | | Donegal |
| McBARRON | Catherine | wife | na | na | | | Tirhugh |
| McBARRON | James | son | 7 | | | | Templecarn |
| McBARRON | Patrick | son | 5 | | | | Bolelshil |
| McBARRON | Mary | dau | 2 | | | claimant, m. DALY | |
| | | | | | | | |
| McBRIDE | John | head | na | na | 0258547 | | Donegal |
| McBRIDE | Cecilia | wife | na | na | | | Raphoe N |
| McBRIDE | Margaret | dau | 9 | | | | Raymoghy |
| McBRIDE | Edward | son | 8 | | | | Kincraigy |
| McBRIDE | John | son | 7 | | | | |
| McBRIDE | Thomas | son | 5 | | | | |
| | | | | | | | |
| McBRIDE | Michael | head | 62 | na | 0258547 | | Donegal |
| McBRIDE | Frank | son | 36 | | | absent | Kilmacrenan |
| McBRIDE | Mary | dau | 32 | | | absent | Clondahorky |
| McBRIDE | Catherine | dau | 30 | | | absent | Castledoe |
| McBRIDE | Ann | dau | 28 | | | absent | |
| McBRIDE | Sophia | dau | 10 | | | | |
| McBRIDE | Rose | dau | 8 | | | claimant | |
| McBRIDE | Rose | wife | 32 | | | nee SHERIDAN, d. date na | |
| | | | | | | | |
| * McCAFFERTY | Margaret | gr/d | 6 | | 0258547 | with gr/f James HEGARTY | |
| | | | | | | | |
| McCALLION | James | head | na | na | 0258547 | | Donegal |
| McCALLION | Mary | wife | na | na | | | Inishowen W |
| McCALLION | Mary | dau | 14 | | | | Muff |
| McCALLION | John | son | 12 | | | | Eskaheen |
| McCALLION | Hugh | son | 9 | | | | |
| McCALLION | Kathleen | dau | 6 | | | | |
| McCALLION | James | son | 3 | | | claimant | |
| McCALLION | Anne | dau | 6 m | | | | |

1851 Irish Census Abstracts (locations in the Republic of Ireland) from Old Age Pensions records held at PRONI, transcribed from LDS film – see also 1841/1851 combined Abstracts and Appendix.

| | | | | | | |
|---|---|---|---|---|---|---|
| McCALLION | Patrick | head na | 1826 | 0258546 | | Donegal |
| McCALLION | Esther | wife na | 1826 | | nee DOHERTY | Raphoe N |
| McCALLION | John | son | 24 | | | Clonleigh |
| McCALLION | Mary | dau | 21 | | claimant | Mulnaveagh |
| McCALLION | James | son | 18 | | | |
| McCALLION | Margaret | dau | 14 | | | |
| McCALLION | Patrick | son | 9 | | | |
| McCALLION | Michael | son | 9 | | d. 1846 | |
| McCALLION | Matilda | dau | 4 | | d. 1847 | |
| McCALLION | Robert | son | 3 | | d. 1847 | |
| | | | | | | |
| McCALLION | William | head na | na | 0258547 | | Donegal |
| McCALLION | Mary | wife na | na | | | Inishowen E |
| McCALLION | William | son | 13 | | | Moville Lr |
| McCALLION | Grace | dau | 12 | | | Meenletterbale |
| McCALLION | Michael | son | 9 | | | |
| McCALLION | Margery | dau | 6 | | claimant Madge? | |
| McCALLION | Patrick | son | 3 | | | |
| | | | | | | |
| McCAN | Thomas | head | 35 | 1842 0258547 lab | | Dublin County |
| McCAN | Abby | wife | 35 | 1842 | Mary per claimant | Castleknock |
| McCAN | Mary | dau | 8 | | Finglas school | Finglas |
| McCAN | Bridget | dau | 4 | | | Town of Talka |
| McCAN | Hugh | son | 2 | | claimant, McCANN | |
| | | | | | | |
| McCAUL | James | head na | 1839 | 0258547 | | Donegal |
| McCAUL | Catherine | wife na | 1839 | | nee McKELVEY | Raphoe S |
| McCAUL | Susan | dau | 11 | | | Donaghmore |
| McCAUL | Margaret | dau | 9 | | | Sessiagh |
| McCAUL | Mary | dau | 7 | | | |
| McCAUL | James | son | 5 | | | |
| McCAUL | Daniel | son | 1 | | claimant | |
| | | | | | | |
| McCAULEY | John | head | 32 | 1844 0258547 | | Donegal |
| McCAULEY | Mary | wife | 42 | 1844 | (age sic) | Inishowen E |
| McCAULEY | John | son | 6 | | | Moville Up |
| McCAULEY | Mary | dau | 2 | | | Drung |
| McCAULEY | Ann | dau | 9 m | | d. 1847 | |
| | | | | | | |
| McCLOSKEY | Daniel | head na | 1831 | 0258547 | | Donegal |
| McCLOSKEY | Sarah | wife na | 1831 | | | Kilmacrenan |
| McCLOSKEY | Andrew | son | 17 | | | Clondahorky |
| McCLOSKEY | Cornelius | son | 12 | | | Dunfanaghy |
| McCLOSKEY | Daniel | son | 10 | | claimant | |
| McCLOSKEY | John | son | 7 | | | |
| McCLOSKEY | Sarah | dau | 4 | | | |
| McCLOSKEY | Margaret | dau | 1 | | | |
| McCLOSKEY | Edward | son | 11 | | d. 1848 | |
| McCLOSKEY – | | | | | See Julia GILES, relationship na | |
| | | | | | | |
| McCLOSKEY | Hugh | head | 36 | 1836 0258547 | | Donegal |
| McCLOSKEY | Sarah | wife | 33 | 1836 | | Raphoe S |
| McCLOSKEY | Catherine | dau | 15 | | | Stranorlar |
| McCLOSKEY | Patrick | son | 7 | | claimant | Ballybofey |
| McCLOSKEY | Elisha | dau | 5 | | | |
| McCLOSKEY | Hugh | son | 1 | | | |
| McCLOSKEY | Edward | son | 7 | | d. 1842 | |
| McCLOSKEY | Elisha | dau | 1 | | d. 1848 | |
| McCLOSKEY - | | | | | See Eleanor BOYLE, lodger | |

| | | | | | | |
|---|---|---|---|---|---|---|
| McCOLLUM | Charles | head na | 1843 0258546 | or MALCOLM | | Donegal |
| McCOLLUM | Eliza | wife na | 1843 | | | Inishowen W |
| McCOLLUM | Mary Jane | dau 8 | | | | Inch |
| McCOLLUM | Serah | dau 5 | | | | Grange |
| McCOLLUM | William | son 3 | | | | |
| McCOLLUM | Eliza | dau 1 | | Elizabeth, claimant m. McINTYRE | | |
| | | | | | | |
| McCORMICK | John | head na | na 0993107 | | | Donegal |
| McCORMICK | Alice | wife na | na | | | Raphoe S |
| McCORMICK | Henry | son 12 | | | | Donaghmore |
| McCORMICK | Nancy | dau 10 | | | | Owennagadragh |
| McCORMICK | Patrick | son 4 | | claimant | | |
| McCORMICK | Sarah | dau 2 | | | | |
| McCORMICK | John | son 1 m | | | | |
| McCORMICK | Sarah | dau 1 | | d. date na | | |
| | | | | | | |
| McCOULE | Charles | head 32 | 1842 0258547 | | (Tyrone?) | Donegal |
| McCOULE | Fanny | wife 27 | 1842 | nee GALLAGHER per Cl. not fd. | | Boylagh |
| McCOULE | Mary | dau 8 | | Mary? | | Templecrone |
| McCOULE | Margaret | dau 5 | | | | Acres |
| McCOULE | Owen | son 3 | | | | |
| McCOULE | Ann | dau 1 | | (see next record) | | |
| | | | | | | |
| McCOULE | Charles | head na | 1842 0258546 | employers Pat CARLIN & Joseph Thompson | | Donegal |
| McCOULE | Fanny | wife na | 1842 | | (Donegal?) | Tyrone |
| McCOULE | Ellen | dau 8 | | Ellen? | | Strabane |
| McCOULE | Margaret | dau 5 | | claimant, m. O'NEILL | | Learmount |
| McCOULE | Owen | son 3 | | | | Stranagalwilly |
| McCOULE | Anne | dau 1 | | (duplicate record?) | | |
| | | | | | | |
| McCREADY | Charles | head na | 1829 0258547 | m. 1829/1841 | | Donegal |
| McCREADY | Magy | wife na | 1841 | | | Tirhugh |
| McCREADY | Susan | dau 18 | | | | Donegal |
| McCREADY | Edward | son 16 | | | | Donegal Town |
| McCREADY | Citty | dau 13 | | Kitty? | | The Diamond |
| McCREADY | Sally | dau 11 | | | | |
| McCREADY | Phillip | son 9 | | | | |
| McCREADY | Ibby | dau 4 | | | | |
| McCREADY | Charles | son 1 | | | | |
| | | | | | | |
| McCREADY | George | head na | na 0258546 | | | Donegal |
| McCREADY | Anne | wife na | na | | | Raphoe S |
| McCREADY | George | son 11 | | | | Kilteevoge |
| McCREADY | Jane | dau 9 | | | | Meenahorna |
| McCREADY | Mary | dau 4 | | Mary Ann, Cl. spells McCREEDY | | |
| McCREADY | Rebecca | dau 4 | | | | |
| | | | | | | |
| McCREEY | John | head 48 | 1824 0258547 | McCREARY? | | Donegal |
| McCREEY | Jane | wife 46 | 1824 | | | Raphoe S |
| McCREEY | Peggy | dau 22 | | | | Donaghmore |
| McCREEY | Fanny | dau 21 | | | | Tirinisk |
| McCREEY | Andrew | son 15 | | absent | | |
| McCREEY | John | son 12 | | | | |
| McCREEY | Jane | dau 10 | | Anne Jane Cl. spells McCREARY | | |
| | | | | | | |
| McCRUDDEN | John | head na | 1828 0258547 | | | Donegal |
| McCRUDDEN | Catherine | wife na | 1828 | | | Raphoe |
| McCRUDDEN | Catherine | dau 15 | | | | Convoy |
| McCRUDDEN | Margaret | dau 11 | | | | Convoy Town |

| | | | | | | | |
|---|---|---|---|---|---|---|---|
| McCRUDDEN | Mary | dau | 6 | | | claimant, m. CAMPBELL | |
| McCRUDDEN | William | son | 4 | | | d. 1844 | |
| | | | | | | | |
| McCUE | Patrick | head | 40 | 1818 | 0258546 | wid | Donegal |
| McCUE | Peggy | dau | 14 | | | | Raphoe S |
| McCUE | Peter | son | 12 | | | claimant | Urney |
| McCUE | Sarah | dau | 8 | | | | Dreenagh |
| McCUE | Kitty | wife | 40 | | | d. date na | |
| | | | | | | | |
| McDAID | John | head | na | 1844 | 0258546 | | Donegal |
| McDAID | Sarah | wife | na | 1844 | | | Inishowen W |
| McDAID | Owen | son | 6 | | | | Fahan Up |
| McDAID | Bridget | dau | 4 | | | | Drumadooey |
| McDAID | Julia | dau | 2 | | | claimant | |
| | | | | | | | |
| McDERMOTT | George | head | 42 | 1835 | 0258547 | McDERMOD on census | Donegal |
| McDERMOTT | Catherine | wife | 40 | 1835 | | | Raphoe N |
| McDERMOTT | Bernard | son | 15 | | | | Clonleigh |
| McDERMOTT | Anne | dau | 13 | | | | Springhill |
| McDERMOTT | George | son | 10 | | | claimant, spells McDERMOTT | |
| McDERMOTT | Edward | son | 7 | | | | |
| McDERMOTT | Mary | dau | 4 | | | | |
| | | | | | | | |
| McDEVITTE | Charles | head | na | na | 0258546 | | Donegal |
| McDEVITTE | Ann | wife | na | na | | nee McBRIDE | Kilmacrenan |
| McDEVITTE | James | son | 2 | | | | Kilmacrenan |
| McDEVITTE | Susan | dau | 1 | | | claimant | Cranford |
| | | | | | | | |
| McDOWELL | Charles | head | na | na | 0258547 | | Donegal |
| McDOWELL | Mary | wife | na | na | | | Inishowen W |
| McDOWELL | Rebecca | dau | 15 | | | | Burt |
| McDOWELL | Isabella | dau | 13 | | | | Moness |
| McDOWELL | Anne | dau | 11 | | | | |
| McDOWELL | John | son | 9 | | | | |
| McDOWELL | Richard | son | 7 | | | | |
| McDOWELL | William | son | 5 | | | claimant | |
| McDOWELL | Charles | son | 3 | | | | |
| McDOWELL | Mary Jane | dau | 9 m | | | | |
| | | | | | | | |
| McEHREE | Andrew | head | na | na | 0258547 | surname spelling checked | Donegal |
| McEHREE | Grace | wife | na | na | | | Kilmacrenan |
| McEHREE | Catherine | dau | 11 | | | | Kilmacrenan |
| McEHREE | Mary | dau | 9 | | | | Currin |
| McEHREE | Fanny | dau | 7 | | | | |
| McEHREE | Bridget | dau | 5 | | | | |
| McEHREE | Pat | son | 4 | | | | |
| McEHREE | Sally | dau | 2 | | | claimant | |
| McEHREE | Manus | son | 6 m | | | illegible | |
| | | | | | | | |
| McELHINNEY | James | head | 30 | 1844 | 0258547 | | Donegal |
| McELHINNEY | Catherine | wife | 31 | 1844 | | Kate | Raphoe S |
| McELHINNEY | Thomas | son | 6 | | | claimant | Donaghmore |
| McELHINNEY | James | son | 3 | | | | Sessiagh Long |
| | | | | | | | |
| McELHINY | Patt | head | 51 | 1825 | 0258547 | laborer | Donegal |
| McELHINY | Thomas | brot | 55 | n.m. | | | Raphoe S |
| McELHINY | Michael | son | 20 | | | in America | Convoy |
| McELHINY | Margaret | dau | 14 | | | | Lettermore |
| McELHINY | Mary | dau | 10 | | | | |
| McELHINY | Anne | dau | 9 | | | | |

| | | | | | | |
|---|---|---|---|---|---|---|
| McELHINY | Mary | wife | 50 | | d. 1844 | |
| McELHINY | John | son | 3 m | | d. 1844 | |
| McELIHINY | Magy | dau | 19 | | d. 1847 | |
| McELHINY | Susan | dau | 16 | | d. 1849 | |
| | | | | | | |
| McFADDEN | Charles | head | na | 1846 0258547 | | Donegal |
| McFADDEN | Ellen | wife | na | 1846 | Nelly | Kilmacrenan |
| McFADDEN | Catherine | dau | 3 | | | Raymunterdoney |
| McFADDEN | John | son | 1 | | | Ray |
| | | | | | | |
| McFADDEN | Shane | head | 45 | 1831 0258546 | wid | Donegal |
| McFADDEN | Sophia | dau | 18 | | | Kilmacrenan |
| McFADDEN | Manus | son | 16 | | | Mevagh |
| McFADDEN | Fred | son | 14 | | Fonigle | Doagh |
| McFADDEN | Michael | son | 12 | | | |
| McFADDEN | Grace | dau | 10 | | | |
| McFADDEN | Shaun | son | 8 | | | |
| McFADDEN | Madge | dau | 2 | | claimant, m. KELLY | |
| | | | | | | |
| McGEAGHAN | Patrick | head | na | na 0258547 | | Donegal |
| McGEAGHAN | Rose | wife | na | na 0993107 | nee KELLY | Inishowen E |
| McGEAGHAN | Rose | dau | 3 | | claimant, m. McCARRON | Clonca |
| McGEAGHAN | John | son | 3 | | | Templemoyle |
| McGEAGHAN | Michael | son | 1 | | | |
| | | | | | | |
| McGILL | John | head | na | na 0258547 | | Donegal |
| McGILL | Mary | wife | na | na | | Raphoe N |
| McGILL | Edward | son | 6 | | | Taughboyne |
| McGILL | James | son | 4 | | | Kinnacally |
| McGILL | Pat | son | 1 | | claimant | |
| | | | | | | |
| McGINLEY | Daniel | head | na | na 0993107 | | Donegal |
| McGINLEY | Margaret | wife | na | na | | Raphoe N |
| McGINLEY | Susanna | dau | 28 | n.m. | Shusana | Clonleigh |
| McGINLEY | Margaret | dau | 25 | | | Millsessiagh |
| McGINLEY | Hugh | son | 17 | | | |
| | | | | | | |
| McGINLEY | Patrick | head | na | na 0258546 | | Donegal |
| McGINLEY | Mary | wife | na | na | | Kilmacrenan |
| McGINLEY | Celty | dau | 16 | | dau? | Clondahorky |
| McGINLEY | Fanny | dau | 13 | | | Carrownamaddy |
| McGINLEY | Peggy | dau | 11 | | | |
| McGINLEY | Mary | dau | 9 | | | |
| McGINLEY | Michael | son | 3 | | d. 1849 | |
| | | | | | | |
| McGLINCHEY | Timothy | head | na | 1830 0258547 | | Donegal |
| McGLINCHEY | Jane | wife | na | 1830 | | Raphoe S |
| McGLINCHEY | Sarah | dau | 18 | | | Convoy |
| McGLINCHEY | Ann | dau | 15 | | | Drumgumberland |
| McGLINCHEY | Mary | dau | 13 | | | |
| McGLINCHEY | Thomas | son | 8 | | | |
| McGLINCHEY | Jane | dau | 6 | | | |
| McGLINCHEY | James | son | 6 m | | claimant | |
| | | | | | | |
| McGLINCHY | Robert | head | na | na 0258547 | | Donegal |
| McGLINCHY | Rose | wife | na | na | nee MONAGHAN | Raphoe N |
| McGLINCHY | Bernard | son | 20 | | | Taughboyne |
| McGLINCHY | John | son | 17 | | | Kilgort |
| McGLINCHY | James | son | 14 | | | |
| McGLINCHY | Margaret | dau | 11 | | | |

| McGLINCHY | William | son | 7 | | | | |
|---|---|---|---|---|---|---|---|
| McGLINCHY | Isabella | dau | 4 | | | | |
| McGLINCHY | Robert | son | 9 m | | | claimant | |
| | | | | | | | |
| McGLYNN | John | head | na | 1843 | 0258547 | | Donegal |
| McGLYNN | Mary | wife | na | 1843 | | | Boylagh |
| McGLYNN | Hugh | son | 6 | | | | Inniskeel |
| McGLYNN | Mary | dau | 4 | | | | Tievedeevan |
| McGLYNN | Bridget | dau | 2 | | | | |
| McGLYNN | Anne | dau | 1 | | | d. 1846 | |
| | | | | | | | |
| McGOLDRICK | Michael | head | na | na | 0993107 | | Donegal |
| McGOLDRICK | Mary | wife | na | na | | | Raphoe S |
| McGOLDRICK | Mary | dau | 14 | | | | Urney |
| McGOLDRICK | Susan | dau | 10 | | | | Graffy |
| McGOLDRICK | John | son | 8 | | | | |
| McGOLDRICK | James | son | 6 | | | | |
| McGOLDRICK | Patrick | son | 3 | | | Patrick? | |
| McGOLDRICK | Rose | dau | 2 w | | | Rose Ann, claimant, m. DUNLEVY | |
| McGOLDRICK | Michael | son | 3 | | | d. date off page | |
| | | | | | | | |
| McGOWAN | James | head | na | 1830 | 0258546 | | Donegal |
| McGOWAN | Bridget | wife | na | 1830 | | | Tirhugh |
| McGOWAN | Andrew | son | 21 | | | absent | Inishmacsaint |
| McGOWAN | Thady | son | 15 | | | | Ballyshannon |
| McGOWAN | Pat | son | 14 | | | | The Rock or |
| McGOWAN | James | son | 12 | | | | Eastport |
| McGOWAN | Thomas | son | 10 | | | claimant | |
| McGOWAN | Mick | son | 9 | | | | |
| McGOWAN | Joseph | son | 2 | | | d. 1849 | |
| | | | | | | | |
| McGOWAN | William | head | na | na | 0258547 | | Donegal |
| McGOWAN | Sarah | wife | na | na | | nee GALLAGHER | Raphoe N |
| McGOWAN | Mary | dau | 7 | | | | Raymoghy |
| McGOWAN | Catherine | dau | 2 | | | claimant, m. RODDEN | Carricknamart |
| | | | | | | | |
| McGRORTY | Hugh | head | 60 | 1821 | 0258547 | wid | Donegal |
| McGRORTY | Sarah | dau | 22 | n.m. | | | Inishowen E |
| McGRORTY | Daniel | son | 19 | | | | Moville Up |
| McGRORTY | Ellen | dau | 16 | | | | Cooly |

McGRORTY – See Fanny LOGUE, gr/dau, with Hugh McGRORTY in 1851 Census (father
James LOGUE, mother Mary McGRORTY, per claimant)

| McGRORTY | Robert | head | na | 1829 | 0258547 | m. 1829/1831/1850 | Donegal |
|---|---|---|---|---|---|---|---|
| McGRORTY | Mary | wife | na | 1850 | | | Kilmacrenan |
| McGRORTY | Robert | son | 20 | | | | Killygarvan |
| McGRORTY | Biddy | dau | 1 | | | | Elly |
| McGRORTY | Susan | wife | 50 | | | d. date off sheet | |
| | | | | | | | |
| McGUINESS | James | head | na | na | 0993107 | | Monaghan |
| McGUINESS | Eliza | wife | na | na | | | Monaghan |
| McGUINESS | James | son | 6 | | | | Thallon |
| McGUINESS | Mathew | son | 4 | | | | Seaveagh |
| McGUINESS | Seria | dau | 2 | | | | |
| | | | | | | | |
| McGUINNESS | Pat | head | 73 | na | 0258545 | | Louth |
| McGUINNESS | Ann | wife | 77 | na | | | Dundalk |
| McGUINNESS | Paddy | son | 38 | 1844 | | | Ballymascanlan |
| McGUINNESS | Biddy | D/L | 30 | 1844 | | | Ballymascanlan |
| McGUINNESS | Bridget | gr/d | 12 | | | claimant, mother Mary per claimant | |

| | | | | | | | |
|---|---|---|---|---|---|---|---|
| McGUINNESS | John | gr/s | 7 | | | | |
| McGUINNESS | Arthur | gr/s | 5 | | | | |
| McGUINNESS | Owen | gr/s | 3 | | | | |
| | | | | | | | |
| McHUGH | Michael | head | 50 | na | 0258547 | | Leitrim |
| McHUGH | Margaret | wife | 40 | na | | | Rosclogher |
| McHUGH | Winnie | dau | 18 | | | | Killasnet |
| McHUGH | James | son | 16 | | | | Glebe |
| McHUGH | Catherine | dau | 14 | | | | |
| McHUGH | Martin | son | 12 | | | Martin? light entry, claimant? | |
| McHUGH | John | son | 9 | | | | |
| McHUGH | Philip | son | 6 | | | | |
| McHUGH | Margaret | dau | 3 m | | | | |
| | | | | | | | |
| McKANE | William | head | 39 | 1840 | 0258547 | | Donegal |
| McKANE | Margareet | wife | 38 | 1840 | | | Raphoe N |
| McKANE | William | son | 9 | | | | Clonleigh |
| McKANE | John | son | 7 | | | claimant | Porthall |
| McKANE | Mary Ann | dau | 5 | | | | |
| McKANE | Mary | dau | 1 m | | | d. 1845 | |
| McKANE | Patrick | son | 2 | | | d. 1851 | |
| | | | | | | | |
| McKELVIE | John | head | 50 | 1837 | 0258547 | claimant says James | Monaghan |
| McKELVIE | Eliza | wife | 40 | 1837 | | claimant says Elizabeth | Cremorne |
| McKELVIE | Sarah | dau | 13 | | | | Ballybay |
| McKELVIE | Thomas | son | 12 | | | | Tonyglassan |
| McKELVIE | William | son | 8 | | | claimant, spells McKELVEY | |
| McKELVIE | James | son | 5 | | | | |
| McKELVIE | Mary | dau | 3 | | | | |
| McKELVIE | John | son | 8 m | | | | |
| McKELVIE | John | aon | 1 m | | | d. 1843 | |
| | | | | | | | |
| McKENNA | Charles | head | na | 1840 | 0258547 | | Monaghan |
| McKENNA | Rose | wife | na | 1840 | | | Trough |
| McKENNA | Ann | dau | 10 | | | | Errigal Trough |
| McKENNA | Elenor | dau | 9 | | | | Aghaderry |
| McKENNA | Charles | son | 7 | | | | |
| McKENNA | Owen | son | 5 | | | | |
| McKENNA | Rosey | dau | 3 | | | | |
| McKENNA | Patt | son | 9 m | | | | |
| | | | | | | | |
| McKERNAN | Bernard | head | na | 1827 | 0258547 | | Cavan |
| McKERNAN | Mary Ann | wife | na | 1827 | | | Tullygarvey |
| McKERNAN | Ellen | dau | 21 | | | | Tumna |
| McKERNAN | Mary | dau | 19 | | | | Cootehill |
| McKERNAN | Ann | dau | 16 | | | | Bridge St. |
| McKERNAN | William | son | 14 | | | | |
| McKERNAN | Jane | dau | 10 | | | | |
| McKERNAN | Bernard | son | 3 | | | | |
| | | | | | | | |
| McKINLEY | Catherine | head | 28 | 1839 | 0258547 | wid | Donegal |
| McKINLEY | John | son | 11 | | | | Raphoe N |
| McKINLEY | Margaret | dau | 8 | | | claimant, m. SWEENEY | Raphoe |
| McKINLEY | James | son | 6 | | | | Ardvarnock Glebe |
| McKINLEY | Michael | husb | 27 | | | d. date illegible | |
| | | | | | | | |
| * McLAUGHLIN | Bridget | visi | 60 | | 0258547 | with John CRUMLISH | |

1851 Irish Census Abstracts (Republic of Ireland locations) from Old Age Pension records held at PRONI, transcribed from LDS film – see also 1841/1851 combined records and Appendix.

| McLAUGHLIN | Denis | head na | na | 0258547 | | Donegal |
|---|---|---|---|---|---|---|
| McLAUGHLIN | Catherine | wife na | na | | | Inishowen E |
| McLAUGHLIN | Patrick | son | 16 | | | Culdaff |
| McLAUGHLIN | William | son | 15 | | | Balleeghan Up |
| McLAUGHLIN | Anne | dau | 12 | | | |
| McLAUGHLIN | Mary | dau | 10 | | | |
| McLAUGHLIN | John | son | 9 | | | |
| McLAUGHLIN | Charles | son | 8 | | | |
| McLAUGHLIN | Denis | son | 5 | | | |
| McLAUGHLIN | Susan | dau | 3 | | | |
| McLAUGHLIN | James | son | 1 | | | |
| McLAUGHLIN | Catherine | dau | na | | deceased in 1851 | |
| McLAUGHLIN | Grace | dau | na | | deceased in 1851 | |
| | | | | | | |
| McLAUGHLIN | Henry | head na | na | 0258547 | | Donegal |
| McLAUGHLIN | Isabella | wife na | na | | | Tirhugh |
| McLAUGHLIN | Mary | dau | 10 | | | Kilbarron |
| McLAUGHLIN | Ellen | dau | 8 | | | Kildoney Glebe |
| McLAUGHLIN | Pat | son | 4 | | | |
| McLAUGHLIN | Lizzie | dau | 2 m | | | |
| | | | | | | |
| McLAUGHLIN | Matthew | head na | na | 0258547 | | Donegal |
| McLAUGHLIN | Catherine | wife na | na | | | Tirhugh |
| McLAUGHLIN | William | son | 10 | | | Donegal |
| McLAUGHLIN | Sarah | dau | 8 | | | Donegal Town |
| McLAUGHLIN | John James | son | 10 m | | claimant | Church St. |
| | | | | | | |
| McLAUGHLIN | Neil | head na | na | 0993107 | | Donegal |
| McLAUGHLIN | Cicely | wife na | na | | | Inishowen E |
| McLAUGHLIN | Rose | dau | 18 | | age 8? | Culdaff |
| McLAUGHLIN | Kate | dau | 12 | | | Balleeghan Up |
| McLAUGHLIN | Patrick | son | 12 | | claimant | |
| McLAUGHLIN | Ann | dau | 10 | | | |
| McLAUGHLIN | James | son | 8 | | | |
| McLAUGHLIN | Grace | dau | 6 | | | |
| McLAUGHLIN | Mary | dau | 2 | | | |
| | | | | | | |
| McLAUGHLIN | Patrick | head na | na | 0258547 | | Donegal |
| McLAUGHLIN | Sarah | wife na | na | | | Inishowen W |
| McLAUGHLIN | Susan | dau | 5 | | | Fahan Up |
| McLAUGHLIN | Neal | son | 1 | | | Castlequarter |
| | | | | | | |
| McLAUGHLIN | Thomas | head na | 1834 | 0258547 | | Donegal |
| McLAUGHLIN | Bella | wife na | 1834 | | nee WOODS per claimant not fd. | Inishowen E |
| McLAUGHLIN | James | son | 16 | | | Moville Up |
| McLAUGHLIN | Mary Ann | dau | 14 | | | Whitecastle |
| McLAUGHLIN | Cecily | dau | 12 | | | |
| McLAUGHLIN | Bernard | son | 10 | | | |
| McLAUGHLIN | George | son | 6 | | | |
| McLAUGHLIN | Thomas | son | 4 | | | |
| McLAUGHLIN | Catherine | dau | 3 | | | |
| | | | | | | |
| McLAUGHLIN | William | head na | na | 0258547 | | Donegal |
| McLAUGHLIN | Elizabeth | wife na | na | | nee DENNISON per claimant not fd | Inishowen W |
| McLAUGHLIN | Eliza | dau | 2 | | | Burt |
| McLAUGHLIN | William | son | 6 m | | | Speenoge |
| | | | | | | |
| McLAUGHLIN | William | head na | na | 0258547 | | Donegal |
| McLAUGHLIN | Molly | wife na | na | | | Inishowen W |
| McLAUGHLIN | Mary | dau | 14 | | | Fahan Up |

| | | | | | | | |
|---|---|---|---|---|---|---|---|
| McLAUGHLIN | Edward | son | 13 | | | | Letter |
| McLAUGHLIN | Susan | dau | 10 | | | | |
| McLAUGHLIN | Sarah | dau | 1 | | | | |
| | | | | | | | |
| McLOUGHLIN | Richard | head | 50 | 1821 | 0258546 | | Donegal |
| McLOUGHLIN | William | son | 24 | | | absent | Inishowen |
| McLOUGHLIN | Susan | dau | 22 | | | | Burt |
| McLOUGHLIN | Margaret | dau | 20 | | | | Mulleny |
| McLOUGHLIN | James | son | 17 | | | absent | |
| McLOUGHLIN | Betty | dau | 15 | | | | |
| McLOUGHLIN | Richard | son | 13 | | | | |
| McLOUGHLIN | Anne | dau | 10 | | | claimant, m. DUMIECE | |
| McLOUGHLIN | Ann | wife | 50 | | | d. 1846 nee DOHERTY | |
| | | | | | | | |
| McMACKIN | James | head | 35 | na | 0258547 | | Donegal |
| McMACKIN | Mary | wife | 37 | na | | | Inishowen W |
| McMACKIN | Charles | son | 12 | | | | Muff |
| McMACKIN | Michael | son | 9 | | | | Three Trees |
| McMACKIN | John | son | 2 | | | | |
| | | | | | | | |
| McMENAMIN | Daniel | head | 35 | 1840 | 0258547 | | Donegal |
| McMENAMIN | Hanah | wife | 32 | 1840 | | | Raphoe S |
| McMENAMIN | Sarah | dau | 11 | | | | Donaghmore |
| McMENAMIN | Biddy | dau | na | | | age illegible | Egglybane |
| McMENAMIN | Mary | dau | 7 | | | | |
| McMENAMIN | Patrick | son | na | | | absent | |
| McMENAMIN | Patrick | son | na | | | d. data illegible | |
| | | | | | | | |
| McMENAMIN | Edward | head | 36 | 1849 | 0258546 | | Donegal |
| McMENAMIN | Margaret | wife | 28 | 1849 | | | Raphoe S |
| McMENAMIN | Sarah | moth | 57 | 1804 | | nee QUINN | Donaghmore |
| McMENAMIN | Patrick | brot | 27 | n.m. | | | Belalt |
| | | | | | | | |
| McMENAMIN | Patrick | head | 34 | 1846 | | | Donegal |
| McMENAMIN | Jane | wife | 33 | 1846 | | | Raphoe S |
| McMENAMIN | Catherine | dau | 3 | | | claimant, m. McGOLDRICK | Donaghmore |
| McMENAMIN | Hugh | son | 2 | | | | Belalt |
| McMENAMIN | A. Jane | dau | 3m | | | | |
| McMENAMIN | Charles | brot | 28 | | | | |
| | | | | | | | |
| McNALLY | John | head | na | na | 0258546 | | Monaghan |
| McNALLY | Nancy | wife | na | na | | | Trough |
| McNALLY | James | son | 19 | | | | Donagh |
| McNALLY | Mary | dau | 15 | | | | Toneycoogan |
| McNALLY | Betty | dau | 12 | | | | |
| McNALLY | Bridget | dau | 9 | | | | |
| McNALLY | Margaret | dau | 5 | | | | |
| McNALLY | Sarah | na | 5 | | | claimant, surname DO -----, m. McCAFFREY | |
| | | | | | | | |
| McNAUGHT | James | head | na | na | 0258547 | | Donegal |
| McNAUGHT | Margaret | wife | na | na | | | Inishowen W |
| McNAUGHT | William | son | 17 | | | | Fahan Up |
| McNAUGHT | Mary | dau | 15 | | | | Ballynahone |
| McNAUGHT | Margaret | dau | 14 | | | | |
| McNAUGHT | John | son | 12 | | | | |
| McNAUGHT | James | son | 8 | | | | |
| McNAUGHT | Ann | dau | 5 | | | | |
| McNAUGHT | Hugh | son | 2 | | | claimant | |

| NEILLIS | Neil | head | 50 | 1833 | 0258547 | m. 1833/1843 | Donegal |
|---|---|---|---|---|---|---|---|
| NEILLIS | Bridget | wife | 40 | 1843 | | | Templecarn |
| NEILLIS | John | son | 7 | | | | Tirhugh |
| NEILLIS | Philip | son | 5 | | | | Grousehall |
| NEILLIS | Bridget | dau | 3 | | | claimant, spells NELIS | |
| | | | | | | | |
| NIXON | George | head | 60 | 1811 | 0258547 | m. 1833/1843 | Donegal |
| NIXON | Sarah | wife | 59 | 1811 | | | Raphoe S |
| NIXON | Francis | son | 25 | 1847 | | | Donaghmore |
| NIXON | Isabella | D/L | 27 | 1847 | | | Carricknamanna |
| NIXON | Elizabeth | gr/d | 3 | | | Eliza Jane, claimant, m. ELLISON | |
| NIXON | Robert | gr/s | 2 | | | | |
| NIXON | George | gr/s | 1 | | | | |
| NIXON | John | son | 18 | | | | |
| | | | | | | | |
| O'BRIEN | Hugh | head | na | na | 0258545 | | Donegal |
| O'BRIEN | Martha | wife | na | na | | | Kilmacrenan |
| O'BRIEN | Mary | dau | 10 | | | | Aughnish |
| O'BRIEN | James | son | 9 | | | | Fortstewart |
| O'BRIEN | Sarah | dau | 7 | | | | |
| O'BRIEN | John | son | 6 | | | | |
| O'BRIEN | Hugh | son | 4 | | | | |
| O'BRIEN | Henry | son | 6 m | | | claimant | |
| | | | | | | | |
| O'DONNELL | James | head | na | 1846 | 0258547 | | Donegal |
| O'DONNELL | Betty | wife | na | 1846 | | | Boylagh |
| O'DONNELL | Mary | dau | 9 | | | claimant, m. McNAUGHT | Templecrone |
| O'DONNELL | John | son | 4 | | | | Meenmore |
| | | | | | | | |
| O'DONNELL | Neal | head | 54 | 1832 | 0993108 | | Donegal |
| O'DONNELL | Ann | wife | 54 | 1832 | | nee SWEENEY? | Kilmacrenan |
| O'DONNELL | Catherine | dau | 18 | | | | Tullaghobegly |
| O'DONNELL | Donal | son | 11 | | | | Dore |
| O'DONNELL | Mary | dau | 8 | | | | |
| O'DONNELL | Maggy | dau | 7 | | | claimant Madge? | |
| | | | | | | | |
| O'DONNELL – | | | | | | See also DONNELL | |
| | | | | | | | |
| O'GRADY | Thomas | head | na | na | 0258547 | | Limerick |
| O'GRADY | Ann | wife | na | na | | nee HOGAN | Owneybeg |
| O'GRADY | Patrick | son | 18 | | | | Abington |
| O'GRADY | Eliza | dau | 16 | | | | Knocknagorteeny |
| O'GRADY | Henry | son | 13 | | | | |
| O'GRADY | Mary | dau | 10 | | | | |
| O'GRADY | John | son | 9 | | | claimant | |
| O'GRADY | James | son | 6 | | | | |
| O'GRADY | Thomas | son | 3 | | | | |
| O'GRADY | William | son | 1 | | | | |
| | | | | | | | |
| PARK | John | head | na | 1844 | 0258546 | | Donegal |
| PARK | Mary | wife | na | 1844 | | nee MILLS per claimant not found | Raphoe N |
| PARK | Robert | son | 5 | | | | Raymoghy |
| PARK | Jane | dau | 2 | | | | Lismoghry |
| | | | | | | | |
| PARKE | James | head | na | na | 0258547 | | Donegal |
| PARKE | Kate | wife | na | na | | nee DOHERTY | Kilmacrenan |

| | | | | | | | |
|---|---|---|---|---|---|---|---|
| PARKE | Nancy | dau | 15 | | | or Annie | Conwal |
| PARKE | William | son | 11 | | | | Ballymacool |
| PARKE | Barney | son | 9 | | | | |
| PARKE | Bridget | dau | 7 | | | | |
| PARKE | Mary | dau | 5 | | | | |
| PARKE | James | son | 1 | | | claimant | |
| | | | | | | | |
| PAYNE | Joseph | head | 40 | 1831 | 0258546 | m. 1831/1842 | Donegal |
| PAYNE | Bridget | wife | 32 | 1842 | | nee O'HARA | Raphoe N |
| PAYNE | Andrew | son | 18 | | | | All Saints |
| PAYNE | Elizabeth | dau | 15 | | | absent | Ballyhaskey |
| PAYNE | Thomas | son | 11 | | | | |
| PAYNE | Joseph | son | 11 | | | | |
| PAYNE | Robert | son | 9 | | | | |
| PAYNE | Mary | dau | 7 | | | claimant, m. REID | |
| PAYNE | Lettisha | dau | 5 | | | | |
| PAYNE | Sarah | dau | 3 | | | | |
| PAYNE | Catherine | dau | 1 | | | | |
| | | | | | | | |
| PEACOCK | William | head | na | na | 0258547 | | Leitrim |
| PEACOCK | Anne | wife | na | na | | | Rosclogher |
| PEACOCK | George | son | 12 | | | claimant | Killasnet |
| PEACOCK | Margaret | dau | 10 | | | | Milltown |
| PEACOCK | Eliza | dau | 8 | | | | |
| PEACOCK | Richard | son | 5 | | | | |
| PEACOCK | Rebecca | dau | 2 | | | | |
| | | | | | | | |
| PERRY | John | head | na | 1838 | 0258547 | head constable R.I.C. | Kerry |
| PERRY | Ann | wife | na | 1838 | | | Iveragh |
| PERRY | Ann | dau | 12 | | | | Caher |
| PERRY | Ellen | dau | 10 | | | | Cahirsiveen |
| PERRY | Katherine | dau | 7 | | | claimant, m. WYNNE | Police Barracks |
| PERRY | Henry | son | 5 | | | | |
| PERRY | John | son | 3 | | | | |
| PERRY | Willliam | son | 9 m | | | | |
| | | | | | | | |
| POLLOCK | Isaac | head | na | na | 0258547 | | Donegal |
| POLLOCK | Mary | wife | na | na | | | Raphoe |
| POLLOCK | Fanny | dau | 24 | | | | Donaghmore |
| POLLOCK | James | son | 23 | | | | Castlefinn |
| POLLOCK | Nancy | dau | 20 | | | | |
| POLLOCK | Samuel | son | 18 | | | | |
| POLLOCK | Joseph | son | 16 | | | | |
| POLLOCK | Kitty | dau | 12 | | | | |
| POLLOCK | Martha | dau | 7 | | | claimant, m. BRYSON | |
| | | | | | | | |
| PORTER | James | head | na | na | 0258546 | | Donegal |
| PORTER | Rebecca | wife | na | na | | | Inishowen W |
| PORTER | Robert | son | 13 | | | | Burt |
| PORTER | John | son | 12 | | | | Carrrowreagh |
| PORTER | Charles | son | 11 | | | | |
| PORTER | James | son | 10 | | | | |
| PORTER | Nancy | dau | 7 | | | | |
| PORTER | William | son | 6 | | | | |
| PORTER | Elizabeth | dau | 5 | | | | |
| PORTER | Thomas | son | 2 | | | claimant | |
| | | | | | | | |
| PRESCOTT | Alexander | head | na | na | 0258547 | | Monaghan |
| PRESCOTT | Isabella | wife | na | na | | nee PURDY per claimant not fd | Dartree |
| PRESCOTT | Annie | dau | 20 | | | | Killeevan |

| | | | | | | | |
|---|---|---|---|---|---|---|---|
| PRESCOTT | Mary Jane | dau | 15 | | | | Newbliss Town |
| PRESCOTT | Matilda | dau | 13 | | | | |
| PRESCOTT | Eliza | dau | 11 | | | | |
| PRESCOTT | Sarah | dau | 9 | | | | |
| PRESCOTT | Isabella | dau | 4 | | | | |
| PRESCOTT | Alexander | son | 2 | | | | |
| | | | | | | | |
| QUINN | Ellen | head | 46 | 1833 | 0258547 | nee DUNLEAVY | Donegal |
| QUINN | James | son | 15 | | | absent | Raphoe |
| QUINN | Margaret | dau | 13 | | | | Donaghmore |
| QUINN | Mary | dau | 10 | | | | Ballyarrell |
| QUINN | James | son | 7 | | | | |
| QUINN | Nancy | dau | 5 | | | Annie, claimant, m. TIMONEY | |
| QUINN | Hugh | husb | 49 | | | d. 1849 | |
| QUINN – See | | | | | | Esther DUNLEAVY, M/L? | |
| | | | | | | | |
| QUINN | Peter | head | 38 | 1835 | 0258547 | m. 1835/1846 | Donegal |
| QUINN | Ann | wife | 30 | 1846 | | Hannah? nee McLAUGHLIN per | Raphoe S |
| | | | | | | claimant not found | Donaghmore |
| QUINN | James | son | 13 | | | | Goland |
| QUINN | Pat | son | 11 | | | | |
| QUINN | Ann | dau | 4 | | | | |
| QUINN | Biddy | dau | 1 | | | | |
| QUINN | Margaret | dau | 1 | | | | |
| | | | | | | | |
| REILY | Thomas | husb | 36 | 1835 | 0258547 | absent | Donegal |
| REILY | Catherine | head | 35 | 1835 | | nee BOYLE per claimant not found | Raphoe S |
| REILY | Thomas | son | 13 | | | | Donaghmore |
| REILY | Elenor | dau | 11 | | | | Carricknashane |
| REILY | Edward | son | 9 | | | | |
| REILY | Margaret | dau | 7 | | | | |
| REILY | Denis | son | 4 | | | | |
| | | | | | | | |
| RITCHIE | Samuel | head | na | na | 0258546 | | Donegal |
| RITCHIE | Hannah | wife | na | na | | | Kilmacrenan |
| RITCHIE | John | son | 5 | | | claimant | Tullyfern |
| RITCHIE | Jane | dau | 3 | | | | Glenkeen |
| | | | | | | | |
| SHANNON | Mary | head | na | 1844 | 0993107 | | Sligo |
| SHANNON | William | son | 4 | | | claimant | Leyny |
| SHANNON | Mary | dau | 2 | | | | Killoran |
| | | | | | | | Coolaney |
| | | | | | | | |
| SHARKEY | John | head | 59 | 1811 | 0258546 | | Donegal |
| SHARKEY | Marcella | wife | 59 | 1811 | | Madge? | Boylagh |
| SHARKEY | Sheelah | dau | 28 | | | | Templecrone |
| SHARKEY | Unity | dau | 25 | | | | Kincaslough |
| SHARKEY | Grace | dau | 20 | | | | |
| SHARKEY | John | son | 15 | | | | |
| | | | | | | | |
| SHARKEY | William | head | na | na | 0258546 | | Donegal |
| SHARKEY | Sarah | wife | na | na | | | Inishowen W |
| SHARKEY | William | son | 8 | | | | Burt |
| SHARKEY | John | son | 6 | | | | Speenoge |

| SHARKEY | Sarah | dau | 1 | | | | |
|---------|-------|-----|---|---|---|---|---|
| SMITH | William | head | 38 | 1835 | 0258547 | | Donegal |
| SMITH | Mary | wife | 31 | 1835 | | | Kilmacrenan |
| SMITH | Eliza | dau | 14 | | | | Gartan |
| SMITH | Catherine | dau | 13 | | | | Meenawilligan |
| SMITH | Mary | dau | 10 | | | | |
| SMITH | William | son | 9 | | | | |
| SMITH | Peggy | dau | 7 | | | | |
| SMITH | Martha | dau | 5 | | | also Margaret 5? Cl. m. PROCTOR data off page | |
| SMITH | Rebecca | dau | 2 | | | | |
| STEEL | John | head | na | na | 0258546 | | Donegal |
| STEEL | Letitia | wife | na | na | | | Inishowen E |
| STEEL | James | son | 15 | | | | Moville Up |
| STEEL | William | son | 14 | | | | Cabry |
| STEEL | Anne | dau | 12 | | | | |
| STEEL | George | son | 10 | | | | |
| STEEL | Mary | dau | 8 | | | claimant, m. MORRIS | |
| STEEL | Dan | son | 6 | | | | |
| STEEL | John | son | 4 | | | | |
| STEEL | Jane | dau | 2 | | | | |
| STEVENSON | Andrew | head | na | 1845 | 0258547 | | Donegal |
| STEVENSON | Ann | wife | na | 1845 | | | Raphoe N |
| STEVENSON | Andrew | son | 9 | | | | Clonleigh |
| STEVENSON | Robert | son | 4 | | | | Gortindorch |
| STEVENSON | Eliza | dau | 2 | | | claimant | |
| STEVENSON | William | son | 3 m | | | | |
| STEVENSON | Mary | dau | 3 m | | | | |
| * SUMMERVILLE | Jane | gr/d | 4 | | 0258547 | with Thomas DAY, gr/f | |
| SWEENEY | James | head | na | na | 0258547 | | Donegal |
| SWEENEY | Mary | wife | na | na | | | Inishowen W |
| SWEENEY | Sarah | dau | 8 | | | | Fahan Up |
| SWEENEY | James | son | 18 m | | | | Crislaghmore |
| SWEENEY | Michael | head | na | na | 0258547 | | Donegal |
| SWEENEY | Catherine | wife | na | na | | | Raphoe N |
| SWEENEY | James | son | 13 | | | | Raymoghy |
| SWEENEY | Michael | son | 12 | | | | Castledowey |
| SWEENEY | Thomas | son | 9 | | | | |
| SWEENEY | Catherine | dau | 6 | | | | |
| SWEENEY | Margery | dau | 1 | | | | |
| SWETE | Benjamin | head | na | na | 0258547 | | Cork W R |
| SWETE | Annie | wife | na | na | | nee DUNSCOMBE | Muskerry W |
| SWETE | George S. | son | 12 | | | George Samuel | Kilmichael |
| SWETE | Margaret | dau | 10 | | | | Greenville |
| SWETE | Charles D. | son | 8 | | | | |
| SWETE | Samuel | son | 5 | | | | |
| SWETE | Annie | dau | 3 | | | claimant, m. MACKLIN | |
| TAITE | William | head | 80 | 1809 | 0258547 | widower | Donegal |
| TAITE | Jain | dau | 40 | n.m. | | | Raphoe S |
| TAITE | Robert | son | 27 | 1847 | | widower | Donaghmore |

| TAITE | Margaret | gr/d | 2 | | | | Ballynacor |
|-------|----------|------|---|----|----|----|----|
| TAITE | William | head | 32 | na | | d. 1848 | |
| TAITE | Jain | moth | 72 | na | | d. 1849, wife? nee HEGARTY? per claimant not found | |
| TAITE | Anna | head | 22 | na | | d. 1851 | |
| | | | | | | | |
| THOMPSON | John | head | 35 | 1837 | 0258547 | | Donegal |
| THOMPSON | Rachel | wife | 36 | 1837 | | | Inishowen W |
| THOMPSON | Rebecca | dau | 12 | | | | Burt |
| THOMPSON | James | son | 10 | | | | Carrowreagh |
| THOMPSON | Andrew | son | 7 | | | claimant | |
| THOMPSON | Martha | dau | 5 | | | | |
| THOMPSON | Humphrey | son | 3 | | | | |
| THOMPSON | Peggy Ann | dau | 10 m | | | | |
| | | | | | | | |
| TINNEY | Charles | head | 63 | na | 0258546 | wid | Donegal |
| TINNEY | Charles | son | 26 | n.m. | | | Tirhugh |
| TINNEY | Mary | dau | 18 | | | | Donegal |
| TINNEY | Susan | wife | 63 | | | d. 184- | Milltown |
| | | | | | | | |
| TOLAND | John | head | na | na | 0258545 | | Donegal |
| TOLAND | Margaret | wife | na | na | | | Raphoe N |
| TOLAND | Ann | dau | 3 | | | | All Saints |
| TOLAND | John | son | 1 | | | | Ardee |
| | | | | | | | |
| TREANOR | Anne | head | 60 | 1827 | 0258547 | wid | Monaghan |
| TREANOR | Catherine | dau | 20 | | | | Trough |
| TREANOR | Michael | son | 19 | | | absent | Errigal Trough |
| TREANOR | Arthur | son | 17 | | | | Bragan |
| TREANOR | James | husb | 55 | | | d. 1850 (sheet 9) | |
| | | | | | | | |
| TREANOR | Edward | head | 35 | 1846 | 0258547 | | Monaghan |
| TREANOR | na | wife | 33 | 1846 | | given name illegible | Trough |
| TREANOR | Rose | na | 16 | | | | Errigal Trough |
| TREANOR | James | fath | 70 | | | d. 1847 | Bragan |
| TREANOR | Rose | moth | 76 | | | d. 1849 (sheet 22) | |
| TREANOR – See | | | | | | Bridget CONNOLLY, serv | |
| | | | | | | | |
| WALSH | James | head | 31 | 1845 | 0258547 | | Donegal |
| WALSH | Ann | wife | 27 | 1845 | | nee GALLAGHER | Boylagh |
| WALSH | Mary | dau | 5 | | | claimant, spells WELSH, m. WARD | Templecrone |
| WALSH | Nelly | dau | 3 | | | | Ardmeen |
| WALSH | Mary | moth | 60 | | | | |
| | | | | | | | |
| WASSON | James | head | na | na | 0258547 | | Donegal |
| WASSON | Eliza | wife | na | na | | | Raphoe |
| WASSON | William | son | 14 | | | | Raymoghy |
| WASSON | Margaret | dau | 10 | | | | Castledowey |
| WASSON | James | son | 8 | | | | |
| WASSON | Isabella | dau | 7 | | | | |
| WASSON | Catherine | dau | 5 | | | claimant, m. GRAHAM | |
| WASSON | Chumbert | son | 4 | | | | |
| | | | | | | | |
| WATT | James | head | na | 1837 | 0258547 | | Donegal |
| WATT | Rebecca | wife | na | 1837 | | | Inishowen W |
| WATT | Jane | dau | 11 | | | | Fahan Up |
| WATT | Sam | son | 10 | | | | Maghera Beg |
| WATT | William | son | 6 | | | | |

| WATT | Mary | dau | 6 | | | claimant | |
|------|------|-----|---|---|---|---------|---|
| WATT | Isabella | dau | 1 | | | | |
| | | | | | | | |
| WELSH | James | head | 40 | 1841 | 0258547 | | Donegal |
| WELSH | Margaret | wife | 27 | 1841 | | | Raphoe N |
| WELSH | John | son | 9 | | | | Clonleigh |
| WELSH | Sarah | dau | 8 | | | claimant, m. McDERMOTT | Ballindroit Town |
| | | | | | | | |
| WILSON | Charles | head | 41 | na | 0258547 | | Monaghan |
| WILSON | Sarah | wife | 30 | na | | | Dartree |
| WILSON | Mary | dau | 4 | | | | Ematris, Boyher |
| WILSON | Sarah | dau | 3 | | | | & Drummula |
| WILSON | Letticia | dau | 2 | | | | Rockorry V |
| WILSON | Charles | son | 4 m | | | | Monaghan St. |
| | | | | | | | |
| WILSON | John | head | na | 1835 | 0258547 | | Donegal |
| WILSON | Rebecca | wife | na | 1835 | | | Raphoe N |
| WILSON | John | son | 15 | | | | Raymoghy |
| WILSON | Elizabeth | dau | 13 | | | | Lismoghry |
| WILSON | Catherine | dau | 11 | | | claimant | |
| WILSON | Alexander | son | 9 | | | | |
| WILSON | Jane | dau | 7 | | | | |
| WILSON | Frances | dau | 4 | | | | |
| WILSON | Robert | son | 1 | | | | |
| | | | | | | | |
| WILSON | Joseph | head | na | na | 0258547 | | Donegal |
| WILSON | Annie | wife | na | na | | | Raphoe N |
| WILSON | Sarah | dau | 4 | | | | Taughboyne |
| WILSON | Joseph | son | 2 | | | | Cloghfin |
| WILSON | Thomas | son | 2 | | | age 2 months? | |
| | | | | | | | |
| | | | | | | | |
| YOUNG | Robert | head | na | 1830 | 0258547 | | Donegal |
| YOUNG | Margaret | wife | na | 1830 | | | Kilmacrenan |
| YOUNG | Jane | dau | 18 | | | | Tullyfern |
| YOUNG | William | son | 16 | | | claimant | Fawninoughan |
| YOUNG | Elizabeth | dau | 14 | | | | |
| YOUNG | Robert | son | 12 | | | | |
| YOUNG | Catherine | dau | 10 | | | | |
| YOUNG | Isabella | dau | 8 | | | | |
| YOUNG | James | son | 5 | | | | |
| YOUNG | William A. | son | 16 | | | William Andrew, d. date na | |
| | | | | | | | |
| YOUNG | Robert | head | 28 | 1841 | 0258547 | | Donegal |
| YOUNG | Mary | wife | 27 | 1841 | | | Raphoe S |
| YOUNG | Alex | son | 7 | | | | Donaghmore |
| YOUNG | John | son | 5 | | | | Ballybun |
| YOUNG | Eliza | dau | 3 | | | claimant, m. EWING | |
| YOUNG | Robert | son | 6 m | | | | |
| YOUNG | Eliza | dau | 2 m | | | d. 1843 | |

1851 Irish Census Abstracts (Republic of Ireland locations) from the Old Age Pension records held at PRONI, transcribed from LDS film – see also 1841/1851 combined Abstracts and Appendix.

## APPENDIX FOR THE 1851 IRISH CENSUS ABSTRACTS
from Old Age Pension records held in Belfast at the Public Record Office of Northern Ireland
for Republic of Ireland locations

Samuel AULL head m. 1848, Margaret wife, Mary Jane Aull or HEESLETT 2 dau
(claimant), John 1 son, William 2 months son.
    Annagola, Kilmore, Monaghan, <u>Monaghan</u>, 0258547

John BELL 27 head m. 1851, Sarah 33 wife m. 1839/1851, Eliza STEWART 11 step dau,
John 9 step son, Sarah 7 step dau, Ellen Stewart 4 step dau (claimant m. CHAMBERS), Alex
Stewart 2 step son. DEC: Alexander Stewart 40 (1st husband of Sarah Bell) d. 1850.
    Drumhaggart, Burt, Inishowen W, <u>Donegal</u>, 0258547

Dan BOYLE 33 head m. 1840, Susan 31 wife (nee GALLAGHER), Mary 6 dau (claimant m.
O'NEIL), Dan 2. DEC: James 1 month d. 1839, Boyle (given name checked) 6 son d. 1841.
    Carrickaghmore (not found), Templecrone, Boylagh, <u>Donegal</u>, 0258546

Isaac BROWN 60 head, Samuel KILPATRICK 30 relative, m. 1845, Eliza Kilpatrick 22
niece m. 1845, Eliza Kilpatrick 3 relative (claimant Elizabeth m. EWART?), Samuel
Kilpatrick 1 relative.
    Corraskea, Aghnamullen, Cremorne, <u>Monaghan</u>, 0258547

Bridget CAMPBELL 50 head wid m. 1811, John 30 son, Bridget 28 dau, Paddy 27 son,
James McCUE (claimant says McHUGH) 6 gr son; ABS: Grace 23 dau.
    Mullanmore, Inniskeel, Boylagh, <u>Donegal</u>, 0258547

Henry CRAIG head m. 1849, Margaret wife, John 1 (not claimant).
    Castruse, All Saints, Raphoe N, <u>Donegal</u>, 0258547

Thomas CROSSAN 60 head m.1810, Mary 57 wife, Thomas 35 son, Alexander 23 son, Ann
17 dau, Joseph 11 son, Mary LOGUE 8 gr dau (claimant, m. MAGEE); ABS: William 33 son,
Cunningham 27 son, Samuel 25 son. DEC: Catherine Crossan 37 dau d. 1842. (Neil Logue
and Catherine parents per claimant.)
    Carrickmore, Taughboyne, Raphoe, <u>Donegal</u>, 0258547

William CROZIES 28 head m. 1850, Alicia 31 wife, Margaret I. 3 mo; step children: William
DOUGLAS 12 (claimant?), James 10, Mary A. C. 7, Richard 5. DEC: James Douglas 53
wife's husband d. 1847.
    Tullyvanus, Muckno, Cremorne, <u>Monaghan</u>, 0993107

Denis CURRIN 40 head m. 1837, Margaret 50 wife m. 1817/1837, step children MULLIN:
Catherine 22, Edward 18, Henry 16; Sarah CURRAN (sic) 8 dau (claimant, m. McGRATH),
Edward GALLAGHER 15 lodger; ABS: step children: Susan 24, Mary 22, Benjamin 20.
    Ballylast, Urney, Raphoe S, <u>Donegal</u>, 0258547

Daniel DORRION 30 head m.1847, Margaret 21 wife, Jonathan 2 son. DEC: Edward 18
months d. 1849.
    Cornagill, Aghanunshin, Kilmacrenan, <u>Donegal</u>, 0258547

James GARY head m. 1849, Mary (nee CAHILL) wife, Mary 1 month dau (claimant Mary Ann b. Mar. 25, 1851).

No. 8 Lisburn St. 89th Reg. Foot, Linen Hall Barracks, Dublin City, Dublin, 0258547

Tom HARODEN head, Anne wife, Susan 17 dau, Tom 13, James 11, Mary 7 (claimant, m. McCARRON), Willie 5.

Drummore, All Saints, Raphoe N, Donegal (Dromore, Clonleigh?), 0258547

Edward HOMES 24 head m.1850, Elin 34 wife m. 1830 or 1833/1850; step children GILL: Mary 17, Ann 13, Sally (Sarah) 10, Michael 7, Catherine 5 (claimant m. McDONNELL), William Homes 22 mo son, Michael Gill 85 wife's F/L m. 1800 wid. Dec: John Gill 38 1st husband carpenter d. 1847.

Ballymacarry Lr, Fahan Lr, Inishowen W, Donegal, 0258547

James KERR 62 head m. 1816, Ann 50 wife, Bernard 34 son wid m.1840, James 9 gr son, Bernard 7, James 4 (claimant James McNAMEE? parents Michael and Bridget, gr/f James Kerr per claimant). DEC: Catherine 25 D/L d. 1849.

Cashel Place, Mulnagung, Clonleigh, Raphoe N, Donegal, 0258547

Jeria (sic) MARTIN 60 head n.m., Martha 60 sister, Fanny 54 sister, John McMONAGLE 19 serv, William KENNEDY 14 serv, Isabella JOHNSTON (nee LEEPER) 40 m. serv, Ruth Johnston (Cl. m. RIDDALL) 4 lodger, Margret 2 lodger; ABS: Robert Johnston 35 serv.

Drummucklagh, Taughboyne Raphoe N, Donegal, 0258547

James MILKIN 60 head m.1823, Mary 52 wife, Anne McMAHON 34 lodger m. 1835, John McMahon 15 lodger, Margaret McMahon 5 lodger (claimant, m. KEENAN).

Shanco or Killeevan Glebe, Killeevan Parish, Dartree, Monaghan, 0258547

Peter MOAN (sic) head, Bridget wife (nee BOYLAN), John 4 son (claimant), James 3 son, Margaret 2 dau.

Legnacreeve (or Monaghan Town?), Monaghan, Monaghan, Monaghan, 0258547

Maggie MULLIN 76 head, John Mullin son m. 1849, Grace D/L, James 1 son (claimant).

Carnamoyle, Muff, Inishowen W, Donegal, 0258546

John McCANDLESS head, Anne wife, George 6 son, James 4 son (Cl. uses MITCHELL).

Aghaglassan, Culdaff, Inishowen E, Donegal, 0258547

James McCURRIN (CAIRN per claimant) 33 head m. 1848, Sarah (nee TONER) 35 wife m. 1838/1848; step children (?) DONAGHY: John 11, Pat 10, James 9, Sarah 8, Margaret 7, Ellen 6, William 5, ------ McCURREN (sic) 1 dau. DEC: William Toner 87 F/L d. 1843, Mary Ann Donaghy 6 dau (step dau?) d. 1843.

Drumskellan, Muff, Inishowen W, Donegal, 0258546

Patrick McMANUS 32 head m. 1848, Grace 29 wife, Patrick 2 (not claimant).

Loughfad, Templecarn, Tirhugh, Donegal, 0258547

Peter McLOONE 40 head m. 1838, Bridget 44 wife, Anne 12 dau, Bridget 12 (claimant), Peter 8, Eloner 6, Rose 2; step children: Catherine MOLLOY 20, Patrick 18, Mary 16.

Meenmore E, Inishkeel, Boylagh, Donegal, 0258547

Darby QUINN 60 head m. 1816, Nancy 55 wife, Denis 34 son, Eloner O'DONNEL 30 dau m. 1834 (1844?), Nancy O'Donnel 6 gr dau (claimant Ann m. McCORMICK, says parents Ellen and Anthony); ABS: Hugh 32 son, Anthony O'Donnel 35 S/L.
    Carricknashane, Donaghmore, Raphoe S, <u>Donegal</u>, 0258547/0993107

Patrick SHIELS head m.1840, Isabella (nee McLAUGHLIN) wife, Margaret 7 dau (claimant born in Elagh More, Templemore, N. W. Lib., Lon'derry), Susan 5 dau. DEC: Charles 10 son d. 1842, Mary Jane 1 week old d. 1850.
    Skeoge, Burt, Inishowen W, <u>Donegal</u>, 0258547

John THOMPSON head m. 1845, Mary Ann wife, Robert 5 son, William 2 son (claimant), Thomas 1 month son.
    Two locations given: Rivory, Urney, Loughtee Upper, <u>Cavan</u>, (family found here) and Ennislare, Lisnadill, Fews Lr, <u>Armagh,</u> 0258547

Unity TOURISH head, brother James CREANOR m. 1831 (data off page), Margaret 16, George 6, Mary Anne 4 (claimant, m. BROWN, says father James Creanor).
    Mulnaveagh, Clonleigh, Raphoe N, <u>Donegal</u>, 0993107

Owen WALSH head m. 1838, Bridget wife (nee McNALLY per claimant not found), Rose 9, John 7, Patrick 6, James 2; ABS: Edward 11 son, Elizabeth 4 dau.
    Lisnafeddaly, Magheross (Carrickamacross?), Farney, <u>Monaghan</u>, 0993107

James WATSON 40 head m. 1835, Margaret/Peggy (nee CANNON) 30 wife, Mary J. 10 dau, James 8, Bell 6, Thomas 4 (claimant), Margaret 6 months.
    Slanvally (not found), Donaghmore, Raphoe S, <u>Donegal</u>, 0258546

James WILSON 55 head m. 1820, Isabella 46 wife, James Henry 22 son m. 1850, Sarah 22 D/L m. 1850, Isabella Jane KELLY 6 gr dau.
    Corkish, Bailieborough, Clankee, <u>Cavan</u>, 0258547


**********************


Transcript of <u>Certified Copies</u> of portions of some returns from the 1851 Census of Ireland, copies held at PRONI in Belfast, Northern Ireland, locations in the Republic of Ireland:

Andrew CUNNINGHAM 34 head m. 1841 farmer RW b. Co Louth, Margaret 30 wife RW b. Co <u>Armagh</u>, John 15 months son b. Co Louth.
    Co <u>Louth</u>, Lr Dundalk, Faughart, Dungooly

Dominick DONLAN 34 m. 1838 smyth, Bridget 32 wife, Michael 3 son.
    Co <u>Roscommon</u>, Mullinshee (near Frenchpark)

John EARLS 40 head m. 1837 foreman tailor RW b. Co <u>Fermanagh</u>, Teresa A. 33 wife RW b. Dublin, Teresa A. 2 dau b. Dublin.
    Co City of <u>Dublin</u>, St. Peter Parish, New St.

Transcription of Certified Copies of a portion of some returns of the 1851 Census of Ireland held at the National Archives, Dublin, Ireland

Martin ASHE 35 m. 1844 farmer RW E&I, Ellen 23 wife, Mary 6 dau, Catherine 3 dau, Margret 3 mo dau, Johanna Ashe 76 mother wid m. 1801, David ALMOND 50 m. 1830 serv farm lab RW E&I, Timothy GALLWAN(?) 25 serv n.m. farm lab RW E&I, John CAHALLANE (sic) 20 serv farm lab, Catherine BARRETT 14 h serv. DEC: Francis Ashe 28 brother cattle dealer d. Autumn 1843 apoplexy, Martin Ashe 70 father farmer d. Winter 1847 consumption, Johanna Ashe 2 dau d. Autumn 1849 smallpox.
    Co Kerry, Corkaguiny Barony, Ballinvoher Parish, Aughills (Aughils) Townland

John BRYAN 38 m. 1831 messenger, Mary 33 wife, Rose 5 dau in school.
    City of Dublin County, St. Nicholas Within Parish, City of Dublin, Municipal Ward of Merchants Quay St., Angel Alley

Thomas CAINE 46 m. 1832 farmer RW, Mary 40 wife RW, Francis 2 son.
    Co Leitrim, Leitrim, Kiltoghert, Knocknasowna

Patt CALLAGHAN 46 m. 1843 land owner, Biddy 28 wife, Catherine 6 mo dau, Anne HIGGINS 14 h serv. DEC: Mary Callaghan 2 dau d. Winter 1846 smallpox, Winifred 3 dau d. Winter 1846 smallpox, Beesy (sic) 9 mo dau d. Autumn 1849 convulsions.
    Co Sligo, Corran, Drumratt (Drumrat), Knocknagore

Thomas CARR 35 m. 1841 house painter RW b. Naul, Co Meath, Mary 36 wife dressmaker RW b. Ratrath, Co Meath, Patrick 1 son b. Maynouth.
    Co Kildare, Salt North, Laraghbryan, Maynooth S.

Anne CLEARY 50 wid m. 1828 broker RW b. Co Dublin, Denis 18 son letter press printer RW b. City of Galway. DEC: William Clary (sic) 48 husband lower press printer d. Spring 1846 decline.
    Co City of Dublin, St. Peter Parish, City of Dublin, Municipal Ward of Mansion House, Kevin St. Lower

Patt CONNELL 53 wid m. 1831 farmer RW, James 7 son. DEC: Anne 40 wife d. Spring 1845 consumption.
    Co Meath, Moyfenrath Lr, Rathcore, Ballynaskea

Bernard CONROY 51 m. 1828 carpenter and builder RW b. Co Cavan, Margret 39 wife b. Co Dublin, Maria Conroy 15 dau b. Co Dublin.
    Co City of Dublin, St. Thomas Parish, Dublin, Montjoy Ward Townland, Ballybough Rd.

Judy CREGG 51 wid m. 1815, Michael 31 son n.m. lab RW Irish, John 21 son n.m. lab RW Irish, Thomas 15 son lab, Patt 13 son; ABS: Ann 18 dau serv in Leitrim, Mary DOWD 32 dau no trade in Roscommon, Sera McDONALD 24 dau no trade in Roscommon, Patt McDonald 4 gr son in Roscommon. DEC: James 2 son d. Spring 1843 colic, Patt Cregg 52 husband pensioner d. Summer 1847 swelling in foot, Bridget 17 dau d. Autumn 1847 decay.
    Co Roscommon, Frenchpark, Tibohine, Portahard (Portaghard)

Martin CURRY 30 m. 1848 farmer, Bridget 24 wife, Margaret 18 mo dau.
Co Mayo, Costello, Knock, Knockroe

John DALY 32 m. 1839 farmer RW, Katy 38 wife RW, Anne 6 dau.
Co Sligo, Tirerrill, Kilmactranny (Kilmactranry), Derraughonlaugh

Mary DALY 42 m. 1821 beggar, Mary 10 dau beggar, Betty 7 dau. DEC: Michael Daly 48
husband lab d. Spring 1849 consumption.
Co Kerry, Magonihy (Magunihy), Kilcummin, Maulyarkane

Patt DWYER (Patrick Dwyre on front page) 33 m. 1840 picture frame maker RW b. Co
Dublin, Ellen 34 wife R, Mary 7 dau in school.
Co City of Dublin, Dublin, St. Michan Parish, Municipal Ward Inns Quay, Mary's
Lane

Peter DWYER 40 m. 1841 taylor, Bridget 32 wife, Bridget 4 dau.
Co Sligo, Tireragh, Skreen (Skeen), Soodry

Peter EAGAN 50 m. 1833 orsler (sic) b. Co Westmeath, Bridget 50 wife dressmaker b. Co
Longford, Michael Eagan 17 son errand boy RW b. Co Longford.
Co Longford, Shrule, Forgney, Forgney

Thomas EGAN 37 m.1848 farmer, Honour 27 wife R E&I, James 2 son.
Co Mayo, Costello, Aghamore, Caher

John ELMES 45 m. 1834 vicar of St. John's RW b. Bandon, Co Cork, Marian 37 wife RW b.
Ennis, Co Clare, John Blair Elmes 15 son RW, b. Ennis, Co Clare, Thomas 13 son RW b.
Ennis, Co Clare, Mary King Elmes 12 dau RW b. Co Limerick, Elizabeth Jane 9 dau RW b.
Co Limerick, Stephen William 6 son R b. Co Limerick, Robert Henry 5 son b. Co Limerick,
(these taught at home), Charles Frederick 3 son b. Co Limerick, Michael Fitzgerald Elmes 1
son b. Co Limerick, Georgina Susan 4 mo dau b. Co Limerick, Bridget MAYNE 30 nurse
n.m. b. Co Clare, Eliza HARTIGAN 17 parlour serv RW b. Co Limerick, Julia SWITZER 14
serv RW b. Co Limerick. DEC: Martha (Matha?) Ann Elmes 18 mo dau d. Spring 1844 water
on the brain. (See also 1841.)
Co Limerick, City of Limerick Barony, St. John's Parish, St. John's Square

Thomas ENNIS 45 m. 1822 blacksmith RW b. Co Dublin, Mary 43 wife nurse, Thomas 6 son
in school.
Co City of Dublin, Dublin, St. Nicholas Without Parish, Municipal Ward of
Merchants Quay, Bonnys Lane

Pat GEARTY 60 m. 1815 farmer RW, Mary 60 wife, Thomas 33 son m. 1849 lab RW, Mary
26 D/L R, Alicce (sic) Gearty 1 gr dau.
Co Roscommon, Ballintober North Barony, Tarmonbarry (Termonbarry) Parish,
Clonmore (Cloonmore) Townland

Thomas GILLERAN 35 m. 1845 farmer R b. Co Westmeath, Bridget 26 wife R b. Co Meath,
Owen 5 son b. Co Westmeath.
Co Meath, (Demi) Fore, Moylough, Oldcastle, Milltown

Christopher GRANGER 37 m. 1838 lab RW b. Co Kildare, Margaret 31 wife R, Patt 7 son in school b. City of Dublin.
Co City of Dublin, Dublin, St. Catherine Parish, Marrowbone Lane

John KEARANS (Kearon on front page) 42 m. 1841 fisherman, Mary 30 wife, Serah Kearons (sic) 2 dau.
Co Wicklow, Arklow Barony, Arklow Parish, Arklow St.

Barny KELLY 35 m. 1845 farmer, Mary 27 wife spins flax, John 4 son.
Co Roscommon, Roscommon, Lissonuffy, Granaghan (Dillon)

Thomas KENNADY (sic) 61 m. 1814 roadmaker and lab RW, Elizabeth 55 wife R, John 25 son n.m. working with spade RW, Patt 21 son spade work RW, Vallentin 18 son spade work RW, Bridget 15 dau spade work RW, Mary 10 dau spade work R. DEC: Jane 21 dau d. Winter 1843 decline, Marsella 20 dau d. Autumn 1848 pain in the head.
Co Dublin, Balrothery East, Lusk, Balcunnin

John KENNEDY 32 n.m. farmer & whincutter, deaf and dumb; ABS: Catherine Kennedy 57 mother hk gone to America, Denis 25 brother lab in America, Richard 23 brother stone cutter in America, Bridget Kennedy 20 sister spinster gone to America. DEC: Patrick Kennedy 60 father farmer d. Summer 1842 evill (sic).
Co Dublin, Balrothery East, Balrothery Parish, Bow-hill (Bowhill)

Mary Anne KENNEDY 48 wid m. 1829 R, Marsella 20 dau spinster RW, Thomas 7 son ploughman RW, Catherine BIRMINGHAM 8 cousin R. DEC: Anne Kennedy 13 dau in school d. Winter 1848 fever, James 11 son in school d. Winter 1848, Jane 8 dau d. Winter 1848 fever.
Co Dublin, Balrothery East, Balrothery, Stephenstown

Eleanor LALLY 80 wid m. 1819 farmer, Margaret 2 dau (sic).
Co Galway E R, Tiaquin, Killescobe, Rahins

William LAMBERD 72 m. 1800 shoemaker, Ally DUGAN 30 dau m. 1845, Phil Dugan 56 S/L m. 1845 house carpenter RW, Phil Dugan 5 gr son.
Co Wexford, Forth, Rosslare, Burrow

Thomas LEONARD 46 m. 1832 shop porter RW b. Co Dublin, Eliza 40 wife washerwoman, Mary 6 dau.
Co City of Dublin, Dublin, St. Michan Parish, Mun. Ward Inns Quay, Charles St.

Patrick LOUGHLIN 40 m. 1836 gardener lab R b. Co Dublin, Bridget 43 wife serv, Mary 2 dau b. Dublin.
Co City of Dublin, Dublin, St. Peter Parish, Municipal Ward of R, Rosses Court, Gr. Longford St.

Patrick MAGHAN 30 m. 1837 road lab, Mary 29 wife, Catherine 1 dau.
Co Dublin, Rathdown, Stillorgan, Stillorgan North

Patt MARTIN 50 m. 1845 RW Irish, Scelia 30 wife R & spell Irish, Michael 5 son R English.
Co Galway E K, Longford, Abbeygormacan, Corbally More

John MOLLOY (Malloy on front page) 42 m. 1828 foreman in a steam packet R b. Co Dublin, Margaret 42 wife R, Stephen 11 son R.
Co City of Dublin, Dublin, St. Thomas Parish, Municipal Ward Mounjoy, Courtney Place.

Thomas MULCAHY 39 m. 1843 landholder RW E&I b. Co Tipperary, Eliza 34 wife RW b. Co Kilkenny, Tresa (sic) 7 dau Miss Wilkinson's school RW.
Co Tipperary S. R., Clanwilliam, Clonpet, Ballyglass Up lst Townland

Patt MULLADY (Mulleady on front page) 42 m. 1840 farmer RW, Mary 32 wife spins & sews R, Ann 5 dau.
Co Meath, Navan Lr, Donaghmore, Donaghmore

John MULVEY 38 m. 1839 lab RW, Eliza 30 wife spinner R, John 9 son.
Co Leitrim, Kiltubride (Kiltubbrid), Bunrevagh

Margaret MURPHY 44 m. 1829 wid sewing & knitting, Biddy 17 dau sewing and knitting.
Co Wexford, Scarawalsh, Tomb (Toome), Camolin

Peter MURREY 40 m. 1830 farmer, Bridget MURRY (sic) 40 wife, Michael Murry 4 son.
Co Galway W R, Ballymoe, Ballynakill, Knockmascahill

Cornelius (Corniles on front page) NEWMAN 29 wid m. 1845 turner RW, Catherine 4 dau. DEC: Anne 20 wife d. Autumn 1849 cholera.
Co City of Dublin, City of Dublin, St. Michan Parish, Church St.

Patrick NOONAN 30 m. 1840 cabinetmaker RW b. Co Galway, Sera 28 wife RW b. Co Kilkenny, Kate 9 dau school b. Co Kilkenny.
Co Tipperary N. R., Ikerrin, Roscrea, Town of Roscrea, Glebe View

Lawrence O'CONNELL 36 m. 1837 tallow chandler RW b. Co Meath, Anne 31 wife RW b. City of Dublin, John 10 son b. City of Dublin.
Co City of Dublin, City of Dublin, St. Michan Parish, Municipal Ward Inns Quay, Linen Hall St.

Richard REID (signed Read) 39 m. 1838 provision dealer RW b. Co Dublin, Eliza 29 wife R b. Dublin, Eliza 6 dau R b. Co Dublin.
Co City of Dublin, City of Dublin, St. Michan Parish, Municipal Ward Arran Quay, Church St.

Michael RYAN 35 m. 1841 farm lab RW, Mary 40 wife, Mary 6 dau school.
Co Clare, Bunratty Lr, Tomfinlough, Newmarket Townland, N. Market on Fergus (rural portion)

William RYAN 50 m. 1820/1839 hoopmaker, Mary 30 wife, Margret 9 dau, Jane 2 dau.
Queens County, Stradbally, Stradbally, Stradbally


Appendix for the 1851 Irish Census Abstracts from Old Age Pension records held in Belfast at PRONI, for Republic of Ireland locations

Matt SAVAGE 25 m. 1850 lab, Thomas 24 brother m. 1850 boatman R, Anne 27 S/L m.1850.
    Co Sligo, Tyrerill (Tirerrill), Killerry, Correy (Correagh)

Timothy SCANLON 40 m. 1847 farmer RW Irish, Catherine 30 wife RW Irish, Margaret 4 dau.
    Co Limerick, Shanid, Rathronan, Athea Lr

Charles SMYTH 37 m. 1833 lab R b. Co Cavan, Letitia 38 wife spinster R b. Co Monaghan, Eliza 9 dau b. Co Cavan.
    Co Cavan, Clankee, Knockbride, Corweelis

Judith SPELLMAN 48 wid m. 1825 huckster R, Mary A. 6 gr dau in school. DEC: Michael Spellman 50 husband corn dealer d. Summer 1848 fall from horse.
    Co Galway, City of Galway, St. Nicholas Parish, Bridge St.

Denis SULLIVAN 32 n.m. farmer, Johanna 54 mother wid m. 1811 spinning flax, John 23 brother n.m. agricultural lab. DEC: Johanna Sullivan 20 sister serv d. Summer 1847 fever.
    Co Kerry, Magonihy, Kilcummin, Manlyarkane

Patt TOWEY 29 m. 1839 farmer RW I, Mary 29 wife RW I, Catherine 9 dau.
    Co Sligo, Coolavin, Kilfree, Doon

Michael VEALE 68 m. 1815 wid farmer, Nicholas 27 son farmer, Mary 25 dau farmer, Briget 23 dau, Ellen 21 dau, Margaret (age na) step mother m. 1811 wid, James WHELAN 18 serv, John RYAN 17 serv, Mary WALSH 50 beggar. DEC: Ellen Veale 69 wife d. Winter 1847 decline.
    Co Waterford, Deries within Drun Barony (Decies within Drum), Ardmore Parish, Ballinhardon (Ballynaharda) Townland

Nicholas VEALE 52 m. 1827 farmer, Mary 50 wife, Michael 21 son, Patrick 17 son, Thomas 15 son, Mary 13 dau in school, Nicholas 10 son in school, Francis 54 brother wid m. 1826 Anne Veale 17 niece, Cornelius HARRINGTON 18 beggar b. Co Cork.
    Co Waterford (Decies within Drum Barony), Ardmore Parish, Ballinhardon (Ballynharda) Townland

Richard WALLACE 34 m. 1839 sailor R, Mary 34 wife RW, Catherine 6 dau in school.
    Co Limerick, City of Limerick, St. Mary Parish, Municipal Ward Thormond Bridge, Nicholas St.

James WALSH 46 m. 1830 lab R, Bridget 43 wife R, Bridget 5 dau.
    Co Wexford, Scarawalsh, Kilrush, Ballyrankin

Note: Place of birth same as residence except where noted.

Transcription of extracts from the 1851 Census returns for COUNTY KILKENNY and COUNTY WATERFORD from the E. Walsh Kelly transcriptions held at the Genealogical Office, Dublin, Ireland

Barony of Gowran, Parish of Clara, Townland of Ballinamona:

1. Richard DOOLEY 68 n.m. farmer, Patrick 56 brother, Mary 33 m. 1840 brother's widow, Mary 9, Patrick 7, Laurence 6, James 4, niece and nephews. DEC: John 47 brother d. Summer 1847, Andrew 9 d. Summer 1850.

4. William HART 65 m. 1817, Margaret (LANNON) 64 wife, Walter 25, Bridget (MURPHY) 28 dau m. 1847, Philip Murphy 34 S/L, Elizabeth 4, Mary 2, Margaret 10 mo, their children; ABS: Patrick (age na) son carpenter in America.


Barony of Gowran, Parish of Clara, Townland of Churchclara:

1. John KEEFE (age na) m. 1814 wid, Margaret 30 m. 1849, Andrew GIBBS 2 gr son. DEC: Statia FENNELLY 76 wid d. Spring 1850.

2. James KEEFE 29 m. 1845, Catherine 28 wife, Anastasia 5, Margaret 2.

4. Henry KEEFE 60 m. 1824 wid, Ellen 19, Martin 17, Catherine 15, Mary 13, Philip 11, John 9, Johanna 7. DEC: Mary 45 wife, John 52 brother, Andrew 45 brother, all d. Summer of 1846, Ann 80 mother d. Autumn 1846, Ann 22 dau d. Autumn 1848.

6. Mary KELLY 55 spinster, James 53 brother, Ann HEFFERNAN (age na) sister m. 1838, Mary 8 niece, John 6 nephew. DEC: Mark 72 father d. Spring 1844, Honor 70 mother d. Autumn 1845, John Kelly 4 nephew and John 50 brother d. Winter 1847.

7. Michael KEEFE 42 m. 1851, Bridget 28 wife, one serv.

8. Nicholas KEEFE 53 m. 1840, Margaret 29 wife, Ann 10, Bridget 8, Catherine 6, Mary 4, Philip 1, three serv. DEC: John 50 and Andrew 40 brothers d. Summer 1844, Ann 76 mother d. Autumn 1846, John 8 months d. Spring 1849.


Barony of Gowran, Parish of Clara, Townland of Clarabricken:

1. Martin KELLY 40 m. 1842, Mary 34 wife, John 8, Bridget 6, James 4, Mary 3, Thomas 2 months.

2. Edmund HART 64 m. 1821 farmer, Catherine 50 wife, Margaret 17, Jane (or James) 13, eight serv. DEC: (since 1841) Agnes 1 week d. Summer 1844, Catherine 18 d. Winter 1848 paralyzed.

6. Patrick HART 64 m. 1816 farmer, Johanna 58 wife, Patrick 23, Teresa 21, Bridget 17, three serv; ABS: James 25 clerk in America, Matthew 21/27 clerk in P. O. in Australia, Edmund 16 in business in Dublin, Ellen 19 in Dublin. DEC: Mary 84 mother d. 8.3.43, Catherine 18 d. Sep 1849.

7. Patrick HART 62 m. 1811 mason, Elizabeth 59 wife, James 19, Elizabeth 15, Elizabeth FITZPATRICK 5 gr dau; ABS: Johanna 32 serv in America, Bridget (age na), Ellen 26 in service in Kilkenny, Margaret 24 serv in America. DEC: Catherine 18 d. Winter 1846, Edward 26 mason d. Winter 1846.

9. Mary HART (age na) m. 1833 wid farmer, James 15, Maria 13, two indoor serv and 7 outdoor serv; ABS: Margaret 17 at school in Kilkenny.

10. Richard HART 53 m. 1826 farmer, Ellen 48 wife, James 25, Nicholas 23, Margaret 20, Johanna 19, Richard 16, Elizabeth 10, two indoor and six outdoor serv, two lodgers (one blind beggar). DEC: three serv and one lodger.

Barony of Gowran, Parish of Clara, Townland of Clifden and Rathgarron:

4. Patrick BLANCHFIELD 40, Mary 38 wife, five outdoor and four indoor serv.

7. Walter HART 50 m. 1830, Mary (RYAN) 53 wife, Mary 18, Ellen 15. DEC: Margaret 30 sister d. Spring 1847.

Barony of Gowran, Parish of Clara, Townland of Comegan:

2. Anthony BYRNE 42 m. 1826 farmer, Ann 41 wife, Elizabeth 18, Mary 16, Ann 14, Teresa 11, Michael 10, Anthony 8, Richard 6, Elizabeth 70 m. 1802 wid mother, two indoor and three outdoor serv.

Barony of Gowran, Parish of Clara, Townland of Kilmagan:

5. Matthais (sic) KEEFE 70 m. 1812, Elinor 67 wife, Andrew 29, Michael 24, Judy GRANT 24 serv.

6. Philip KEEFE 75 m. 1808 wid, Martin 41 m. 1842, Margaret 42 his wife, Mary 8, Bridget 7, Catherine 6, Philip 4, Andrew 2, their children, John RYAN (age na) ploughboy, Mary BRENNAN 17 serv; ABS: Andrew 38, Matthais 35, James 31, John 28, Bridget 25, all in America.

7. Mary BRENNAN (age na) m. 1820 wid, Martin 24, Catherine 18, Mary 14, Margaret 8, James 6; ABS: Kyran 29, Thomas 19 in Australia. DEC: James 56 husband d. Winter 1847.

14. Mary KELLY 64 m. 1817 wid, Margaret 22, Mary m. 1850, Michael MURPHY 28 S/L; ABS: Michael 30 in America, Thomas 24 and Margaret 22 in Kilkenny.

15. Margaret KELLY 50 m. 1824 wid, Mary 20, John 18, Bridget 17 niece; ABS: Patrick 23 in Police Force in Co Clare. DEC: Martin 58 husband d. Spring 1849, Thomas 14 and Bridget 12 d. Autumn 1850.

Barony of Iverk, Parish of Aglish, Townland of Aglish North:

1. John DOODY 31 m. 1838 farmer, Anty 37 wife, Peter 11, Thomas 9, Richard 6, Margaret 3, James 1, Thomas Doody 32 B/L(sic), 3 serv.

2. Nicholas IRISH 36 m. 1850 farmer, Bridget 33 wife, Ann NEILL m. 1816 M/L, Margaret FARRELL 22 S/L, Patrick Farrell 60 nephew (sic), Larry O'HARA 38 nephew, Mary WALSH 4 visitor, 2 serv. DEC: Ed. Farrell 60 F/L d. Autumn 1842.

3. Ed. DOODY 40 m. 1851 farmer, Mary 30 wife, 3 serv.

4. John DOODY 48, m. 1849 farmer, Margaret 42 wife, William 1, Johanna 2 months. DEC: William 1 and Nora 6 months d. Spring 1850.

5. John DOODY 75 m. 1816 farmer, Mary 60 wife, Edmund 33. DEC: Alice 28 d. Spring 1850.

6. Kate PHELAN 45 n.m. dealer, Joany BRODERS 35 aunt, 2 lodgers.

7. Patrick PHELAN 67 m. 1813 farmer, Margaret 64 wife, Walter 29, Nelly 28 D/L, Peter 26, Patrick 22, Michael 18, Margaret 6, Patrick 4, Kate 2, Bridget 2 months, grandchildren, Kate POWER 45 m. 1829, John Power 14, visitors, one serv; ABS: Thomas 24 son clergyman and Andrew (age na) fisherman (?) in America.

8. Walter FEWER 60 n.m., Mary 64 sister, Margaret 62 sister, William 46 brother m. 1841, Alice 44 S/L, Thomas 42 brother, Anty 9 and Mary 6, nieces, Richard 3 months nephew, 2 serv. DEC: Richard 2 nephew d. Spring 1850.

9. Ed. FEWER 55 m. 1826 farmer, Mary 50 wife, Bridget 20, Kate 18, Mary 16, Joany 14, James 12, Anty 10, Richard 7, Ed. DELAHUNTY 55 m. 1820 wid, John CONNOLLY 55 m. 1823 wid, Peter PHELAN 26 cousin, William WALSH 26 cousin.

10. John GRANT 35 m. 1847 smith, Margaret 25 wife, Kate 3, Anty 8 months, Anty WALSH 80 M/L, Mary Walsh 7 cousin; ABS: Bridget McDONALD 30 S/L in service in New York, Ed. McDonald 60 B/L smith in America. DEC: Richard McDonald 50 F/L d. Spring 1848.

11. Patrick BARRY 71 m. 1820 basketmaker, Michael 30 son m. 1846, Kate 28 D/L. DEC: Margaret 60 wife d. Spring 1846, two infants d. 1848.


Barony of Iverk, Parish of Aglish, Townland of Aglish South:

1. Mary WALSH 70 m. 1798 wid publican, John 35, Nicholas 30, Nicholas GUINAN 35 nephew, Nora 65 sister (listed last, entry unclear); ABS: Geoffrey 36 railway lab in America, Edmund 32 railway lab in America. DEC: Walter 40 publican d. Spring 1845.

2. John FENNELLY 60 m. 1830 weaver, Mary 60 wife, Thomas 19, Patrick 16, Nancy FARRELLY 30 S/L, Kate REILLY 26 niece, Mary PENDER 8 niece. DEC: Thomas Fennelly 80 father d. Autumn 1844.

3. (or 2.a) Thomas WALSH 50 m. 1830 farmer, Nora 40 wife, Walter 19, Richard 17, James 16, Mary 12, Margaret 10, Nicholas 8, John 6, Michael 3, Johanna Walsh 50 S/L, one serv. (Nichlaus)

4. Richard KEEFE 42 m. 1836 farmer, Anty 40 wife, Mary 23, Anty 20, Ellen 18, Joany 14, Margaret 12, Kate 11, one serv.

5. Walter WALSH 60 m. 1819 farmer, Kate 61 wife, Mary 26, Alice 25, Edmund 32 m. 1845, Mary 30 D/L, Walter 5 gr son, Joany 3 gr dau, one serv. DEC: Kate 6 and William 3 d. Spring 1850. (Broders?)

6. Nicholas WALSH 33 m. 1847 farmer, Anty 24 wife, Walter 2, Patrick 22 brother, Bridget 21 sister, Mary 12 cousin, one serv. DEC: Walter 60 father and Nora 21 sister d. Summer 1845 and 1847. (Moores)

7. James WALSH 38 m. 1850 farmer, Kate 23 wife, Michael 11 visitor, 4 serv. DEC: Walter 72 father and Edmund 40 brother d. Spring 1842 and 1847.

8. Thomas WALSH 35 m. 1840 farmer, Anty 32 wife, John 8, Margaret 6, Kate 4, Ellen 2, Richard 60 uncle, 4 serv. DEC: John 70 father and Margaret 68 mother d. Autumn 1846 and Spring 1846. (Shawnells)

9. John WALSH 21 lab, Margaret (FLEMMING) 54 wid mother, Kate 18 sister; ABS: Nicholas GUINAN 32 lab, Laurence (Guinan) 26 in America. DEC: Betty (Guinan) 60 mother d. Spring 1843.

10. Mary MILLER 40, Margaret 10, Kate 7, Robert 5, Alice 3; ABS: Thomas 17 and William 15 working in Co Kilkenny, James 40 husband in America.

11. Ellen McDONALD 50 m. 1822 wid, Mary 13, Bridget 60 S/L.

12. Margaret MAHER 29 dressmaker, Ellen GRANT 62 m. 1810 wid visitor, Judy Grant 25 visitor, Ellen Grant 14 visitor.

13. James KELLY 34 m. 1848 lab, Mary 28 wife, Johanna 1, Johanna 23 sister, Kate KEEFE 70 m. 1800 M/L. Dec: Peter 48 father, Joany 49 mother, Matrin (sic) (Martin?) 60 uncle d. Winter 1846, 1845 and 1850.

14. Michael QUINN 40 m. 1849 lab, Johanna 34 wife, Bridget 6, Joany 5, Kate 2. DEC: Joany 60 mother and Thomas 60 father d. Autumn 1848 and Spring 1850.

15. Thomas HANLON 50 m. 1833 farmer, Joany 48 wife, Ed. 17, John 15, Anty 11, Kate 10, Richard WALSH 30 B/L, 3 serv.

16. Richard WALSH 45 m. 1842 shoemaker, Mary 32 wife, Walter 6, Mary 4, Thomas 3, Michael 1.

17. Richard WALSH 60 m. 1825 farmer, Margaret 55 wife, Ellen 28, Mary 26, Joany 23, Kate DOHERTY 32 m. 1846 dau, John Doherty (age na) S/L, Richard 4, Mary 3, William 6 months, grandchildren, one serv. (Hack)

18. John WALSH 57 m. 1837 farmer, Ellen (QUINN) 37, Walter 13, William 12, Kate 10, Thomas 8, Richard 7, James 5, Mary 2, John 9 months, William Quinn 65 m. 1812 F/L, Mary (DUNPHY) 63 M/L, Ed. Quinn 60 B/L, eight serv. (Pope)

19. Walter WALSH 45 m. 1838 farmer, Mary 36 wife, Kate 12, Ann 10, Walter 7, Maria 3, Richard 1, five serv. Dec: Richard 1 son d. Winter 1842.

20. ED. CONNOLLY 26 m. 1845 lab, Nancy 24 wife, Patrick 4, James 2, Johanna 73 m. 1810 wid mother. DEC: James 50 father d. Spring 1848.


Barony of Iverk, Aglish Parish, Glengrant Townland:

1. William REDDY (age na) m. 1841 farmer, Ellen 40 wife, Samuel 7. DEC: John 18 brother d. 1847, Mary 1 dau d. 1848.

2. John KELLY 48 m. 1835 lab, Mary 40 wife, Judy 14, Thomas 10, Kate 8, Ed. 5, William 3, Daniel 32 brother, Johanna 76 m. 1801 mother. DEC: Thomas father d. 1844, Anty 64 aunt d. 1848.

3. John WALSH 70 n.m. farmer, Mary QUILTY 50 m. 1822 sister, Robin Quilty 24 nephew, Ellen Quilty 22 niece; ABS: Mary Quilty 27 niece in America. DEC: Mary Walsh 51 sister d. 1850.

4. James WALSH 65 m. 1820 farmer, Anty 60 wife, Richard 27, William 25, Joany 23, Margaret 21, James HEARNE 4 gr son. Dec: Ellen 81 mother d. Autumn 1843.

5. Margaret KEEFE 56 m. 1825 wid, Ellen 24, Mary 22, Thomas 20, Margaret 14. DEC: Peter 50 husband d. Spring 1847.

6. Thomas KEEFE 44 m. 1827 farmer, Jane 36 wife, Peter 12, Judy 9, Samuel 4, John 60 brother, Robert 50 brother. DEC: Joany 80 mother d. 1847, Samuel infant d. 1844.


Barony of Iverk, Aglish Parish, Mountneill Townland:

1. Johanna DOYLE 50 m. 1834 farmer, Thomas WALSH 18 son, Michael 14, Ed. 12, Philip 9, Anty 7, 4 serv. DEC: William Walsh 52 husband d. Winter 1845, fell from a car, Margaret Walsh 70 M/L d. Winter 1848.

2. John NOLAN 64 m. 1810 lab, Kate 62 wife, Patrick 28 m. 1847, Mary 27 D/L, Mary 3, Kate 2, grandchildren, Nancy 32 dau.

3. Edmund QUINN 30 m. 1848 farmer, Anne 19 wife, Anty 1, Ally 42 M/L m. 1831, Mary 17 S/L, Margaret 9 S/L, Ed. 11 B/L, one serv.

4. John WALSH 76 m. 1807 wid tailor, Ann 30, Rebecca 24, Patrick 30 m. 1842, Margaret 28 D/L, John 7, Thomas 5, Ann 3, Mary 1. DEC: Ambrose 26 son d. 1844 decline.

Barony of Iverk, Aglish Parish, Portnahully Townland:

1. Patrick PHELAN 63 m. 1820 farmer, Bridget 60 wife, Ed. 28, Judy 26, Richard 24, Kate 21, one visitor.

2. Thomas WALSH 60 m. 1833 farmer, Margaret 53 wife, Peter 21, John 17, Kate 15, Joany 13, Richard 8, Ellen Merry 20 cousin, 3 serv. DEC: Anty 21, Mary 16 and (Anty) Ellen 11 d. 1846 and 1847, Anty 80 mother d. Winter 1849..

3. John DELAHUNTY 34 m. 1846 farmer, Richard 4, James 8 months, 9 serv; ABS: Alice 30 wife, Mary 5 in Waterford, Anty WALSH 18 (rel. na) in service. DEC: David 1 son d. Autumn 1850.

4. Honor DOYLE 28 m. 1839 b. Co Tipperary, Mary 2, John 9 months, 4 serv; ABS: Thomas 32 husband printer in Dublin, William Doyle 54 B/L in America. DEC: Patrick Doyle 86 F/L d. Winter 1850, Mary 76 M/L d. Autumn 1841, John 24 B/L clerk d. Winter 1847, Mary 45 S/L d. Winter 1848.

5. John PHELAN 64 m. 1818 farmer, Thomas 35 m. 1828, Margaret 30 D/L, John 12, Margaret 10, Mary 8, Ellen 6, William 3, Joany 9 months, 2 serv.

6. Michael WALSH 55 m. 1810 wid farmer, John QUINN 37 S/L m. 1837, Mary 39 dau, Kate 14, Mary 12, Michael 10, Nora 8, James 7, Edmund 4, Margaret 2, Anty 6 months, one visitor. DEC: Margaret Quinn 2 gr dau d. Winter 1847.

7. Ed. DOYLE 47 m. 1834 farmer, Kate 37 wife, Anty 16, Thomas 14, Margaret 12, Ed. 10, Walter 7, Joany 4, Mary 2.

8. Joany CONNOLLY 40 m. 1832 wid lab, James 17 working, Joany 14, Anty 12. DEC: Anty 60 mother d. Spring 1847.

9. Richard BARRY 30 m. 1837 lab, Kate 42 wife, Margaret BRENNAN 12 S/L, Richard Brennan 10 B/L, John 20 B/L working, Michael 19 B/L working, Mary 17 S/L working, Anty 14 S/L working. DEC: Patrick infant d. 1850.

10. John BRENNAN 46 fisherman. DEC: Patrick 41 brother d. 1850, Kate 48 sister d. 1850.

11. John MURRAY 40 m. 1835 agriculturist, Kate 45 wife, Mary 12, Ed. 7. DEC: Margaret 60 mother d. Summer 1848.

12. James QUIRK 36 m. 1843 lab, Ellen 36 wife, Thomas 6, Mary 4, James 2.

13. Patrick DOOLAN 58 m. 1830 lab, Mary 60 wife, Mary 28 m. 1846 dau, Anty CUMMINS 4 gr dau, William Cummins 3 gr son; ABS: Margaret 20 working, Kate 17 working, Nora 22 and Ann 19 in America.

Transcription of extracts from the 1851 Census returns for County Kilkenny and County Waterford from the E. Walsh Kelly transcriptions held at the Genealogical Office, Dublin, Ireland

Barony of Iverk, (Ballincurra Parish), Ballincour otherwise Ballincurra Townland:

1. Edward or Edmond DUNPHY 34 n.m. farmer RW E&I, Ellen 69 m. 1814 wid mother, Elizabeth CUNNINGHAM 13 serv.

2. Edmond WALSH 40 m. 1846 mower, Anastasia 40 wife, Catherine 35 S/L n.m. strawplatter, Mary 2 dau.

3. James WALSH 76 m. 1820 farm lab, Mary 67 wife, Michael 27 lab, Walter 23 lab, Alice 29 strawplatter, Ellen 26 strawplatter, Thomas 4 son (sic).

4. William WHELAN 52 m. 1832 farmer, Anastasia 55 wife, William 4 son, Catherine 40 S/L hk, James 42 brother ploughman, Anastasia NOONAN 14 niece at convent school.

5. James FOLEY 34 m. 1841 farm lab RW E&I, Honor 34 wife, Mary 10, Richard 8, Joany 6; ABS: Alice 6 months with an aunt in Co Kilkenny. DEC: Thomas 2 son d. 1850, Andrew 18 months son d. 1850.

6. Michael WALSH 36 m. 1836, Allice 30 wife, Walter 5, Mary 5, Judy 2, John Walsh 5 nephew, Ellen 30 sister nursing. DEC: Walter 80 father farmer d. 1848 decline, Mary 70 mother d. 1848 decline, Allice 31 sister serv d. 1848 decline..

7. Cornelius KEHOE 60 m. 1820 farm lab, Mary 60 wife, David 20; ABS: Michael 25 son in America. DEC: Thomas 23 son d. 1847 fever.


Barony of Iverk, Portnascully Parish, Ballygorey Townland:

5. Michael WALSH 54 m. 1819 wid, Thomas 28, Anty 26. Alice 21, John 14. DEC: Mary 80 m. 1795 mother d. 1847, Margaret (age na) dau d. 1847.

15. James WALSH 57 m. 1837 Joany 52 wife, Anty 17.

16. Michael WALSH 50 m. 1825, Anty 52 wife, Mary 30, Richard 21. DEC: Bridget 85 mother d. Spring 1851.


Barony of Iverk, Portnascully Parish, Clasharow (Clasharoe) Townland:

1. Richard WALSH 35 m. 1850 farmer, Ellen 25 wife, Mary 9 months, Joany DUNPHY 60 m. 1815 wid M/L, Patrick Walsh 27 brother, Philip 24 brother, 2 serv.

2. Michael WALSH 25 m. 1848 farmer, Bridget 22 wife, Thomas 2, Kyran 6 months, 2 serv. DEC: Mary 84 mother d. Winter 1843, Michael (? sic) brother d. 1848.

3. Richard DEADY 51 m. 1838 farmer, Joany 38 wife, Mary 12, Patrick 10, Ellen 8, Bridget 6, James 3, Patrick 80 father m. 1798 wid.

Barony of Iverk, Portnascully Parish, Luffany Townland:

12. Margaret DUNPHY 56 m. 1815 wid, Patrick 21, Ed. 15, Bridget 45 (sic) niece, Patrick BRENNAN 14 nephew. DEC: John 19 d. Spring 1847.

14. Patrick DUNPHY 62 m. 1846(?) wid, Thomas QUINN 33 S/L m. 1846. Dec: John 95 father d. Spring 1843, Kate 80 mother d. Spring 1845.

Barony of Iverk, Rathkyran Parish, Ballymountain (Ballymantane) Townland:

1. Robert WALSH 54 m. 1221 (sic) wid farm lab, Ned 28 fisherman RW, Catherine 10 attends convent school R, Michael 24 farm lab, Walter 17 farm lab. DEC: Anastasia 54 wife d. 1850 decline.

(Another version of same return: No. 1 Robert WALSH 54 wid, Ed. 28, Michael 24, Walter 17, Kate 10. DEC: Anty 54 wife d. in Dublin 1850. Edmund DEADY 24 m. 1846, Ann 24 wife, James 2. DEC: Thomas 2 d. 1848.)

(No no.) Edmond DEADY 24 m. 1846 farm lab RW E&I, Ann 24 wife RW E&I, James 2. DEC: Thomas 2 son d. 1848 decline.

2. Richard KENNY 45 m. 1827 farm lab RW E&I, Mary 40 wife, Andrew 14, William 8, Margaret COOKE 40 S/L platting straw; ABS: Margaret Cooke 12 her dau, illeg. in Kilkenny h serv.

(On another page: Richard KENNY 45 m. 1827, Mary 40 wife, Ann 14, William 8, Margaret CROKE (sic) 40 S/L, Margaret Croke 12 her dau serv. ill.)

3. Mary WALSH 50 m. 1827 wid Richard 21 farm lab, Anastasia 22 dairy maid, Mary 20, Denis 18. DEC: Patrick 50 husband d. 1846 decline

(Another version: Mary WALSH 50 m. 1827 wid, Anty 22, Richard 21, Mary 20, Denis 18. DEC: Patrick 50 husband d. 1846 decline.)

4. Edmond FEWER 44 m. 1834 thatcher, Judy 44 wife, Thomas 14, Nicholas 12, Mary 10, Catherine 6. DEC: Thomas 68 father d. 1844 farm lab.

(Another version: Edmund FEWER 44 m. 1834 thatcher, Judy 44 wife, Thomas 14, Nicholas 12, Mary 10, Kate 6. DEC: Thomas 68 father d. 1844.)

5. James OSBORNE 48 m. 1833 farm lab RW E&I, Ellen 48 wife, Thomas 14.

6. Johanna NEILL 64 n.m. spinning wool, Margaret 36 niece straw platter. (Another version has John NEILL, bachelor.)

7. Patrick COLLINS 48 m. 1834 wid farm lab, David 16, John 11 or 14, James 7, Ned 5, Anastasia or Anty 3, Mary DOODY 53 m. 1814 M/L hk; ABS: Peter Collins 14 cowboy in Co Kilkenny. DEC: Anastasia 50 wife d. Summer 1848 fever. (two versions)

COUNTY WATERFORD (Locations in parentheses added by transcriber)

Ballydrislane Townland (Drumcommon Parish, Middle Third Barony):

No no. William PHELAN 38 m. 1842, Eliza 28 wife, Michael 8, Nicholas 7, Alice 5, Patrick 3, Ed. 9 months, Eliza 60 mother m. 1808, Michael 28 brother, Jeffry 22 brother, Margaret MURPHY 12 niece, 3 serv. DEC: Mary age 1 week d. Spring 1848.

Ballykinsella Townland (Drumcommon Parish, Middle Third Barony):

4. Michael POWER 31 m. 1848, Kate 23 wife, Mary 3, Kate 18 months

5. Patrick POWER 55 m. 1817, Kate 53 wife, John 28, Thomas 26, Mary 23, Richard 20, Ellen 18, Kate 15, one serv.

7. (?) Michael POWER 41 n.m., Margaret 66 m. 1809 mother, Ed 35, Richard 31, Robert 21, brothers, Mary 38 sister, Bridget 27 sister, Ellen HALLY 80 aunt visitor.

16. Mary POWER 60 m. 1819 wid, Kate 19, Patrick 14; ABS: Geffry (sic) and Richard 22 in England. DEC: Ed. Power 58 husband d. Spring 1847.

Grobally Townland, Upper Drumcannon (Drumcommon? Middle Third Barony):

23. James Oliver WALSH 20 brother of head of family b. Co Kilkenny, Ellen GRIFFITH 65 aunt b. Kilkenny, Bridget CUMMINS 57 serv b. Co Tipperary; ABS: Peter Walsh 24 landed proprietor in Dublin, William Thomas 22 accountant(?) in England, Ann Mary 18 at Miss Ryan's school in Waterford, Walter Hoyle 17 and John Peter 15 at school in Kilkenny, James GRACE 38 serv in Kilkenny. (Children of Peter Walsh of Belline who married secondly Ann Griffith 12.5.1825 and d. 21.11.1859).

26. Johanna GALWAY 84 m. 1790 wid, Ellen SWEENEY 49 dau m. 1832. DEC: Patrick Sweeney 50 S/L tailor d. Summer 1848, William Galway 50 lab d. Summer 1848.

Newtown (Drumcommon Parish? Middle Third Barony):

No no. Daniel CARRIGAN 38 timber merchant, Mary Teresa 38(?) wife, 2 serv. DEC: Daniel 3 son d. Spring 1847, John 5 d. Summer 1844(?).

--uilla:

No no. Nicholas POWER 41 m. 1840, Margaret 35 wife, Ed 10, Kate 9, Mary 7, Bridget 5, Ellen 3, Michael 1, 7 serv. DEC: Ed. Power 77 father d. Spring 1851.

Tramore (Middle Third Barony)

Broad Street

6. John PHELAN 23 n.m. hotel keeper, Matthew 20 brother, Maurice 18 brother, 3 serv. DEC: Ellen 49 mother d. Winter 1842.


Green Lane

1. Patrick POWER 36 m. 1843, Ellen 31 wife, Patrick 6, Ed 5, Ann 2, Richard 1, 7 serv.


Doneraile Place

1. Thomas WALSH 39 m. 1835 tobacco merchant, Kate 35 wife, Margaret 13, James 11, Joseph 9, Mary 6, Thomas 4, Kate 3, Ann 8 months, 2 serv; ABS: John 35 brother sea captain in Cardiff, William 32 brother clerk in America. DEC: John 2 d. Spring 1845.

2. Robert CURTIS 60 m. 1817, Margaret 50 wife, Mary 18.


Main Street

14. Ed. WALSH 60 m. 1814/1830 b. Kilkenny, Margaret 45 wife, Thomas 18, Johanna 16, Ann 10, Ellen 8, Maurice 7, John 4, David 6 months; ABS: Bridget 20, Ed. 13(?). DEC: Martin 1 d. Winter 1849.

16. T. F. STRANGE 38 m. 1845, Mary 30 wife, Rose 3, Agnes 1; ABS: Theodore NEWNES(?) 21 B/L.


Market Street

6. James BUDD 55 m. 1824, Jane 54 wife, James 20, Clara(?) 17, Mary 77 mother m. 1794, Maria BLAKE 26 visitor m. 1845, Lizzie Blake 17 visitor; ABS: Lydia 21 in Waterford. DEC: Mary SLATER 95 mother(?) d. Spring 1843.

11. Patrick FLAHERTY 66 m. 1811, Margaret 60 wife, John 27, Ellen 29, Kate 7; ABS: Richard 37 and Timothy 35 in America.

27. Robert EGAN (or Lyan) 26 n.m., Johanna TREACY 48 wid mother b. Tipperary, Ellen GOUGH (age na) serv.


Old Waterford Road

3. Eliza MOLYNEUX 32 m. 1835 house owner, Eliza 11, Frances 7, Ann 4, Eliza POWER 61 aunt m. 1827 wid, 7 serv; ABS: Henry 43 husband artist in Liverpool.

28. Martin ROCHE 40 m. 1848, Kate 27 wife, Margaret 1, Widow WALSH 60 M/L m. 1811 b. Co Kilkenny.

-108-

30. William FORRISTALL 35 m. 1838, Mary 32 wife, Eliza 12, John 10, Kate 8, Anty 5, Mary 3.

## Patrick Street

21. Walter HALLY 45 m. 1837, Bridget 40 wife, James 13, Mary 12, Nicholas 11, Michael 9, Kate 7, Walter 4, John 2, 6 serv.

## Priest's Road

9. Michael POWER 23, Andrew 17 brother, Mary 16 sister, Johanna 50 mother m. 1823 wid.

## Queen Street

13. James H. KEANEY(?) 41 m. 1843, Louisa 40 wife, Mary Ann 6, James 4, Eliza HOWES 11, Mary Howes 9, nieces, Samuel GRAHAM 4 nephew.

9. Patrick PHELAN 60 m. 1791 wid, builder b. City of Waterford, Ed. 32, Michael 30, Anty 28, Ellen 26. DEC: Two died since 1841.

## St. Leger Place

4. Joseph HEARNE 57 m. 1835 master mariner, Alice 50 wife, Ann CORISH 20 cousin, 2 serv; ABS: Mary (age na), Joseph 14 at school in Waterford.

## Square

2. Mary KEANEY 45 m. 1829 wid, James 14, Andrew 13, Mary 11, Margaret 9; ABS: Ed. 19, John 17. DEC: John 39 husband merchant d. Autumn 1844.

## Strand Street

11. Ed. MORRISSEY 40 m. 1834, Anty 40 wife, Ed. 14, Philip 11.

20. John CORBETT 60 m. 1810 saddler, Ellen 62 wife, William 24 bootmaker, Ann 22 confectioner.

21. John CORBETT 28 saddler (no further data).

Note: All born in county of residence unless otherwise specified.

Thrift Genealogical Abstracts from the 1851 Census for Ireland, Counties
DUBLIN, KILKENNY, LEITRIM, LIMERICK and ROSCOMMON
Republic of Ireland locations only

## COUNTY DUBLIN

BROWNHILL, Deborah (no. 18, no further data).
    Co Dublin, St. Mary's Parish, Lower Ormond Quay

FOX, John, lab (no. 26, no further data).
    Co Dublin, St. Michan's Parish, Upper Ormond Quay

KAVANAGH, Joseph 67 m. 1820 sendor(?) of ink b. Co Carlow, Mary 60 wife b. Dublin,
Mary Anne 30 dau n.m. bonnetmaker b. Dublin; ABS: Christopher 24 son clerk in
Manchester, Mary 20 dau caseworker in Manchester.
    Co Dublin, St. Michan Parish, 61 Beresford St.

SEYMOUR, Joseph 26 m. 1844 police constable b. Co Cork, Ellen 25 wife b. Co Derry,
Horatio 9 months son b. Co Dublin (no. 7).
    Co Dublin, St. Mary's Parish, Lower Ormond Quay

## COUNTY KILKENNY

PHAYER, John R. 38 m. 1835 apothecary RW b. City of Limerick, Catherine 48 wife m.
1825/1835 RW b. Kilkenny, Joseph 14 son in school RW b. Kilkenny, Alexander 12 son in
school RW b. Graig? Mary 7 dau, Maria (Marian?) MAGEE 20 step dau RW b. Graig,
Bridget WHELAN 23 serv b. Kilkenny.
    Co Kilkenny, St. Mary's Parish, City of Kilkenny, Chapel Lane St.

## COUNTY LEITRIM

HUNT, Christopher 45 m. 1829 farmer RW, Sarah 42 RW, George 21 lab, Saragh 12 R,
Robert 10 R, Mary 5, Ann 3, Fanny 8 months. DEC: Fanny Hunt 20 dau d. Summer 1850
decline, Jane 2 dau d. Spring 1845 consumption(?).
    Co Leitrim, (Mohill Barony) Mohill Parish, Curraun Townland

HUNT, George 40 m. 1828 farmer R, Rose(?) 40, Mary Ann 20, Lillian 16, Catherin 10,
William 9. DEC: Joseph 10 d. Spring 1846 (no. 13).
    Co Leitrim (Mohill Barony) Mohill Parish, Curraun Townland

WYNNE, Michael 29 n.m. farmer RW, Daniel HURLY 21 n.m. serv lab, Catherine HUNT 12
serv lab (no. 16).
    Co Leitrim, (Mohill Barony) Mohill Parish, Drumrohoal (Drumraghool) South Tnld

WYNNE, Widow 65 m. 1805 farmer, William 24 son n.m. lab RW, Lillian HUNT 14 serv R;
ABS: Daniel Wynne 28 son in America, Margaret Wynne 28 dau in America, Cathrine
Wynne 20 dau in America. DEC: Thomas Wynne 23 son d. Summer 1847 debility (no. 9).
    Co Leitrim, (Mohill Barony) Mohill Parish, Drumrohoal (Drumraghool) South Tnld

COUNTY LIMERICK

FEORE, Laurence 30 m. 1850 publican RW, Mary Anne 24 RW, Alicia CARROLL 19 S/L
n.m. RW, Johanna Feore 17 sister RW. DEC: Julia Carroll 18 S/L d. spring 1849 decline.
    Co Limerick (Lib of Kilmallock Barony, Sts. Peter & Paul Parish) Killmallock Hill
    Townland (Kilmallvel?)

FEORE, John 54 m. 1816 farmer RW, Alice 25 dau n.m. RW, Margaret 23, Mary 21, Thomas
19 son ploughboy RW, Johanna 17 in school RW, Michael 15 in school RW. DEC: Catherine
Feore 31 dau d. Summer 1844 decline, Honora 12 dau d. Spring 1845 apoplexy.
    Co Limerick (Coshna Barony, Effin Parish) Greyanster Townland (Graiganster Tnld)

FEORE, Martin 75 m. 1811 occupies land RW E&I, Catherine 60 RW E&I, Thomas 28 son
lab RW E&I, Mary 26 dau RW E&I; ABS: John Feore 24 son lab in America.
    Co Limerick (Lib of Kilmallock Barony, Sts Peter & Paul Parish) Culomus Townland

FEORE, Martin 33 m. 1847 clerk of Kilmallvel(?) RW, Catherine 29 RW, Honora 2,
Catherine SLATTERY 22 serv R, Catherine SEXTON 20 serv. DEC: John Feore 1 month
son d. Summer 1849 debility.
    Co Limerick (Lib of Kilmallock Barony, Sts. Peter & Paul Parish) Kilmallock Hill
    Townland

FEORE, Mary 50 m. 1828 making shirts RW E&I, Thomas 20 son field lab RW E&I,
Margaret 18 dau knitting RW E&I, Edward 16 son lab RW E&I, Mary 12 dau RW E&I,
Bridget 8 dau RW, John 5 son; ABS: John Feore 60 husband assistant master auxiliary(?)
poor house in Co Cork.
    Co Limerick Lib of Kilmallock Barony) Sts. Peter & Paul Parish, Ardkilmartin Tnld

PHAYER, William 38 m. 1837 coach builder RW, Ellen 32 wife hk RW, Thomas 25 brother
n.m. coach builder RW, Richard 12 son at Mr. Healy's school RW, Elizabeth 10 dau
Miss Benne's school RW, Jane 9 dau in school RW, Anna 8 dau in school R, William 7 son R,
Henrietta 4 dau, Rebecca 3 dau, Thomas 1 son, Margaret ROSS 30 serv R, Margaret
CRONEN 20 serv R (no. 1).
    Co Limerick, Parish of St. Patrick, Corbally Townland, City of Limerick


COUNTY ROSCOMMON

BARLOW, Anne 60 m. 1830 householder, John 17 son sowing potatoes, George 14 son RW.
DEC: Mary Barlow 14 dau d. Winter 1847.
    Co Roscommon (Athlone Barony, Fuerty Parish) Castlecoote Townland

BREWIN, Michael 50 m. 1834 farmer, Mary 40 R, Matt 14 son lab sowing oats, Mick 7 son
R; ABS: Mathew Brewin 60 brother lab in America.
    Co Roscommon (Athlone Barony, Fuerty Parish) Aghagad Townland

CONNOR, Rose 60 m. 1815 wid eggler, Ellen HIGGINS 20 dau m. 1848, Margaret Higgins
10 mo gr dau, John LEAVY 14 lodger serv; ABS: Thomas Higgins 24 S/L lab in America.
DEC: Patt Connor husband lab d. Spring 1850 asthma.
    Co Roscommon, Ballintober S Barony, Roscommon Parish, Ardnanagh Tnld

CURIE, Patt 40 m. 184- wid lab RW, Mary Curie 9 dau, Margaret QUIGLEY 20 S/L.
    Co Roscommon, Ballintober S Barony, Roscommon Parish, Ardnanagh Townland

HIGGINS, Bridget 70 m. 1811 wid pauper, Nicholas 24 son n.m. pauper partially blind.
DEC: Dennis Higgins 60 husband lab d. Spring 1847 dysentery.
    Co Roscommon, Ballintober S Barony, Roscommon Parish, Ardnanagh Townland

HIGGINS, James 33, Susan 30, Eliza 12 dau, Thomas 10 son, Luke 6 son, Pat 6 son, James 3
son (Bernard?) 6 months old, Mathew REYNOLDS 20 serv, Mary KELLY 20 serv, Bridget
WARD 40 serv. DEC: Malachy Higgins 5 son (no further data).
    Co Roscommon (Ballintober S Barony) Roscommon Parish, Lisnamalt Townland

HIGGINS, John 58 m. 1830 wid farmer RW.
    Co Roscommon (Ballintober S Barony) Roscommon Parish, Lisnamalt Townland

HIGGINS, Luke 67, Catherine 60.
    Co Roscommon (Ballintober S Barony) Roscommon Parish, Lisnamalt Townland

HIGGINS, Patt 42 m. 1839, Mary 32, Denis 10, Patt 3. DEC: Michael 3 son d. Winter 1844
convulsions.
    Co Roscommon, Ballintober S Barony, Roscommon Parish, Ardnanagh Townland

HIGGINS, Thady 74 m. 1820 linen weaver RW E&I, Bridget 61 m. 1802/1820 RW E&I,
John 34 lab RW, Thomas 23, Timothy 21; ABS: Anne Higgins 25 dau serv in Dublin.
    Co Roscommon (Ballintober S Barony) Roscommon Parish, Baleenagarba
    (Ballinagard?) Townland

HIGGINS, Thomas 55 m. 1827 wid farmer RW, Timothy 23 son m. 1848 lab RW, Ellen 24
D/L m. 1848 lab RW, Luke 15 son lab RW, Patt 2 son, Winifred COYLE 18 serv RW; ABS:
James Higgins 20 son lab in America, Ellen 18 dau in America. DEC: Mary Higgins 50 wife
d. Autumn 1848 fever.
    Co Roscommon (Ballintober S Barony) Roscommon Parish, Ardkeel Townland

HIGGINS, Thomas 40, Bridget 24, Thomas 7 son, Patt 5 son, Mary Anne 3 dau, Catherine 2
dau, Ellin 1 month dau, Joseph 1 month son, Bridget BRIAN 18 serv.
    Co Roscommon, Ballintober S Barony (incomplete data)

HIGGINS, William 42, Mary 35, Mary 17, Patt 15, Thomas 12, Michael 8, Catherine 6,
Margaret 4, William 2, Francis 4 months.
    Co Roscommon, Ballintober S Barony (incomplete data)

HOLWELL, Thomas 30 m. 1846 shoemaker RW, Hanna 26 RW, Edward 4 son, Mary Ann 2
dau, Honor MORAN 56 m. 1815 wid M/L R, Edward Moran 18 B/L n.m. RW, Margaret
Moran 15 S/L RW, Anne Moran 12 S/L RW.
    Co Roscommon (Athlone Barony, Fuerty Parish) Creemully & Augagaeheg (Aghagad
    Beg) Townland

KEATING, Honor 54 m. 1831 wid spinning wool, John 20 son lab RW, Mary HARDINAN
21 serv n.m. washing. Catherine CANE 62 m. 1840 lodger serv, Maria CARTY 6 gr mother
(sic); ABS: Mary Keating 22 dau serv in England, Anne Keating 18 dau serv in America.

Co Roscommon (Athlone Barony, Fuerty Parish) Clooneenbane (Clooneenbaun) Tnld

KEATING, John 50 m. 1820/1830 farmer RW E&I, Catherine 40 m. 1830, Margret 22 dau sowing potatoes R, Robert 18 son lab RW, Catherin 16 dau Mrs. Kilias school RW, John 12 son Mrs. McDouglas school RW; ABS: Jane Keating 20 dau in America. DEC: Michael Keating 21 lab d. Autumn 1847 fever, William Keating 21 d. Summer 1850 apoplexy.
    Co Roscommon (Athlone Barony, Fuerty Parish) Creenmully & Aughagaeheg (Aghagad Beg) Townland

KEATING, John 50 m. 1820 lab RW E&I, Jane 48 wife RW E&I, William 20 son lab RW E&I, Patt 17 RW, Mick 15 RW, Luke 13 reads English, Biddy 9 reads English, Mary 5, Margaret DONNELLY 55 m. 1819/1835 wid lodger RW E&I; ABS: Thomas Keating 30 son lab in America, Laurence 27 son lab in America, Timothy 25 lab in America, John 22 son lab in America. DEC: Kitty Keating 8 dau d. Summer 1848 consumption.
    Co Roscommon (Athlone Barony, Fuerty Parish) Clooneenbane (Clooneenbaun) Tnld

KEATING, Kitty 60 m. 1817 wid RW E&I, Biddy 26 dau cutting potatoes RW E&I, John 24 lab R, Peter 20 son lab R, Nelly 18 dau cutting potatoes RW E&I, Mary 16 dau RW E&I, Honor HESLER 20 lodger knitting RW E&I, Kitty McDERMOTT 40 married lodger pauper RW E&I, Biddy McDermott 18 pauper RW E&I, Patt McDermott 14 pauper RW E&I, Ned McDermott 12 pauper RW E&I; ABS: Kitty Keating 28 dau serv in America, Patt 22 son lab in America.
    Co Roscommon (Athlone Barony, Fuerty Parish) Clooneenbane (Clooneenbaun) Tnld

KEATING, Peggy 50 n.m. householder, Catherine McGLINN(?) 10 niece R. DEC: Mary Keating 60 mother d. Spring 1846 decay.
    Co Roscommon, Athlone Barony, Fuerty Parish, Muff Townland

KEATING, Robert 50 m. 1820/1835 farmer RW, Catherine 42 m. 1835 sowing potatoes b. Co Galway, Anne 13 dau R, Cathrine 10 months dau, Mary KILRUE 70 lodger wid beggar b. Co Galway, Ann DEGLY 36 n.m. beggar, Mary FLYNN 10 beggar.
    Co Roscommon (Athlone Barony, Fuerty Parish) Creenmully & Aughagaeheg (Aghagad Beg) Tnld.

MURPHY, John 30 n.m. farmer RW, Michael MURRY 40 lodger m. 1835 lab, Biddy Murry 40 m. 1835 lodger sowing potatoes, Pat Murry 15 lodger sowing potatoes RW, Mary 8 at Mr. Kilran's school R. DEC: Biddy Murphy 60 d. Spring 1849 decay.
    Co Roscommon (Athlone Barony, Fuerty Parish) Castlecoote Townland

MURRAY, Andy 65 m. 1820 farmer RW, Biddy 50 RW, Michael 20 son plowing RW, Ann 18 dau sowing potatoes RW, William 17 sowing potatoes RW, Edward 14 lab sowing oats RW, John 30 son m. 1844 farmer RW, Anne 25 D/L m. 1844 spinning & sewing RW, Biddy 4 gr dau, Mary 3 gr dau, Michael 9 mo gr son; ABS: Thomas Murray 27 lab in America. DEC: Pat 29 son lab & James 26 son lab both d. Summer 1843 decline.
    Co Roscommon (Athlone Barony, Fuerty Parish) Cloonyquin Townland

MURRAY, John 71 m. 1810 farmer RW, Biddy 70 RW E&I, James 28 son farmer RW, Ellen OWENS 24 h serv.
    Co Roscommon (Athlone Barony, Fuerty Parish) Cloonyquin Townland

MURRAY, Martin 60 m. 1827 wid sowing oats RW E&I, Thomas 21 son sowing oats RW
E&I, Mary 13 dau; ABS: Michael 24 son lab in England, Honoria 26 dau serv in America.
    Co Roscommon, Athlone Barony, Fuerty Parish, Emlaghkeaden (Emlaghkeadew)
Townland

MURRAY, Mary 70 m. 1800 wid RW E&I, Pat 45 son n.m. herdsman RW, Honoria 29 dau
n.m. dressmaker RW, Catherine 27 dau m. 1840 wid dressmaker RW, Anne Murray 17 serv
sowing potatoes RW, Patt CURLEY 17 gr son sowing potatoes RW, Mary Anne DAILY 2
mo gr dau b. America. DEC: William Murray 77 husband herdsman d. Autumn 1844 decline.
    Co Roscommon, Athlone Barony, Fuerty Parish, Castlestrange Townland

MURRY, Denis 50 m. 1824 farmer, Catherine 45 knitting, Patt 25 m. 1850 lab, Catherine 21
m. 1850 S/L sewing R, Mary 19 dau lab R, Ellin 14 dau lab R, Margat 12 dau lab R, Honor 10
dau, Michael 8 son, Celia 6 dau, Catherine (age na) niece. DEC: Martin 1 son d. Summer
1847 chincough, Denis 1 son d. Autumn 1848 chincough.
    Co Roscommon, Athlone Barony, Fuerty Parish, Muff Townland

MURRY, Lacky 43 m. 1832 farmer, Biddy 43 b. Co Galway, Mary 17 dau sowing oats, Tom
16 son sowing potatoes RW, Peggy 9 dau Mrs. Kilias school, Anne 7 in school, Malachi 5
son. DEC: Biddy 2 dau d. Summer 1850 decay.
    Co Roscommon (Athlone Barony, Fuerty Parish) Creenmully & Aughagaeheg
(Aghagad Beg) Townland

MURRY, Martin 50 m. 1830 farmer, Ellen 43 lab, John 20 son R, Mary 16 dau, Michael 14
son, Margaret 10 in school, Martin 7 son in school, Honor 5 dau in school; ABS: Pat Murry
18 son lab in Roscommon.
    Co Roscommon (Athlone Barony, Fuerty Parish) Creenmully & Aughagaeheg
(Aghagad Beg) Townland

MURRY, Michael 40 m. 1842 herdsman, Catherine 30, Maria 8 dau in school, James 4, John
3. DEC: Patt HANLY 60 F/L lab d. Spring 1847 dysentery, Ann Hanly 18 S/L d. Winter
1847 pain in hip, John Murry 2 son d. Summer 1847 dysentery.
    Co Roscommon (Athlone Barony, Fuerty Parish) Fuerty Townland

MURRY, Patt 40 n.m. reads Irish, Peggey 70 m. 1801 mother wid, Michael 30 brother m.
1846, Biddy 30 S/L RW, Patt 4 nephew, Denis 2 nephew, Mary 2 months niece.
    Co Roscommon, Athlone Barony, Fuerty Parish, Muff Townland

MURRY, Patt 37 m. 1836 farmer, Honor 37 wife sewing, Mary 12, Ellen 6, Biddy 3,
Catherine 1. DEC: Anne 60 mother d. Autumn 1845 fever, Andrew Murray (sic) 65 father d.
Autumn 1849 spasms in stomach.
    Co Roscommon (Athlone Barony, Fuerty Parish) Aghagad Townland

McDONAGH, John 59 m. 1827 pensioner and schoolmaster RW Irish, Mary HOLWELL 22
visitor n.m. R.
    Co Roscommon (Athlone Barony, Fuerty Parish) Aghagower Townland

QUIGLEY, Michael 55 m. 1831, Mary 50, Martin 18 lab, Thomas 16 lab, Mary 14, Margaret
11, Bridget 8.
    Co Roscommon, Ballintober S Barony, Killteen (Kilteevan) Parish, Newtown Tnld

QUIGLEY, Robert 34 n.m. private. Officers and non-commissioned officers, 14th Regiment of Foot, quartered here Mar 30 1851.
    Co Roscommon, Ballintober S Barony, Roscommon Parish, Town of Roscommon

SMYTH, Jane 57 n.m. shopkeeper RW, Ann BOLDING 30 niece n.m. RW, Mary HIGGINS 25 assistant RW b. Co Galway.
    Co Roscommon (Ballintober S Barony, Roscommon Parish) Roscommon Townland


Note: Locations in parentheses added by the transcriber. Spellings of townlands vary.


********************


The following records are from the Wilson Family transcription held in Belfast at the Public Record Office of Northern Ireland, their number T.372, LDS film 0258608; Republic of Ireland location:

KINGS COUNTY

Smith Massey BERRY 63 m. 1819 wid gentleman farmer, Thomas Francis Berry 31 son n.m., Allan Noble Berry 27 son n.m., Marlboro Parsons Berry son n.m., 2 maids and 2 man serv.
    Kings County (Eglish Barony) Parish of Eglish, Townland of Eglish

Ann CUNNINGHAM 64 m. 1820 housekeeper, Eliza BERRY 2 gr dau.
    Kings County (Eglish Barony) Parish of Eglish, Townland of Eglish

Kavanagh, Joseph, 110
Kavanagh, Mary, 110
Kavanagh, Mary Anne, 110
Keaney, Andrew, 109
Keaney, Ed., 109
Keaney, James, 109
Keaney, James H., 109
Keaney, John, 109
Keaney, Louisa, 109
Keaney, Margaret, 109
Keaney, Mary, 109
Keaney, Mary Ann, 109
Kearans, John, 96
Kearans, Mary, 96
Kearans, Serah, 96
Keating, Ann/Anne, 112, 113
Keating, Biddy, 113
Keating, Catherine, 113
Keating, Honor, 112
Keating, Jane, 113
Keating, John, 112, 113
Keating, Kitty, 113
Keating, Laurence, 113
Keating, Luke, 113
Keating, Margret, 113
Keating, Mary, 112, 113
Keating, Michael/Mick, 113
Keating, Nelly, 113
Keating, Patt, 113
Keating, Peggy, 113
Keating, Peter, 113
Keating, Robert, 113
Keating, Thomas, 113
Keating, Timothy, 113
Keating, William, 113
Keefe, Anastasia, 99
Keefe, Andrew, 99, 100
Keefe, Ann, 99
Keefe, Anty, 102
Keefe, Bridget, 99, 100
Keefe, Catherine, 99, 100
Keefe, Elinor, 100
Keefe, Ellen, 99, 102, 103
Keefe, Henry, 99
Keefe, James, 99, 100
Keefe, Jane, 103
Keefe, Joany, 102, 103
Keefe, Johanna, 99
Keefe, John, 99, 100, 103
Keefe, Judy, 103
Keefe, Kate, 102
Keefe, Margt., 99, 100, 102,
    103
Keefe, Martin, 99, 100
Keefe, Mary, 99, 100, 102, 103
Keefe, Matthais (sic), 100
Keefe, Michael, 99, 100
Keefe, Nicholas, 99
Keefe, Peter, 103
Keefe, Philip, 99, 100

Keefe, Richard, 102
Keefe, Robert, 103
Keefe, Samuel, 103
Keefe, Thomas, 103
Kehoe, Cornelius, 105
Kehoe, David, 105
Kehoe, Mary, 105
Kehoe, Michael, 105
Kehoe, Thomas, 105
Kelly, Anty, 103
Kelly, Barny, 96
Kelly, Bridget, 99, 100
Kelly, Daniel, 103
Kelly, Ed., 103
Kelly, Honor, 99
Kelly, Isabella Jane, 93
Kelly, James, 99, 102
Kelly, Joany, 102
Kelly, Johanna, 102, 103
Kelly, John, 96, 99, 100, 103
Kelly, Judy, 103
Kelly, Kate, 103
Kelly, Margaret, 100
Kelly, Mark, 99
Kelly, Martin, 99, 100, 102
Kelly, Mary, 96, 99, 100, 102
    103, 112
Kelly, Michael, 100
Kelly, Patrick, 100
Kelly, Peter, 102
Kelly, Thomas, 99, 100, 103
Kelly, William, 103
Kennady, Bridget, 96
Kennady, Elizabeth, 96
Kennady, Jane, 96
Kennady, John, 96
Kennady, Marsella, 96
Kennady, Mary, 96
Kennady, Patt, 96
Kennady, Thomas, 96
Kennady, Vallentin, 96
Kennedy, Ann/Anne, 96
Kennedy, Bridget, 96
Kennedy, Catherine, 96
Kennedy, Dennis, 96
Kennedy, James, 96
Kennedy, Jane, 96
Kennedy, John, 96
Kennedy, Marsella, 96
Kennedy, Mary Ann, 96
Kennedy, Patrick, 96
Kennedy, Richard, 96
Kennedy, Thomas, 96
Kennedy, William, 92
Kenny, Ann, 106
Kenny, Andrew, 106
Kenny, Mary, 106
Kenny, Richard, 106
Kenny, William, 106
Kerr, Ann, 92

Kerr, Bernard, 92
Kerr, Catherine, 92
Kerr, James, 92
Kilpatrick, Eliza/Elizabeth, 91
Kilpatrick, Samuel, 91
Kilrue, Mary, 113

Lally, Eleanor, 96
Lally, Margaret, 96
Lamberd, William 96
Leavy, John, 111
Leonard, Eliza, 96
Leonard, Mary, 96
Leonard, Thomas, 96
Logue, Mary, 91
Loughlin, Bridget, 96
Loughlin, Mary, 96
Loughlin, Patrick, 96

Magee, Maria/Marian, 110
Maghan, Catherine, 96
Maghan, Mary, 96
Maghan, Patrick, 96
Maher, Margaret, 102
Martin, Fanny, 92
Martin, Jeria (sic), 92
Martin, Martha, 92
Martin, Michael, 96
Martin, Patt, 96
Martin, Scelia, 96
Mayne, Bridget, 95
Milkin, James, 92
Milkin, Mary, 92
Miller, Alice, 102
Miller, James, 102
Miller, Kate, 102
Miller, Margaret, 102
Miller, Mary, 102
Miller, Robert, 102
Miller, Thomas, 102
Miller, William, 102
Mitchell, James, 92
Moan, Bridget, 92
Moan, James, 92
Moan, John, 92
Moan, Margaret, 92
Moan, Peter, 92
Molloy, Catherine, 92
Molloy, John, 97
Molloy, Margaret, 97
Molloy, Mary, 92
Molloy, Patrick, 92
Molloy, Stephen, 97
Molyneux, Ann, 108
Molyneux, Eliza, l08
Molyneux, Frances, 108
Molyneux, Henry, 108
Moran, Anne, 112
Moran, Edward, 112
Moran, Honor, 112

Walsh, Ned, 106
Walsh, Nicholas, 101, 102
Walsh, Nora, 101, 102
Walsh, Owen, 93
Walsh, Patrick, 93, 102, 103, 105, 106
Walsh, Peter, 104, 107
Walsh, Philip, 103, 105
Walsh, Rebecca, 103
Walsh, Richard, 102, 103, 104 105, 106
Walsh, Robert, 106
Walsh, Rose, 93
Walsh, Thomas, 102, 103, 104, 105, 108

Walsh, Walter, 101, 102, 103, 105, 106
Walsh, Walter Hoyle, 107
Walsh, Widow, 108
Walsh, William, 101, 102, 103, 108
Walsh, William Thomas, 107
Ward, Bridget, 112
Watson, Bell, 93
Watson, James, 93
Watson, Margaret, 93
Watson, Mary J., 93
Watson, Thomas, 93
Whelan, Anastasia, 105
Whelan, Bridget, 110

Whelan, Catherine, 105
Whelan, James, 98, 105
Whelan, William, 105
Wilson, Isabella, 93
Wilson, James, 93
Wilson, James Henry, 93
Wilson, Sarah, 93
Wynne, Cathrine, 110
Wynne, Daniel, 110
Wynne, Margaret, 110
Wynne, Michael, 110
Wynne, Thomas, 110
Wynne, Widow, 110
Wynne, William, 110

Adair, Bridget dau nee Heaver

Boylan, Bridget wife m. Moan (A)
Brown, Julia dau nee Hogan
Brown, Mary Anne dau nee Creanor (Tourish) A
Brown, Mary Anne dau nee Creanor (dupl.)
Bryson, Martha dau nee Pollock
Bryson, Mary wife m. Delany

Cahill, Catherine wife m. Brennan
Cahill, Mary wife m. Gary (A)
Campbell, Margaret dau nee Boner/Bonar
Campbell, Mary dau nee McCrudden
Cannon, Margaret wife m. Watson (A)
Carlin, Betty dau nee Kearney
Carolan, Kitty wife m. Coyle
Chambers, Ellen st/dau nee Stewart (Bell) A
Clifford, Sarah D/L m. Hegarty
Collins, Mary dau nee Green
Craigs, Mary A. dau nee Baldrick
Cullen, Mary dau nee Campbell

Daly, Mary dau nee McBarron
Devlin, Sarah dau nee Cooke
Doherty, Ann wife m. McLoughlin
Doherty, Annie, wife m. Byrne
Doherty, Eliza dau nee Kelly
Doherty, Esther wife m. McCallion
Doherty, Grace dau nee Clarke
Doherty, Kate wife m. Parke
Donnell, Jane wife m. Brannan
Dumiece, Anne dau nee McLoughlin
Dunphy, Mary wife m. Quinn (J. Walsh p. 103)
Dunleavy, Ellen wife/wid m. Quinn
Dunlevy, Rose (Ann) dau nee McGoldrick
Dunscombe, Annie wife m. Swete

Ellison, Eliz./Eliza Jane gr/dau nee Nixon
Ewing, Eliza dau nee Young

Fitzmorris, Bridget wife m. Gorman

Gallagher, Ann wife m. Walsh
Gallagher, Annie dau nee Monaghan
Gallagher, Catherine dau nee Coulter
Gallagher, Magy wife m. Campbell
Gallagher, Sarah wife m. McGowan
Gallagher, Susan wife m. Boyle (A)
Given, Margaret. wife m. Mahon
Graham, Catherine dau nee Wasson

Heffron, Jane wife m. Lytton
Hogan, Ann wife m. O'Grady
Houston, Susan wife m. Dever
Huston, Sarah dau nee Clonoughan
Hutton, Fanny gr/d nee Logue/McGrorty

Johnston, Anne wife m. Kelly

Keenan, Margt. dau nee McMahon (Milkin) A
Kelly, Madge dau nee McFadden
Kelly, Mary wife m. Cannon
Kelly, Rose wife m. McGeaghan
Kilgore, Sarah dau nee Bradley

Lannon, Margt. wife m. Wm. Hart (p. 99)
Lardner, Julia wife m. Hogan
Leich, Betty dau nee Glackin
Leeper, Isabella wife m. Johnston (Martin) A
Lynch, Betty wife m. Doherty

Macklin, Anne dau nee Swete
Magee, Mary gr/d nee Logue (Crossan) A
Maguire, Cath. gr/d nee Coyle (Donnell)
Mallon, Catherine wife m. Hughes
Melvin, Ellen wife m. Kennedy
Merryan, Susanna dau nee Freil
Mitchell, Grace dau nee Doherty
Monaghan, Rose wife m. McGlinchy
Moorehead, Matilda (Jane) dau nee Kincaid
Moran, Marjory dau nee Gillespie
Morris, Mary dau nee Steel
Murphy, Anne dau nee Cannon
Murphy, Bridget dau nee Hart (p. 99)
Murphy, Mary dau nee Lytton
Murtagh, Margaret dau nee Carr

McBarn, Cathrine wife m. Magee
McBride, Ann wife m. McDevitte
McCafferty, Margaret wife m. Coyle
McCaffrey, Sarah rel. na nee Do—(McNally)
McCarron, Ellen dau nee Dever
McCarron, Mary dau nee Haroden (A)
McCarron, Rose dau nee McGeaghan
McClelland, Margaret dau nee Avea
McCormick, Ann dau nee O'Donnel (Quinn) A
McCrossan, Anne/Nancy dau nee Kenedy
McDermott, Sarah dau nee Welsh
McDonnell, Cath. step dau nee Gill (Homes) A
McDowell, Suley (Cecilia?) dau nee Deeney?
McFadden, Ellen wife m. Duffy
McGoldrick, Catherine dau nee McMenamin
McGonagle, Susan wife m. Freil
McGranahan, Sarah dau nee Duffy
McGrath, Sarah dau nee Currin/Curran (A)
McIntyre, Eliza dau nee McCollum
McKelvey, Catherine wife m. McCaul
McLaughlin, Isabella wife m. Shiels (A)
McLaughlin, Rose dau nee Boyle
McMenamin, Biddy dau nee Byrne
McNaught, Mary dau nee O'Donnell
McNully, Mary wife m. Catterson

O'Donnell, Eloner dau nee Quinn (A)

O'Hara, Bridget wife m. Payne
O'Neil, Mary dau nee Boyle (A)
O'Neil, Margaret dau nee McCoule

Proctor, Martha dau nee Smith

Quinn, Ellen wife m. John Walsh (p. 103)
Quinn, Elizabeth dau nee Butler
Quinn, Sarah mother m. McMenamin

Reid, Mary dau nee Payne
Riddall, Ruth dau nee Johnston (Martin) A
Rodden, Catherine dau nee McGowan
Russell, Jane wife m. Kincaid
Ryan, Mary wife m. Walter Hart (p. 100)

Sheridan, Rose wife m. McBride
Steele, Fanny dau nee Ferren
Stevenson, Martha wife m. Cresswell
Sweeney, Margaret dau nee McKinley

Taylor, Bridget dau nee Byrne
Timoney, Nancy/Annie dau nee Quinn
Toner, Sarah wife m. McCurrin (A)

Ward, Mary dau nee Walsh
Warren, Ellen dau nee Hughes
Wilson, Margaret dau nee Mahon
Woods, Mary Ann dau nee Connolly
Wynne, Katherine dau nee Perry

Note: A or (A) indicates location in Appendix

# PART THREE

Killeshandra Parish, County Cavan – 1841 Census Surnames

# SURNAMES LISTED IN THE 1841 CENSUS FOR KILLESHANDRA PARISH, COUNTY CAVAN, IRELAND

A filmed copy of the census for this parish, the only complete existing original parish-wide census for the year 1841, was found on LDS films 0100831-00100838 (2,285 households, approximately 15,000 person). The original records are held by the National Archives, Dublin, Ireland. At this time (January 1998) pre-publication copies of transcriptions and indexes of this portion of the 1841 Census of Ireland may be found in various libraries: the National Library of Ireland, Dublin, the Family History Library of the Latter-day Saints in Salt Lake City, Utah, the Allen County Public Library in Fort Wayne, Indiana, the Pennsylvania Historical Society, Philadelphia, Pennsylvania and the Cavan County Public Library, Cavan Town, County Cavan, Ireland.

This list may be helpful in ascertaining if it is worth pursuing research in this parish. Some of the surnames are for families and others may be for relatives or servants. The surnames underlined have the more numerous entries.

Abbot, Adams, Akens/Akin/Akins, Allen, Alwell, <u>Anderson</u>, Archibold, Argyle, Arington, Arkerson, Arkinson, <u>Armstrong</u>, Arnold, Arwen, Atkins, Aughultry

Bagland, Bailey, Baird, <u>Baker</u>, Ballam, Banan/Bannan/<u>Bannon</u>, Bannott, Barker, Barn, Barrett, Bartley/Bartly, Barton, Baseter, Battesty, Baxter, Baylan/Baylon, Bearer, Bearlot, <u>Beatty</u>/Beaty, <u>Beck</u>, Beirne, Belhenry, <u>Bell</u>, <u>Bennet</u>/Bennett/Bennit/Bennitt, Berrane, Berrney, <u>Berry</u>/Bery, Biggar/<u>Bigger</u>, Biggs, Birney

<u>Black</u>, <u>Blair</u>, Blakely, Blarkny. Bleakely/Bleakley/<u>Bleakly</u>, Blosset, Bohan, Bohanan, Bolan, Bonden, Booth, Boston, Bothwell, Bourk, Bowen, Bows, <u>Boyd</u>/Boyde, Boylan, <u>Boyle</u>, Boylen/Boylin, Braday, Braden, Bradford, Bradly, <u>Brady</u>, Braison, Brannan/Branon, Breaden, <u>Bready</u>, Brean, <u>Bredy</u>, <u>Breen</u>, Brennan, Breslan, Briody, Brison, Brogan, Brooks, Brouster, <u>Brown</u>, Bruce, Bruin, Burdet, Burhage, Burke, <u>Burns</u>, Burrows, Byrne

Cadan, Cadders, Cadwin, Caffary/Cafferry/Caffery/Caffray/Caffrey/Caffry/Cafrey, Cahill, Caill (sic), Cain, Calaher/Calahers, Calders, Caldwell, Callaghan, Callery, Cambell/Camble, Camel, <u>Camp</u>, Campbele/<u>Campbell</u>, Canaughty, Cane, Canfield, Cannon, Carabin,/<u>Carbin</u>/ Carbon/Carbone, Carbura, Carmichael, Carn, Carney, Carothers, Carrol/<u>Carroll</u>, Carte, Carthright/Carthrite/<u>Carthwright</u>/Cartwright, Carty, Casaday/Casidy/<u>Cassady</u>/<u>Cassidy</u>, Cathcart, Causgrove, Cavana, Ceelagher, Ceery

Chaday, Chadwick, Charters, Christie, Church, Cimmons, Clail, Clandenen/Clandinan/ <u>Clandinen</u>, Clark/<u>Clarke</u>, Clary, Cldal (sic), Clearken, Cleary, Cleminger, Clemments/ Clemons, Clendennin/Clendenning, Clerken, Clifforty, Clindinnang (sic), Clingin/Clinging, Clinton, Coar, Cobane, Coby, Coil, Colaher, Coldwell, Cole, Collom, Collons, Column, Conaghty, Conaly, Conaughty, Conely/Conlay/Conley, Conlin/Conlon, Conly, Connaghty, Connally/Connele/Connelly/Connlly(sic)/<u>Connolly</u>, Connor, Conoley, Conway, Cook/<u>Cooke</u>, Cooney, Corbet/Corbett, Corbey/Corby, Corcoran, Coreran (sic), Corkins, Cornan, Corr, Corray, Cortney, Cosgrave/Cosgrove, Costello/Costelloe, Costola, Coulson, Coulter, <u>Courtney</u>, Cowan, <u>Cox</u>, Coyl/<u>Coyle</u>

Crague, Cranston, <u>Crawford</u>, Creague, Creamer, Creed, Crethers, Crist, Crofton, Cromby, Cronan, Cronogue, Crosby, Crosin/<u>Crossan</u>/Crossen/Crosson, Crotty, Crow, Crumby,

Crummy, Cull, Cullen, Cullion, Cullum, Culm (sic), Cumesky, Cumins, Cumiskey, Cummins, Cunningham, Curean, Curigan, Curley, Curneen, Curren, Currey, Currian, Currin, Currnan, Curry

D'Arcy, Dacod, Daily/Daly, Danagho, Dannon, Danohoe, Darby, Darcy, Darling, Darting, Daudle, Daughterty, Davis, Dawsey, Deacon/Decons, Degnan/Degnen, Degonan, Delamere/ Delamore/Delimor/Dellamare/Delmore, Dempsay/Dempsey, Develin/Devellin, Devine, Devlin, Dierne, Dignan, Dillan, Dininy/Dinneny

Dodson, Dogan, Dogherty/Doghterty/Doherty, Doil, Dolan/Doland/Dolen/Dolin, Dolle, Donaghoe/Donahoe/Donahoo, Donal, Donaldson, Donavan/Donavin, Doneley, Donen, Donery, Donevan, Donnelly/Donnely, Donoehe/Donoeho/Donoghoe/Donoho/Donohoe/ Donohoo/Donoohoe, Dooan (sic), Doogan, Doolady, Doonan, Dorsey, Doud, Dougan, Dougherty, Douglas, Dowling, Downer, Downes, Downey, Doyl/Doyle, Drapar/Draper, Drenan, Drum/Drumn, Dudley, Duffy, Dugan/Duggan, Duigenan/Duignan, Dulamare/ Dulamere, Dunary, Duncan, Dunery, Dunken/Dunkin, Dunlap/Dunlop, Dunn, Dunnary/ Dunnory, Dyer, Dygnan

Eakins, Early, Egan, Egleston, Eliott, Elis, Ellies, Elliott, Ellis/Elliss, English, Ennis, Errington, Ervin/Erwen/Erwin

Fagon, Fair, Fairagh, Fallis, Fallon, Faney, Fannan, Farel, Faris, Farlay/Farley/Farly, Farnin, Farrel, Farreley, Farrell/Farrelle, Farrelly, Farrill, Farry, Favers, Fay, Fee, Fegan, Fenigan, Ferguson, Fernin, Ferns, Fethorsten

Fielding, Finegan/Finigan, Finlay/Finley/Finly, Finnagan/Finnegan, Finnelly, Finnigan Fitchpatrick, Fitzimmons, Fitzimons, Fitzpatrick, Fitzsimmons, Flack, Flagherty/Flaherty, Flanagan/Flanigan, Fleming/Flemming, Flin, Flood/Flud, Flynn, Folbley, Folles/Follis, Forbes/Forbis, Forster, Forsythe, Foster, Fox, Fraser/Frazer, French, Frieragh, Friery, Frimmel, Frost, Fulton, Fury, Fyfe

Gaffnay/Gaffney/Gafney, Gahagan/Gahaghan, Gainer, Galaher, Gallagen, Gallagher, Gallegan/Galligan, Galloher, Gammell, Ganly, Gannon/Ganon, Garner, Garvey, Gatharin, Gaughagin, Geary/Geery, Geharty/Geherty, Gelhooly, Geoghagan, Georman (sic), Giblin, Gibney, Gibson, Gilece/Gileece, Gilhooly, Gilleece, Gillerlane, Gillis, Gilmore, Gilpin, Gilronan/Gilrownan, Gilroy, Gilsenan, Ginly, Gintie/Ginty, Glohan, Godley, Goff, Golden, Goldrick, Gomby, Good, Goodfellow, Goodwin, Gorman, Gormely/Gormlay/Gormley/ Gormly, Gould, Govern, Graham, Graul, Gray, Green/Greene, Grenan, Greves, Grey, Griffin, Griffith, Grogen, Guin/Guinn, Guinty, Gumley/Gumly, Gunning, Gurty, Guynn

Haddock, Haddon, Hagerty, Hague, Hale, Hales, Hall, Halpin, Hambleton, Hammelton/ Hamilton, Hammel, Hammon, Hanasy, Hands, Handy, Haniffee, Hanisy, Hanlen, Hanley, Hanlon, Hanly, Hanna, Hare, Hariterity, Harity, Harkness, Harlay, Harmon, Harpen, Harper, Harrison, Hart, Harten/Hartin, Hartt, Harvey, Haughton, Haulton, Hays

Heaney/Heany, Hearkin, Heart, Heartin, Heerin, Henderson, Hendrey, Hennishen/Hennison, Henry, Herbert, Heslin, Hetherton, Hewett/Hewit/Hewitt, Hicks, Higgin/Higgins, Hill, Himsworth, Hindry, Hintan, Hix, Hogg, Holaghan, Holdon, Holoughan, Hopkins, Hosset, Hotton, Hough, Houghton, Hourican, Hous, Howe, Hues, Huggans/Huggins, Hughes/Hughs, Hughston, Huitt, Humphrys/Humprys, Hunter, Hussey, Hutchinson/Hutchison, Hylan/ Hyland, Hynds

Ireton, Irwen/Irwin, Iveston

Jackson, Jeble, Jobe, Johnson, Johnston, Jones, Jordan/Jordon, Judge, Jute

Kane, Kealaher, Keane, Kearnan, Keegan, Keek, Keelagher/Keelaher, Keirnan/Keirnon, Keith, Kelaher/Kelehar/Keleher/Kellaher, Kelliot/Kellott, Kelly, Kemp, Kenaday/Kenedy/ Kennady/Kennedy, Kenney/Kenny, Keogan, Keogh, Kernahan, Kernan/Kernen/Kernon, Keron, Kerr, Kerrigan, Kerron, Kerwin, Kiernan, Kilbride, Kilkenny, Killdulay, Killhooly, Killmarton, Killoly/Killooly, Kilpatrick, Kincade, Kinear, King, Kingston, Kinnian, Kittrington, Knipe, Knott, Knowles, Kurnan, Kyle

Laday, Ladon, Lahy, Lanauze, Lang, Langley/Langly, Langue, Lappin, Larnen, Lasley, Latamore/Latimer/Latimore/Lattimore, Laurence, Law, Lawler, Lawsin/Lawson, Leady Leahey, Leavy, Leddie/Leddy, Ledswith, Lee, Leech/Leeche,/Leetch, Leghorn, Lenard, Lench, Lennin, Lennix/Lennox, Leonard, Lester, Levengston, Levisten, Lewis, Liday/Liddy, Lighten, Lilly, Linch, Linnard, Linnon, Linster, Little, Lockhart, Logan, Loney, Looby, Love, Lovett, Low, Ludlow, Lunny, Lynch, Lynden

Macabe, Maclean, Macue, Macusker, Magherin, Magarry, Magauran/Magauvaran/ Magauvran/Magaveran/Magavern/Magavran, Magee, Magennis, Maghan, Maghren, Magierity, Magin, Magines, Maginn, Maginnes, Maglane, Maglew/Magloo/Maglue, Magohan, Magolrick, Magoohan, Magoohity, Magourty, Magoveran/Magovern/Magovrun, Magragh, Magrath, Maguarty, Maguhay, Maguinnes, Maguire, Mahan/Mahon

Mains, Makimson, Malanny, Malcolmson/Malcomson, Malehet, Maler, Mallon, Malloy, Malone, Maloy (sic), Maneely, Manford, Manning, Marron, Marten/Martin/Marton, Massy, Master, Masterson, Matchet, Mathews, Maxwell, Mayberry/Maybury, Medly, Meely, Megure (sic), Menakin, Miginis (sic), Miller, Mills, Minnitt, Mll (sic)

Molloy, Monaghan/Monahan/Monahon/Monaughan, Montgomary/Montgomery/ Montgomray/Montgumary, Monypeny, Mooney/Moony, Moor/Moore, Mordy, Moreton, Moriarty, Morison, Moron, Morray, Morris, Morrison/Morrisson, Morrow, Morten, Mortimer, Morton, Muligan, Mullan/Mullen, Mullegan/Mulligan, Mullin, Mulloy, Mulreany/ Mulreigney/Mulreigny, Mulvey/Mulvy, Murday, Murdock, Murdy, Murfay/Murphey/ Murphy, Murray/Murry, Murtagh, Myers, Mynagh

McAffry/McAfry, McAloon, McAnea, McAniff, McAnna, McAvaney, McAvea, McAveety, McAvey, McAvina, McAvinea, McAvoy, McAweeny, McBride, McBrien/McBrine, McCabe, McCadan, McCafey, McCaffery/McCaffry, McCahal/McCahil/McCahill, McCall, McCann, McCanna, McCanne, McCart, McCartan/McCarten, McCarter, McCathel, McCaul/McCawl, McCawley, McClain/McClean, McCleery, McClenon, McCloone, McClusky, McCollister, McConel/McConell/McConnel/McConnell/McConul, McCormack/McCormick, McCubbin, McCue, McCusker

McDearmid, McDeed, McDeeny, McDermid/McDermot/McDermott, McDole, McDonald/ McDonel/McDonnal/McDonnel/McDonnell, McDool, McDowel/McDowell/McDowill, McElheran, McEnay(?), McEntee, McEntire, McEvay, McEver, McFadden/McFaddin

McGaghran/McGaharn/McGaherin/McGahran, McGann, McGaughran/McGauran, McGauvern/McGauvirn/McGauvrn, McGerrill, McGibney, McGinn, McGinness, McGivney,

McGlaughlin, McGlaun, McGlin, McGloe, McGlorlin, McGlue, McGolrick, McGooghan/ McGoohan, McGoorty/McGourty, McGoveran/McGovern/McGovran/McGovren, McGowan, McGragh, McGrath, McGraw, McGreal, McGreen, McGuire, McGurney, McInerney, McInerny, McInteger, McIntire

McKane, McKearnan, McKeever, McKeirnan, McKena/McKenna, McKenney, McKeon/ McKeone, McKernan/McKerron/McKiernan, McKinly, McKittrick, McKlem, McKnight, McKoan/McKowen/McKown, McLane, McLaughlin, McLean, McMagert, McMaghan/ McMahan, McManas/McManass/McManes/McManis/McMans/McManus, McMichaiel (sic), McMullin, McNama (sic), McNamara, McNeely, McNerney, McNulty, McParthan, McPeague, McPhilips, McRyan, McSharry/McSherry, McSoarla/McSoarley, McTague/ McTeague, McTernan, McVay, McVimur, McVinnue, McVittie

Narroway, Naylor, Neary, Neelly, Neil/Neile, Neithercoat, Nells, Nerway, Nesbet, Nesdale, Nethercut, Newell, Newham, Nicells, Nichol, Nicholson, Nickle/Nicoll/Nicolls, Night, Noble, Nollen, Norton, Norway, Nowlan, Nowles

O'Brien, O'Cane, O'Conner/O'Connor, O'Daniel, O'Donnell, O'Hara, O'Nail/O'Neal/O'Neale/ O'Neil/O'Neill, O'Reilley/O'Reilly, Obryan, Ogle, Oliver, Olwill, Onail, Owen

Parker, Parsons, Paterson, Patison, Patterson, Pattison, Pendergrass, Pennel, Pentland, Peterson/Petterson, Phair/Phare, Phillips, Piercan, Pinkman, Plant, Plunket/Plunkett, Pogue, Pollick/Pollock, Powel/Powell, Prier/Prior, Prunty, Puruson

Quail/Quale, Quillan, Quin/Quinn/Quinne

Rael, Rafferty, Rainnay/Rainney, Rall, Randals, Raymond, Reanny/Reany, Reehill/Rehale/ Rehile/Rehill, Reiley/Reilley/Reilly/Reily, Renals, Renick, Renuk, Reynolds/Reynols, Rialay/ Rialey/Riallay/Rially/Rialy, Rice, Richardson, Richmond, Riehael, Rieley/Rielly/Riely/Rilay/ Riley/Rilly/Rily, Rivers

Roach/Roache, Roark/Roarke, Robbinson, Roberts, Robinson, Roche, Roden, Rodgers, Rodin, Rodney, Roe, Rogers/Roggers, Rollay, Ronan, Roonay, Rork/Rorke, Roseman/ Rosman, Ross, Rourke, Rowan, Rowe, Rowley, Rudden, Ruddy, Ruden/Rudin, Rusk, Rutledge, Ryan

Sadleir, St. Lawrence, Sales, Sandiford, Sands, Saunderson, Saus, Saxton, Scarlet, Scholes, Scorby, Scot/Scott, Seales, Seaman, Shanan/Shanon, Shaugnaughsy/Shaunasey, Shaw, Sheales/Sheals, Shearen, Shenan,/Shenon, Sheridan/Sheriden/Sheridon/Sherridan/Shirden Shiredan/Shirridan, Short, Simonton, Simpson, Skinen/Skinnen/Skinnion, Sleaven, Slemmon/Slemons, Sloan, Slosh, Sloss, Slowey, Smiley, Smith, Smothergile, Smyth, Sorahan, Sorrele, Sorrohan, Southwell, Stanny, Steenson, Stephens, Steward/Stewart, Stinson, Storey/Story, Stretton, Strong, Stuart, Suiter/Suitor, Sulavin/Sulevan/Sullevan/ Sullivan, Sunney, Swan, Sweeney/Sweeny/Swenney, Swift

Taafe/Taffe, Taylor, Tearney/Tearny/Terney, Theckpeny, Thedfart, Thompson/Thomson, Thornton, Tibbs, Tierney, Tilson, Timmens/Timmin/Timmon/Timmons/Timon, Todd, Torney, Trap/Trappe, Travers, Tremble, Troy, Trumble, Tubman, Tuite, Tuley/Tullay/ Tulley/Tully, Tuvan, Tyford, Tygart

Vahey/Vahy, Vance, Vaughan, Veitch, Venton, Victory, Vinson, Vinton

Wag, Waldin, <u>Wallace</u>, Walnuck, Walpole, Walsh, <u>Ward</u>, Warran, Warrant, <u>Warren</u>, Warrington, Waters, Watson, Watters, Watterson, Weare, Weaver, Webster, Weel, <u>Weer/Weir</u>, Welch/Welsh, Whealan, Wheeler, <u>Whelan</u>, <u>White</u>, Whitehead, Whitney, Whittendale, Whyte, Widows, Wier/Wiere, Wiley/Willey, <u>Williams</u>, Williamson, Willis, Willson/<u>Wilson</u>, Winn, Winslow, Wood, <u>Woods</u>, <u>Wren</u>, <u>Wright</u>, <u>Wrin</u>, Write

<u>Young</u>

The most frequent surnames (including variations) encountered in the 1841 Census for Killeshandra Parish, County Cavan, Ireland, are the following, listed with the number of entries found:

| | | | | | |
|---|---|---|---|---|---|
| Armstrong | 154 | Maguire | 100 | McManus | 132 |
| Brady | <u>375</u> | Martin | 117 | Reilly | <u>786</u> |
| Donoghoe | 150 | Masterson | <u>223</u> | Scott | 147 |
| Elliott | 121 | McCabe | 99 | Sheridan | <u>288</u> |
| Johnston | 169 | McCormack | 96 | Wilson | 111 |
| Keirnan | 116 | McKiernan | 100 | | |

The townlands of Killeshandra Parish in 1841 (many variations in spelling):

| | | | |
|---|---|---|---|
| Aghanock | Corr | Drumcullion | Killatawnay |
| Aghavadrin | Corraderren | Drumgoa | Killeshandra |
| Aghullaghy | Corran | Drumgoon | Kiltrasna |
| Ardarrah | Creena Glebe | Drumguird | Kinkeel |
| Ardra | Curlis/Corlis | Drumhart | Lachen |
| Arva (town of) | Dernawil | Drumhillagh | Lahard |
| Aughnacur | Derreskett | Drumkeeran Beg | Laheen |
| Bawn | Derrindrehid | Drumkeeran More | Lossett |
| Behy | Derry | Drumkernan Black | Loughnafin/Rockfield |
| Bohora | Derrygid | Drumkilrosk | Mullaghboy |
| Brankhill | Derrylane | Drumlarny | Ned |
| Bruse | Derrynacross | Dummany | Portaliff/Town Parks |
| Cappagh | Donawell | Drumnawal | Portaliff Glebe |
| Castlepoles | Drumalt | Drumrockady | Portlongfield |
| Clodrum | Drumamry | Drumroe | Portnaquin |
| Cloggy | Drumbery | Drumroosk | Pottle |
| Cloncose | Drumbess | Drumshiney | Quivy |
| Condry | Drumbullion | Drumyouth | Sallaghan |
| Coragh Glebe | Drumcarey | Farrangarve | Shancor |
| Coranea (Glebe) | Drumcohill Lower | Farranseer | Shancroghan |
| Corradownan | Drumcohill Upper | Gartenardress | Tully |
| Corhanagh | Drumcon | Gartylaught | Tycusker |
| Corlespratton | Drumconlister | Gorteen | Woodland |
| Cornafean | Drumcrow | Keelagh | Yewer Glebe |
| Coronary | Drumcrow North | Kilgarve | |

The 1841 Census for the Parish of Killeshandra is complete except for 19 persons unaccounted for in the Townland of Portaliff Glebe.

PART FOUR


Union of Kilworth, County Cork – 1851 Census Surnames

Kilcrumper and Kilworth Parishes with portions of Leitrim and Macroney

A list of surnames in the 1851 Census for four Parishes of
COUNTY CORK, IRELAND, IN THE UNION OF KILWORTH

Following is a list of surnames from a transcription and index of the 1851 Census for <u>two</u>
parishes (Kilcrumper and Kilworth) and <u>portions</u> of <u>two</u> other parishes (Leitrim and
Macroney) of County Cork, Ireland, in the Union of Kilworth (a Church of Ireland unit of
administration) which was published by the Clearfield Company, 200 East Eager St.,
Baltimore, Maryland, 21202, in 1994 (*County Cork, Ireland – A Collection of 1851 Census
Records* by Josephine Masterson). A photostatted copy of the handwritten original, M4685, is
held at the National Archives in Dublin, Ireland; a xeroxed copy was obtained from them.
This information was not available in the U. S. on LDS film. (750 households, 4000 persons.)
Underlined surnames have significant numbers of entries. Some are family surnames and
others are for relatives or servants.

<u>Ahern</u>, Ambrose, Andrews, Armor, Ashby, Atkins

Baker, Baldwin, Banfield, Barrett, <u>Barry</u>, Bassett, Beary, Begly, Bennett, Bermingham (sic),
Bible, Blake, Boland, Bolster, Bonynge, Bourke, <u>Bowen</u>, Bowler, Boyce, Brady, <u>Brien</u>,
Broderick, Bronig, <u>Brouder</u>, Brown/Browne, Brunig, Bryan, Buckly, Bull, Bulman, Burchill,
<u>Burke</u>, <u>Byrnes</u>

<u>Cahill</u>, Caine, <u>Callaghan</u>, Campion, Cane, Carey, Carrol/<u>Carroll</u>, Carthy, <u>Casey</u>, Casheen,
Casheran, Cauley, <u>Clancy</u>, Clarke, <u>Cleary</u>, <u>Clifford</u>, <u>Cody</u>, Coffee, <u>Colbert</u>, <u>Colman</u>, Collins,
Collis, <u>Condon</u>, Connell, Connelly/<u>Connolly</u>/Connoly, <u>Connors</u>, <u>Conroy</u>, Cooney, Coppinger,
Corban, Corbitt, Corency, Cormack/Cormick, Cosgrove, Coskeran, <u>Cotter</u>, <u>Coughlan</u>,
<u>Courtney</u>, Cranwell, Creedon, <u>Cronan</u>, Croneen, Cronin, <u>Crotty</u>, <u>Crowe</u>, Crowly, Cummins,
<u>Cunningham</u>, <u>Curtin</u>

Dalton, <u>Daly</u>, Daniels, Dawson, Dennehy (sic), Devine, Digeen, Dillon, <u>Divine</u>, Doherty,
<u>Donegan</u>, Donoghue/<u>Donoughue</u>, <u>Donovan</u>, Doody, <u>Doran</u>, Dorling, <u>Dorney</u>, Downey, Doyle,
Drake, Driscoll, Duane, Duggan, Dundan, Dunn, Dwyer

<u>Egan</u>, <u>Ellard</u>, Ellaw, Elsworth, English, Erles

Fannesy, <u>Fanning</u>, Farrell, Fawsitt, Fennell, <u>Fennesy</u>, Fenton, Feore, Fey, Fing, Finley, <u>Finn</u>,
<u>Fitzgerald</u>, Fitzgibbon, Fitzpatrick, Flanagan, Flemming, <u>Flynn</u>, <u>Foley</u>, Fouhy, Frazier

Galavan, Galligan, Garrett, Gearey/<u>Geary</u>, Geeleher, <u>Geran</u>, Govld/Govlde (sic), Grant,
<u>Greehy</u>, Green, <u>Griffin</u>, Guinevan

Hackett, Hagarty, Hales, Halloran, Haly, Handley, <u>Hanlon</u>, Hanrahan, Harding, Harrington,
Harris, Hartnetty, Hayes, <u>Heafy</u>, Healy, Heffernan/Heffernon, Hegarty, Hendley, <u>Hennesy</u>,
Henry, Heskin, Hickey, Higgins, Hogan, <u>Holehan</u>, Holmes, Horgan, Hoskin, Howard, Howe,
Hudson, Hughes, Hurley/Hurly, Hurst, Hutchinson, Hyde

Ilard

Johnson, Jones, <u>Joyce</u>

Kane, Keane, Kearney, <u>Keating</u>, <u>Keeffe</u>, <u>Keleher</u>, Kelly, <u>Kennedy</u>, <u>Kenny</u>, Kenrick, Kent,

Keresy, Kinnealy, Knowles

Lande, Lane, Leahy, Leamy, Leary, Lee, Lehane, Lenard/Leonard, Lenehan/Linehan, Lodge, Lomasney, Londregan/Londrigan, Lonergan, Looney, Luby, Lukey, Lynch, Lyons

Mackesy, Madden, Magner, Mahoney/Mahony, Malone, Mangan, Monsergt (sic), Meade, Meagher, Meany, Meara, Miller, Mills, Milton, Moakley, Moher, Molan, Molone, Molony, Molowphy (sic), Montgomery, Moore, Moran, Moriarty, Moroney/Morony, Morrison, Morrogh, Mulcahy, Mullins, Murphy, Murray/Murry, Myles

McAuliffe, McCarthy, McCauley, McCoy, McCraith, McDonald/McDonnell, McEnernay, McGrath, McLean, McMahon, McNamara/McNamarra

Nagle, Neil, Nolan, Noonan, Norcott, Norman, Norris, Nugent, Nunan

O'Brien, O'Connor, O'Donnell, O'Flanagan, O'Hara, O'Leary, O'Neil/O'Neill

Parker, Payne, Pendergast, Pierce, Pigott, Pillon, Pinchon, Pine, Power, Price, Prior

Quinlan, Quinn, Quirk/Quirke

Rankin, Rea, Readey, Really, Redding, Regan, Rial, Rice, Riley, Riordan, Roche, Ronan, Russell, Ryall, Ryan

Saul, Savage, Scanlon, Scully, Sennott, Sexton, Shanahan, Sheedy, Sheehan, Sheely, Sherlock, Simmons, Sinnott, Slattery, Smyth, Spalane, Stack, Stanton, Starkie, Steele, Strapp, Sullivan, Swain/Swaine/Swayn, Sweeny

Teulon, Thompson, Tobin, Toohill, Torbett, Torhill, Touel, Trehy, Troy, Twomy

Veale, Verlin/Verling

Wade, Wall, Walsh, Warner, Waters, Watson, Watts, Whelan, Whibbs, White, Wilkinson, Williams, Woods, Worrell, Wright

Young

The most frequent surnames and their numbers, appearing in this compilation:

| | | | | | |
|---|---|---|---|---|---|
| Ahern | 54 | Flynn | 54 | McCraith | 65 |
| Brien | 96 | Hennesy | 44 | Quinn | 44 |
| Casey | 86 | Joyce | 32 | Rice | 65 |
| Clancy | 51 | Keeffe | 33 | Roche | 70 |
| Condon | 67 | Lyons | 30 | Ryan | 64 |
| Courtney | 39 | Mahony | 48 | Sullivan | 65 |
| Daly | 46 | Moher | 31 | Tobin | 36 |
| Fitzgerald | 49 | Murphy | 44 | Walsh | 68 |

Additional information, omitted from M4685, was obtained from National Archives manuscript 999/643.

## SOURCES

Old Age Pension records were filmed by the Genealogical Society of Utah in Salt Lake City; the 0258500 series filmed in 1959, the 0993000 series filmed in 1977. Microfilms of the original records are at PRONI, T.550. Permission to publish was obtained from the Director of the Public Record Office of Northern Ireland, Dr. Anthony Malcomson. The LDS film numbers are 0258526-0258548 and 0993086-0993108. The Irish Free State/Republic of Ireland records were found on films 0258546-0258548 and 0993086-0993108.

Information from the burnt fragments of the 1841 Census records was found on LDS film 0100816. The originals (available for viewing under supervision) are at the National Archives, Dublin, Ireland, listed in their reading room in the Pre-1901 Censuses Catalogue and the filmed records are on their film N1837, which is also the National Library of Ireland film number.

Information from the Certified Copies of portions of some returns from the 1841 and 1851 Censuses for Ireland was found on LDS film 0101767. Microfilmed copies of the originals are at the National Archives, Dublin, their M5248. Gregory O'Connor, Archivist at the National Archives, supplied xeroxed copies of records, not found on LDS film, from which information was extracted and incorporated in this compilation.

Information for the 1841 Census abstracts for County Galway, Loughrea Town, was obtained from the National Archives, Dublin, who hold this transcription, a private accession, their number M150/2. Not found on LDS film.

The information from the 1841 and 1851 E. Walsh Kelly transcription was obtained from LDS film 0100158. The manuscript is held by the Genealogical Office, Dublin, Ireland, their reference GO Mss. 683-86. The use of this material is courtesy of the Chief Herald of Ireland.

The 1841 and 1851 Thrift Genealogical Abstracts were found on LDS film 0596418. The National Archives hold a copy of this family transcription, their numbers 4845-4946, 5026 and 4947-5008, 5029. Permission to publish National Archives holdings was granted by the Director, Dr. David V. Craig. NA reference numbers provided by Gregory O'Connor, Archivist.

The Killeshandra Parish surnames were taken from a pre-publication copy of *A Transcription and Index of the 1841 Census for Killeshandra Parish, County Cavan, Ireland.*

The surnames from a portion of the 1851 County Cork Census were taken from *County Cork, Ireland – A Collection of 1851 Census Records*, by Josephine Masterson, published in 1994 by the Clearfield Company, 200 East Eager St., Baltimore, MD, USA, 21202; available from the publisher.

REFERENCES: (maps, spellings, geographical locations, available records):

*Irish Genealogy – A Record Finder*, edited by Donal F. Begley, Heraldic Artists Ltd., Dublin 2, Ireland, 1981, Mount Salus Press Ltd., Dublin 4, Ireland

*Tracing Your Irish Ancestors – The Complete Guide,* by John Grenham, published by Gill and Macmillan Ltd., Dublin 8, Ireland, 1992, and Genealogical Publishing Co. Inc., Baltimore, MD 21202, 1993

*Census of Ireland, 1851, General Alphabetical Index to the Townlands and Towns, Parishes and Baronies of Ireland,* edited by Alexander Thom, 87 & 88 Abbey St., Dublin, 1861

*Census of Ireland, 1871, General Alphabetical Index to the Townlands and Towns, Parishes and Baronies of Ireland,* edited by Alexander Thom, Dublin, 1877 (found on LDS film BGL 104 item 5)

*Picturesque Ireland,* John Savage, LL.D. editor, Thomas Kelly publisher, New York, 1884

*Scotch-Irish Family Research Made Simple,* revised edition, by R. G. Campbell, Summit Publications, Munroe Falls, Ohio, 1992


LOCATION OF INDEXES